indonesia

1984

No. 38 (October)

© 1984, Cornell Southeast Asia Program

NOTE FROM THE EDITORS

The Editors for the October 1984 issue of *Indonesia* are Audrey Kahin and Benedict Anderson. Associate Editors are Roberta Ludgate and Dolina Millar.

Prospective contributors should submit their manuscripts in a typewritten, *double-spaced* format (*including footnotes*), with footnotes and other stylistic conventions in accordance with the University of Chicago *Manual of Style*. A short statement of the author's institutional affiliation and status should be included with the original manuscript as these will be needed for "List of Contributors" in case of eventual publication. Please address all correspondence to: *Indonesia*, Cornell Modern Indonesia Project, 102 West Avenue, Ithaca, New York 14850.

Contributors will receive 10 complimentary reprints of their articles and one copy of the issue in which their article appears. Additional reprints may be ordered at cost at the time a manuscript is accepted for publication. Abstracts of articles published in this journal may be found in *Excerpta Indonesica*, which is published semiannually by the Centre for Documentation on Modern Indonesia, Royal Institute of Linguistics and Anthropology, Leiden.

The price of a subscription to *Indonesia* is $14.00 per year, or $7.50 per issue.

ISBN: 978-0-87727-838-2

CONTENTS

RELIGION AND POLITICS

The Contraction and Expansion of the *"Umat"* and the Role of the Nahdatul Ulama in Indonesia *Sidney Jones*	1
Death and the History of Islam in Highland Aceh *John R. Bowen*	21
Repression and Regroupment: Religious and Nationalist Organizations in West Sumatra in the 1930s *Audrey R. Kahin*	39
The Political and Social Language of Indonesian Muslims: The Case of *Al-Muslimun* *Howard M. Federspiel*	55
Pancasila as the Sole Foundation *Sjafruddin Prawiranegara*	74
Government and Mission in the Torajan World of Makale-Rantepao *Terance Bigalke*	85
The Logic of *Rasa* in Java *Paul Stange*	113
Tales from the Island of Roti, compiled by D. Manafe Translated by *Thomas John Hudak*	135

Review Article

Second Thoughts About a History of Batavia *Tony Day*	147

THE CONTRACTION AND EXPANSION OF THE "UMAT" AND THE ROLE OF THE NAHDATUL ULAMA IN INDONESIA

Sidney Jones

One of the most powerful concepts in Islam is that of the *umat* (Arabic *umma*), the universal community of the faithful to which every Muslim belongs. The *haj* is probably the single most important means of making that concept a concrete reality, but except for the haj few Muslims experience the universality of the umat directly. For most, there is a narrower, more relevant community that helps define an individual's identity as a Muslim. This point was brought home forcefully in a recent article by Abdurrahman Wahid on the changes in meaning that Arabic loan words have undergone in Indonesian.[1] Thus *tarbiah*, which in Arabic means training or education in the broadest sense, has come to have the very specific meaning of Islamic education as taught in an institution. Likewise, Wahid asserts, umat has come for all practical purposes to mean the membership of the particular Muslim social, educational, or political organization to which an Indonesian Muslim belongs. In fact, it is not the definition of the word which has changed, but the nature of the community through which an Indonesian experiences his or her own membership in the umat. Looking at how the community, the relevant umat if you will, has changed over time for the Javanese, suggests that what has come to be called an Islamic resurgence may be simply the widening of the community most directly relevant to Muslim self-identity. It also suggests that beyond signifying the stifling of political participation the decline of Islamic political parties in Indonesia has implications for fundamental questions of Islamic identity.

Two factors affect the scope of the relevant Muslim community (hereafter referred to as "umat," the use of quotation marks indicating that this is a contrived use of the term and is to be distinguished from the universal community). One factor is the local political and economic environment in which the "umat" exists, the second, the international Islamic environment to which it relates. To some extent, the more the global umat approaches political reality, the more outward looking the local "umat" will be.

Umma in Arabic means "nation" or "people." Since the early days of Islam, then, it has had a political connotation, for it embraced all those who accepted the Will of God as expressed in the *shari'a* or Islamic law and thus gave rise to the need for institutions to enforce that law. The Will of God could only be implemented through a political order.[2] While religious and secular authority in the Islamic world diverged soon after Mohammed's death, the existence of the umma as a political community remained a necessary and powerful fiction,

---

1. Abdurrahman Wahid, "Kata Sama, Arti Berbeda," *Tempo*, August 20, 1983.
2. Fazlur Rahman, *Islam* (Chicago: University of Chicago Press, 1979), p. 3.

because it was only in the umma that ultimate truth resided. As the Prophet was reported to have said, "My community shall never agree on an error."[3]

If infallibility and universality together accounted in part for the endurance and strength of the concept of the umat, another factor was the concrete reality of Mecca. There was of course the haj, the annual reaffirmation of community, and the duty of every Muslim who could afford it to make the pilgrimage to Mecca gave that city an important role in perpetuating a belief in the physical reality of a global umat. But the fact that, until the surrender of Sherif Hussein to Ibn Saud in 1925, Mecca had always enjoyed special political status under a succession of Arabic, Persian, and Turkic dynasties meant that in a very real sense, there was a capital city for the umat with a ruler, the Sherif, who could receive delegations from other states. More important, perhaps, Mecca housed the religious scholars who acted as ultimate arbiters of differences within the umat and who could confer legitimacy on any Muslim ruler or withdraw it from him. The *ulama* in Mecca were no less guilty of political intrigue than was the Pope in medieval Europe, and the Ottomans, among many others, were past masters at securing favorable *fatwa*.[4] But whatever the foibles of individual scholars, the possibility of an appeal to Mecca for such a fatwa gave credence to the idea of a religio-political authority that transcended the authority of individual Muslim rulers. That authority could be assumed only in the absence of competing political ideologies, and, with the onset of colonialism and nationalism throughout the Islamic world on the one hand, and the end of the Sherifian dynasty and the incorporation of Mecca into the new nation-state of Saudi Arabia on the other, the relation of local Muslim communities to the broader umat would necessarily undergo change.

If changes in the "capital" of the Muslim world affect the scope of the "umat," so too do local political and economic conditions. At the most basic level, relations with the broader Muslim world depend on whether the political unit within which that community lives is Muslim or non-Muslim and, if the latter, whether hostile or sympathetic to Islamic activities and associations. It depends on whether the members of that "umat" define themselves primarily in terms of religion, ethnic group, or nation. It depends on the nature of exchange between the "umat" and the rest of the Muslim world--whether this is primarily economic, religious, or cultural, taking the form of trade, the haj, or mass communications. And it depends on the ability to communicate in a commonly understood language.

With local and international factors in mind, we can look at the evolution of the Javanese "umat." In the following pages, I will briefly examine how these factors may have shaped that "umat" at selected points in history, and how the realignment of the "umat" today is affecting one organization, the Nahdatul Ulama.

---

3. Ibid., p. 78.

4. In 1726, the Ottomans received a *fatwa* allowing them to help fight off an Afghan invasion of Persia, despite the fact that the Afghans, like the Ottomans, were Sunni and the Persians, heretical Shi'a. The fatwa was based on the fact that since the Afghan leader had declared himself "Caliph of the East" there was the danger of the split Caliphate and a threat to the dignity of Islam. Edward G. Brown, *A Literary History of Persia*, vol. 4 (Cambridge: Cambridge University Press, 1924), p. 130.

The Seventeenth Century to the Present

In the seventeenth century, the "umat" for the pious Muslim from Java was the entire Islamic world, a fact made possible by trade and the use of Arabic as a lingua franca in the Indian ocean. In the early part of the century, through trade the coastal states on the major islands of Java, Sumatra, and Sulawesi were well integrated into the Islamic world. There is a long-standing debate as to whether Arabs, Chinese, Gujeratis, or Bengalis first brought Islam to the islands but, as Anthony Johns has noted, the important point is that any of them could have. All mixed with Malay sailors in the ports of the Indian Ocean, which had all the characteristics of "an Arabic-speaking Mediterranean."[5] Muslim scholars from Aceh studied in Mecca, Damascus, Cairo, and elsewhere with sheikhs from the subcontinent and the Maghreb, and major theological debates over Sufism and the relationship between man and Allah were reflected not only in writings of indigenous Muslims but in texts written by renowned Muslim scholars in Mecca for their "Jawi"--that is, Malay-speaking--students.

At the same time, Islam was incorporated into the existing political structure without much disruption of traditional practices, in part because it reached the islands peacefully, through trade, and conversion of local rulers seems to have been for the most part voluntary. In western Sumatra, among the Minangkabau, religious leaders had their own niche in the traditional hierarchy, the mosque stood side by side with the tribal council hall, and legend had it that the Minangkabau world was ruled by three kings: King of Adat, King of Religion (that is Islam), and King of the World.[6] Aceh was already well established as a Muslim state by the time Iskandar Muda ascended to power, and, under Iskandar, it established diplomatic relations with the holy city of Mecca and with the two major Muslim powers of the era, the Ottoman and Mughal Empires.[7] Java was somewhat more problematical, because Islam's place in the great seventeenth-century state of Mataram was variously defined in opposition to the Christian colonial powers, to the heavily Islamicized north coast cities, and to the Hindu-Buddhist states to the east. It was clear, however, that, even in the agrarian interior of Central Java where the Mataram court lay, Islam was a necessary component of kingship, and Sultan Agung saw himself as a Muslim ruler. Not only did he declare a *jihad* against Bali and the easternmost part of Java which had not yet converted to Islam,[8] but, more telling perhaps, he sent an ambassador to Mecca to legitimize his claim to the title of Sultan. In doing so, he allowed himself to become caught up in the Anglo-Dutch rivalry for influence over Eastern trade, because it was the English, undoubtedly hoping to strengthen an indigenous ruler against the Dutch, who provided the ships in which the Sultan's envoys made their

---

5. Anthony Johns, "Islam in Southeast Asia: Reflections and New Directions," *Indonesia* 19 (April 1975): 39.

6. Taufik Abdullah, *Schools and Politics: The Kaum Muda Movement in West Sumatra* (Ithaca: Cornell Modern Indonesia Project, 1971).

7. Anthony Johns, "Islam in the Malay World," in *Islam in Asia*, ed. Johns (Boulder: Westview Press, 1983), p. 121.

8. D. G. E. Hall, *A History of Southeast Asia* (New York: Macmillan, 1955), p. 314.

journey.⁹ But apart from playing into the hands of a colonial power, the Sultan's move did serve to acknowledge the existence of a bond between Java and the Islamic heartland which was based on a common religion but which had wider cultural and political implications. To quote Johns, "the Islamic tradition represented the world of intellectual life and culture outside of Java; and Arabic was as well-known by those who participated in this world as Dutch was among their equivalents two centuries later."¹⁰ It was therefore only natural that, after being exposed to the strength of the European powers, the Sultan would seek to strengthen his own hand by formally requesting an Islamic title not from the Ottoman Sultan, but from the ruler of Mecca.

Compared with the seventeenth century, the "umat" for Javanese Muslims at the end of the nineteenth century has become much narrower. Javanese Muslims no longer define themselves as Muslims in relation to Islamic culture writ large, but in relation to those who speak Malay--the community known in Mecca as the Jawah. One important factor in this change is that, with control of Indian Ocean trade passing from Arabs and Arabic-speakers to Europeans, Arabic was transformed into a purely religious language for most Javanese, and their interaction with other Muslims, even in Mecca, was largely restricted to those who spoke Malay.

In some ways the Mecca phenomenon was ironic, because it was precisely the increase in the numbers of people from the Indies making the pilgrimage that led to a contraction of the relevant "umat," even within the holy city itself. The fluent Arabic speakers, the longtime residents, and the well-established *imam* of Malay and Indies origin found themselves interacting increasingly with fellow-Malay speakers. The reason was not just that there were more Malays to speak to, thanks to improvements in transportation that made the journey to Mecca safer, shorter, and perhaps less costly. It was also because of the employment opportunities that the increased numbers made possible, such as guiding pilgrims, lodging and feeding them, and teaching those who wished to prolong their stay beyond the pilgrimage season. For all of these tasks, a knowledge of Malay was essential. The economic links binding Malay speakers to one another operated not only within Mecca, but between Mecca and the Indies as well. There was a good market in the archipelago for products from the Middle East, and one of the most important of these was books.

> This phenomenon [the reliance of the Indies Muslims on "spiritual nourishment" from Mecca] can be discerned in the hand-books used in teaching in Moslim schools in Java, Sumatra, and Borneo. The latest literary publications in Mekka soon drive out the teaching material brought formerly from Mekka, and among the merchandise exported out of Mekka which finds a ready market, figure above all, printed books, the authors of which are either Jâwah settled in Mekka or Mekkan professors specially esteemed by Jâwah.¹¹

---

9. H. J. DeGraaf, "Southeast Asian Islam in the Eighteenth Century," *Cambridge History of Islam* (Cambridge: Cambridge University Press, 1971), p. 149.

10. Johns, "Islam in Southeast Asia," p. 48.

11. C. Snouck Hurgronje, *Mekka in the Latter Half of the 19th Century* (Leyden: Brill, 1931), p. 258.

If in the "capital" of the Islamic world, the "umat" for the Javanese had come to be defined primarily in terms of language and place of origin, the same was true on Java, but for very different reasons. For one thing, the "umat" on Java no longer embraced the political elite. The Dutch colonial state had given an administrative unity to the islands that once composed a host of individual states and sultanates, and political and Islamic authority were now completely separate; the Dutch governor-general did not need to send an emissary to Mecca to legitimate his position. The Dutch refusal to accord Islam even a symbolic place in the colonial government was reflected in the deterioration of relations between the religious elite and the indigenous Javanese political elite through whom the Dutch ruled. Fear of organized Islam made colonial authorities unwilling to give even the symbols of traditional power to aristocrats or *priyayi* with strongly Muslim sympathies. A kind of selection process was thus at work. The religious elite, for its part, distrusted the association of the priyayi with the Christian authorities, but they themselves had no independent channel of communication to the Dutch.[12] The priyayi, as their political authority was sapped, devoted more and more of their time to the refinement of arts and language, developing the artificial, flowery, and excessively Sanskritized high-status *krama inggil* and turning to pre-Islamic themes for dance and drama.[13] The gap between political and religious elites thus increased as neoclassical Javanese culture flourished. The gap was widened even further by the emergence of a competing school system to that of the traditional religious teachers, the *kyai*, in their rural *pesantren*. Until the appearance of Dutch schools designed to train some of the aristocracy for civil service careers, Javanese princes and sons of Muslim traders alike had been sent to pesantren, and if the education they received more resembled initiation into mystic secrets than instruction in Islamic legal principles, its authenticity as *Islamic* education was not questioned by either group. By drawing the priyayi sons out of the pesantren, the Dutch schools removed one important cultural link between *santri* and priyayi.

Developments in the Islamic world also served to separate the two. It may have been their consciousness of the broader umat and the fact that they no longer had ties to the political center on Java, that led Javanese Muslims to look toward Mecca, and to a lesser degree the Ottoman Empire as their center. Most Javanese may not have had a clear idea of where "Stamboul" was, but they knew it mattered, and the Jawah in Mecca followed the course of the Russo-Turkish war of 1877-78 with interest as an example of the conflict between Christianity and Islam.[14] Javanese identification with the Islamic side of the struggle undoubtedly fueled and was fueled by their dislike of the Dutch and their contempt for the Javanese aristocrats through whom the Dutch ruled.

In the differences that emerged in cultural orientation and education between the priyayi and the self-conscious Muslim in Java lie the beginnings of the distinction that exists to this day between "practicing" and "nominal" Muslims, with the political elite falling in the latter category. It is important to recall that this division, which has led those for whom Islam is the organizing principle of daily life to consider themselves a beleaguered and politically

---

12. Heather Sutherland, *The Making of a Bureaucratic Elite* (Singapore: Heinemann Books, 1982), p. 29.

13. Benedict R. O'G. Anderson, "Sembah-Sumpah" (unpublished paper, 1981).

14. Snouck Hurgronje, *Mekka*, p. 260.

impotent minority amidst a majority of nominally Muslim *abangan*, is of relatively recent vintage. It was Dutch policy that effectively removed the local political elite from membership in the relevant "umat"; indeed, to a large extent, it was thanks to the Dutch that one could define oneself as a Muslim in opposition to the aristocracy and bureaucracy. There was nothing inherent in the culture of the Indies that made this outcome inevitable.

One more point is worth making here before taking another historical leap. It was in the latter part of the nineteenth and early part of the twentieth centuries that Islamic reformist ideas from Cairo, inspired by the teachings of Mohammed Abduh and Rashid Rida began reaching the Indies. In reading accounts of Indonesian Islam, it often seems as though this reformism represented the first real intellectual development to reach the island from the Middle East. Nothing could be further from the truth. Virtually every major theological or doctrinal debate in the Islamic heartland had an effect on Islamic thinking and scholarship in the Indies through the Jawah who studied in Mecca. One reformist wave which had a profound impact particularly on Java, Sumatra, and the southern part of Kalimantan was the Naqshbandi reform movement which reached the Indies in the late nineteenth century and affected almost every Sufi *tarekat*.[15] One of the reasons Abduh-inspired reformism became such a force in the islands was that the Dutch policy toward the priyayi prevented them from establishing a working relationship with it, as they had with earlier such waves. The *modus vivendi* of customary practice and Islam, of religious and secular authority, had been permanently altered.

During the first decades of the twentieth century, the "umat" for the Javanese became increasingly coterminous with the Dutch East Indies. If in Cairo or Mecca where many Southeast Asian Muslims studied, the important community was still one's fellow Malay speakers, in the Dutch East Indies it was one's fellow Indonesians. For a brief period, even the antagonism between religious and political elites was subsumed by opposition to the Christian Dutch. As the country's first mass-based nationalist organization, Sarekat Islam, demonstrated quite clearly, "native" and "Muslim" were synonymous, in the same way as were "Dutch" and "Christian" or even "Chinese" and "Confucian."

If the "umat" for the first time had geographic boundaries reflecting the extent of Dutch control, there were conflicting claims to represent that "umat" which were gradually institutionalized into organizations with branches throughout the Indies: Muhammadiyah, established in 1913 representing reformism; and the Nahdatul Ulama, set up thirteen years later, representing traditional orthodoxy.

The Muhammadiyah organization was founded by Kyai Achmad Dachlan, a religious official of the royal court in Yogyakarta, in part to provide modern schooling for children of relatively well-to-do Muslims who were not allowed to attend Dutch schools or those set up at the court. He had been to Cairo and was particularly taken with those aspects of reformist thinking which encouraged establishment of a modern educational system. The schools set up by Muhammadiyah were popular, particularly in urban areas, and spread rapidly--and with them, reformist ideology.

---

15. Hamid Algar, "The Naqshbandi Order: A Preliminary Survey of Its History and Significance," *Studia Islamica* 44 (1976): 123-52.

Reformism, among other things, denied the validity of the principle of *taqlid*, in essence relying on recognized authority for interpretation of the Quran and *hadith*. The Javanese kyai were threatened, in part because the new schools competed with the pesantren, in part because a denial of taqlid denied the kyai's own legitimacy as interpreter of the Shafi'ite *mazhab*, and in part because some traditional practices of the rural kyai were deemed illegal innovations by Muhammadiyah religious leaders. Fierce doctrinal debates raged for over a decade, exacerbated by the uncertainty of the fate of traditional religious shrines in Mecca and Medina under the new Saudi stewardship.

The concern caused in kyai circles by the Saudi takeover reflected apprehension not only over the puritanical bent of the Wahabi-influenced Saudis, but over a possible change in the role of Mecca vis-à-vis the "umat." The Sherifian dynasty had, after all, been an unbroken chain since the days of Mohammed and had enjoyed an autonomous vassal relationship with successive Islamic empires, most recently with the Ottomans. World War I threw the established Islamic order into a state of total confusion; first, the Sherif of Mecca cooperated with the infidel British against the Muslim Turks, and in the aftermath of the war, not only was the Sherif himself overthrown by Ibn Saud, an unknown quantity without the backing of empire, but the Kemalists in Turkey abolished the caliphate. As a result, the umat was probably less of a political reality than at any time since Mohammed. Saudi Arabia and Turkey were separate states, neither of which could make any pretense at domination of the Islamic world. The days of seeking political legitimacy from the rulers of Mecca were not quite over, as competition between Muhammadiyah and the Nahdatul Ulama for the right to represent Indonesia at a world Islamic congress called by Ibn Saud in 1926 attested, but it soon became clear that the legitimacy of the leaders of the local "umat" would henceforth have to be established first within the local political setting.

At this stage, the following characteristics of the Javanese "umat" may be noted:

--It was increasingly extending beyond a narrow religious elite, thanks to increased literacy, publications available in the vernacular, improved transportation, and the focus on education of the two most prominent Muslim socioreligious organizations.

--Its membership was bounded by the borders of Dutch control. This was clear in the race of both Muhammadiyah and NU to open branch offices in every district of the country, and also in the fact that membership was limited, in fact if not by regulation, to Indonesian Muslims. No Thais or Malayans were invited, a significant, if obvious, fact given the importance of the Jawah community.

--It had, at this stage, neither political power nor political aspirations; the center of the "umat" was still, symbolically, Mecca, though the role of Mecca in relation to local Muslim communities was permanently altered.

By the 1950s, the character of the "umat" had changed once more. The Japanese occupation and the years of revolution had muted the differences between the reformists and traditionalists. On Java the Japanese had drawn all Muslim organizations together into a federation called Masjumi and used Muslim leaders from NU and Muhammadiyah to try to mobilize grassroots support for the Japanese war effort. Prominent Muslims had been appointed to positions of political prominence, and thus had been consciously set up as alternatives to the "secular nationalists," led by Sukarno. The Japanese also had given military training to Muslim leaders on Java and established a separate militia under Masjumi. During the revolution, both secular and religious nationalists had been fighting for the same objective, but the autonomous Muslim militias had made it possible to define oneself as a Muslim by fighting there, rather than in the regular army or one of the secular *lasykar*.

Two years after the declaration of independence in 1945, the fragile unity of the "umat" was initially shattered when the Partai Sarekat Islam Indonesia (PSII) split off from the Masjumi. The attempt to preserve a single Muslim party and maintain the degree of cooperation that had existed during the occupation and early war years had thus broken down. In 1952 the NU also seceded to form its own independent party. By the mid-fifties there were different Muslim parties representing the interests of West Sumatra, West Java, East Java, and South Sulawesi and representing the ideological spectrum from Muslim "socialists" to Javanese traditionalists. The differences were highlighted by reactions to the establishment of the Revolutionary Government of the Republic of Indonesia (PRRI) in February 1958 in Padang, West Sumatra, wherein a number of Masjumi members held leading positions. Although not exclusively religious in orientation, the PRRI government developed a distinctly Islamic cast. And the fact that a nationwide organization like the Nahdatul Ulama--in contrast to the Masjumi--made no effort to defend the PRRI, was an indication of how narrow the conception of "umat" had become.

But if regional and political differences had divided the Indonesian "umat," those differences were perpetuated by the fact that there has never been an Islamic institution that could preserve the unity of the "umat" in the absence of an external threat. The islands were never unified under a single Muslim ruler. There is no major Islamic urban center or seat of learning comparable to al-Azhar, Fez, or Aliqarh. There was never an Islamic bureaucratic hierarchy culminating in a single figure able to issue fatwa in the name of Islam (the Shafi'i Mufti in Mecca was flooded with requests for decisions from the Jawah throughout the late nineteenth and early twentieth centuries); the Majelis Ulama is a New Order innovation, though organizations with a similar structure but much less influence had existed under Sukarno. While the absence of such an institutional framework has made Islam less susceptible to government control, it has also increased the likelihood that the "umat" will divide along regional and ideological fault lines.

Because of the way in which confessional lines determined allegiance to political parties in the so-called *aliran* system of the 1950s, membership in a Muslim party served to define one as a practicing Muslim. In a sense, voting for a Muslim party in 1955 was a widely accepted indication of one's piety. It is curious that the depth of one's commitment to a religion could be measured by such a secular mechanism as a national election. Even today, when mention is made of devout Muslims as a minority amidst a more lax majority, the usual reference point is the 1955 elections, the only free national elections Indonesia has ever had, where Muslim parties got approximately 40 percent of the vote. We have no other measure, and no way of indicating whether this relative percentage has changed in the last thirty years.

The "Umat" Today and the Decline of the Nahdatul Ulama

The old Islamic organizations-cum-political parties today have lost their monopoly on representation of Muslim interests, and the leading Muslim activists of the 1980s are distinguished as much by their lack of organizational affiliation as by their identification with Muslims beyond Indonesia's borders. The expansion of the "umat" in Indonesia today can be explained by the same two factors that determined its contraction in earlier periods--changing local political and economic conditions, and a changing international Islamic environment. At the national level, the power of the central government has increased under the New Order, as tolerance for independent political organizations has decreased. The strength of rural Javanese landlords, mainstay of the Nahdatul Ulama, has declined as government economic institutions have made themselves felt at the village level, and as major cash crops such as sugar, tobacco, coffee, and pineapples are increasingly controlled by bureaucratic and military elites rather than by Muslim landlords. At the same time, changes in the international Islamic environment have made it increasingly possible for the state, rather than private Islamic organizations, to represent Islamic interests. Such changes have also resulted in the emergence of different models of the Islamic state, each competing for world recognition, and different centers of Islamic thought, each attracting adherents from around the globe. Mecca is still the holiest city of Islam but in terms of Islamic education, ideology, and political development, there are several aspiring "capitals" for the umat. A third important change in the international Islamic environment has been a shift in the class base of activist Islam from traditional conservative elites to the urban lower middle class.

The recent history of the Nahdatul Ulama demonstrates the effect of all of these changes. Founded in 1926 as the *wadah* for traditionalist Javanese Islam in opposition to Abduh-influenced Muslim reformism, NU had reached its zenith by the late 1960s. Throughout the Sukarno years, it had been an ally of the nationalist party, the PNI, and represented a more amenable form of organized Islam than the more outspoken Masjumi, a reformist party with great strength in the islands outside Java. In return for its willingness to support the government, NU gained control over both the Ministry of Religion and the vast and lucrative haj operations. It also secured a kind of "benign neglect" for the pesantren-based kyai who, as the party's senior authorities, would thus be free from government harassment. NU's active role in the crackdown and massacres of suspected Communists in 1965-66 had led it to expect more rewards from Sukarno's successor than it received, and its relatively strong showing in the 1971 election (18.9 percent of the vote) led some to conclude that its reputation as a party led by opportunists needed some revision.[16]

The results of the election and the campaign that preceded it need to be put in perspective, however, for NU's high profile during the campaign and its vote-getting ability did not represent a break with its cautious past. Any election was a chance to demonstrate the power of Islam, and if not as violent, perhaps, as 1971, the 1955 elections had been just as vocal and heated. In each case, the virulence of the campaign resulted not so much from specific grievances or from the desire to control parliamentary seats or even patronage sources, but from the determination to prove the strength of Islam and Islamic leaders in a government-sanctioned competition.

The grievances of the NU leadership were genuine, as was the bitterness caused by the patently manipulated results, but the willingness to engage in frequent and often harsh criticism of New Order policies that characterized

---

16. Ken Ward, *The 1971 Election in Indonesia: An East Java Case Study* (Clayton, Vic.: Monash Papers on Southeast Asia, No. 2, 1974).

the NU campaign in 1971 dissipated soon after the election. In 1973, the NU leadership agreed to follow Suharto's directive on party simplification and merge with three other parties to form the Partai Persatuan Pembangunan (PPP) or United Development Party, a move made more palatable by the fact that NU was by far the strongest element within the new party. Its three partners were Parmusi, Perti, and the PSII.

Parmusi (Parti Muslimin Indonesia) was the accommodationist rump of the old Masjumi party which had been banned in 1960 for its role in the regional separatist movements. When its leaders pressed for reinstitution of the party prior to the 1971 elections, the government agreed on the condition that none of the old Masjumi leaders hold official posts in the new party. An "acceptable" leadership was finally approved in 1968, and two years later, Jaelani or "Johni" Naro took control of the party in an internal but government-backed "coup." The result was that Parmusi no longer represented any readily identifiable constituency. Such Masjumi elder statesmen as Mohammed Natsir and Mohammed Roem, who still commanded widespread respect and affection, expressed contempt for Naro whom they and many others regarded as a government lackey. And the Muhammadiyah, a leading organizational member of the old Masjumi, specifically rejected Parmusi's claim to be the heir to their old party. Parmusi received 24 parliamentary seats in the 1971 election.

Perti (Persatuan Tarbiah Islamiyah) was a small Sumatra-based party, ideologically akin to NU, but even stricter than NU in its reliance on the Shafi'i school of orthodox Islamic law. Perti had received 24 seats in the 1971 election.

Partai Sarekat Islam Indonesia (PSII) was strongest in Central and West Java. It was the direct descendant of Sarekat Islam, the first mass-based nationalist organization. The leader of PSII was the son of the charismatic founder of Sarekat Islam, Cokroaminoto, but by 1973, the party was beset by a bitter split in the leadership to the point that, when the merger with the other parties was under discussion, it was difficult to determine who in fact represented PSII. In 1971, the party won ten seats in the national Parliament.

Their common Islamic base in no way smoothed over the differences in geographical attachment, doctrine, constituencies, or personal rivalries among the PPP partners, nor did the four *unsur* (elements) lose their individual identities when subsumed in the new party. An arrangement whereby in every subsequent election, each of the four was allotted a percentage of PPP seats based on their performance in the 1971 elections was one factor reinforcing their separateness. NU, with 61 percent of the seats, could thus always overrule the combined strength of the other three, a fact which Parmusi members particularly resented.

The leadership of PPP also reflected a careful effort to accommodate the interests of the different unsur, rather than appeal to the rank and file over unsur divisions. The head, *ketua umum*, of the party was Parmusi leader Johni Naro. Idham Chalid, ketua umum of NU, was PPP president, and Kyai Masykur of NU headed the party's executive council. Despite its ability to act collectively on legislative issues and provide enough of an independent opposition to appeal to critics of the government who were not devout Muslims, PPP was in fact a fragile coalition.

Its fragility was nowhere so clearly demonstrated as in the efforts to construct a candidate list for the 1982 elections which would take the interests of both Parmusi (now called MI to indicate it was no longer an independent party) and NU into account. After several fruitless meetings at which no agreement was reached, Naro on October 27, 1981 took to the National Election Board a list from which were excluded most of the well-known NU activists and government critics, most notably Yusuf Hasyim and Saifuddin Zuhri. Not only were key NU people dropped, but Naro had unilaterally reallocated seats so that NU no longer held an absolute majority. With seven seats eliminated from NU's portion and given to MI, MI and the three smaller unsur combined now had one more seat than NU. The list was immediately accepted by Amir Machmud, chairman of the Board, and NU just as immediately cried foul and threatened to withdraw from PPP.

If, as many suspected, Naro was acting on instructions from above, what were the motives behind the manipulation? In the short run, it was a way, admittedly heavy-handed, of settling a seemingly irreconcilable dispute between MI and NU over names on the candidate list—a dispute that had reduced the already low credibility of the elections. At least with one list, *any* list, the election machinery could crank ahead; without one, it ground to a halt. At the same time, the move weakened PPP's credibility as a party representing both a unified umat and an independent opposition. It was the latter that more immediately concerned the government. The weakness would redound to the benefit of Golkar in 1982, particularly in Jakarta, by reducing the possibility of crossover votes for PPP by disenchanted urban voters who had given PPP a victory in the capital in 1977. The elimination of the most vocal, and, in government eyes, most obstreperous NU leaders was probably a short-term goal in itself.

There were longer-term objectives as well. Naro's action would inevitably intensify the MI-NU rivalry which would lead PPP to go the way of PDI, a party that had been destroyed by internal factionalism one year earlier. This would be consistent with the Suharto government's policy of muzzling all sources of independent political opinion without eliminating the semblance of parliamentary democracy. The president had specifically rejected the idea of a single-party system; what he wanted was a system where all three parties were supportive, obedient, and pliable. Neither PPP nor PDI had been willing to play the game properly despite the cooptation of key leaders. The destruction of the parties by decree would have cost the state legitimacy. Destruction through internal squabbling, carefully orchestrated, would reflect less on the government than on the party leadership.

Naro's backers also undoubtedly realized that the move would ultimately divide NU itself, with the accommodationist recipients of government largesse grudgingly accepting the *fait accompli* and the dispossessed activists clamoring for retaliation. NU, arguably the last mass-based organization in the country with political aspirations, was worrisome, all the more so because its refusal to conform to the New Order ideals of political behavior, so clearly demonstrated in 1971, still showed few signs of weakening. NU had staged a walk-out on a parliamentary debate over Pancasila education in 1978 and in a national conference in 1981, its kyai had explicitly refused to endorse Suharto for a third term or confer on him the title of "Father of Development." It had also protested as unconstitutional a regulation prohibiting civil servants from belonging to political parties. Such defiance was enough to target the organization for reprisal. An internal split within NU would greatly reduce the possibility of any united action from Indonesia's largest Muslim organization.

Government manipulation was only part of the reason for the disorder in NU, however. The preelection moves to discredit PPP and its major component could only have been successful if NU itself was already weak. And it was symptomatic of the changes confronting the organization that, in 1981, NU had no national leaders with the will and authority to mobilize the rank and file. The two top positions in the organization were held by a singularly uncharismatic political novice, Kyai Ali Masyum, and a political hack close to the government, Idham Chalid. It was Kyai Masyum who held the more influential post in the NU's organizational structure.

NU is divided into two major bodies, the legislative council or *syuriyah* consisting of religious scholars or kyai, and the *tanfidziyah* or executive branch, consisting of politicians and religiously trained laymen who handle the day-to-day affairs. It is the head of the syuriyah, the *rais aam*, who wields ultimate authority, a recognition in theory of his outstanding personal qualities and his capacity to determine the legality of any issue according to Islamic law. The syuriyah has veto power over decisions made by the tanfidziyah.

In April 1980, the old rais aam died at the age of 95. This was Bisri Syamsuri, the kyai of Pesantren Denanyar in Jombang and the last of the original founders of NU. He was also the last of a Jombang dynasty that had produced the first two rais aam, Hasyim Asyari and Wahab Chasbullah, and the last person who could mobilize the organization nationally. His death came at a low point in NU fortunes--the Ministry of Religion had passed out of NU hands, "Golkarization" was rapidly depleting the ranks of educated NU members, pesantren enrollment was on the decline, and the head of all Sufi tarekat had just defected to Golkar, raising the spectre of thousands of his followers doing likewise.[17] If ever a strong leader was needed, this was the time, yet the position of rais aam remained vacant for a year-and-a-half, an indication of the difficulty in finding a suitable successor.

There seemed to be no kyai who could fulfill the unwritten qualifications to lead NU, someone who appealed to both East and Central Java, directed an influential pesantren, commanded respect as a religious scholar, and was relatively uncorrupt. Ky. Machrus Ali of Kediri was popular but too close to Gudang Garam, the clove cigarette company, and reputed to be too fond of the good life. Ky. Asad of Situbondo was an East Javanese favorite son, but had no desire to take on a prominent position. After a long and fruitless search, a conference of leading kyai was called in Kaliurang, Yogyakarta, in October 1981, specifically to choose a new rais. Largely through the efforts of the progressive wing of the party headed by Abdurrachman Wahid, a choice was finally

---

17. Since 1957, there has been a federation of "orthodox" *tarekat* orders in Indonesia, the Jamiyyah Ahli Thoriqoh Mu'tabarah (Association of Members of Respected Tarekat Orders). In 1975, Kyai Musta'in Romly of Jombang, son of one of Java's most respected Sufi teachers and son-in-law of the *rais aam* of the Nahdatul Ulama, Wahab Chasbullah, was elected chairman of that body, thus becoming the head of all Naqshbandi-Qadiriyyah orders in Indonesia. Kyai Musta'in, however, was wooed by influential members of the Suharto government and, in return for ten hectares of land and funds to improve his Islamic university in Jombang, Dar al-Ulum, he campaigned for Golkar in the 1977 elections. The blow to NU was especially great because of the tradition of absolute obedience of Sufi followers to their leader--which meant that thousands of Kyai Musta'in's followers also defected to Golkar. NU was forced in 1979 to change the name of the Sufi federation by adding "Nahdliyyin" on the end, meaning NU orders as opposed to those in Golkar. See Zam Dhofier, "The Pesantren Tradition" (PhD dissertation, Australian National University, 1980), pp. 269-86.

made—Ky. Ali Masyum of Krapyak, the large and influential pesantren near Yogyakarta, known both for its Sufi tarekat and its innovative curriculum. Relatively young, not particularly well-known nationally, inexperienced politically, lacking any particular charismatic traits or oratorical ability, Ky. Ali was chosen because he was thought to be innovative and open-minded. He was the technocrat of kyai, someone who could lead NU in new directions along the lines of the development plan worked out at the party congress in Semarang in 1979.

If the new rais could not lead the "umat" because of inexperience and limited exposure, the tanfidziyah head, Idham Chalid, whose experience and exposure were second to none, was not about to lead the "umat" into active opposition or bite the hand that had fed him such delicacies as Kalimantan timber concessions. Idham had held his position in NU since 1956 and was reelected at the Semarang congress. The only other contender for the post in 1979 was Ahmad Syaichu, a hardline, popular, if arrogant, ex-speaker of Parliament, who was known as a sworn enemy of Suharto and a close friend of General Nasution. Syaichu had no chance. Not only were millions of rupiah channeled into the party by the government to bring pro-Idham supporters in from the provinces, but there were stories of Opsus (Special Operations) men putting pressure on delegates in hotel hallways to vote for Idham.[18] He was duly reelected, and his men filled all but two of the key positions in the tanfidziyah. Anti-Idham forces were powerless to halt the pro-Idham steamroller, well-financed and government-backed as it was, and this, too, was an indication of change in the party. The independence and strength of NU had always lain not in Jakarta but in the provincial, pesantren-influenced areas of East and Central Java and Madura. This was partly due to the presence of the most influential kyai in these areas and also to the mass mobilization efforts of the later Sukarno years which depended on grassroots support. Under the New Order, NU, like all other political organizations, had grown much more centralized, much more dependent on Jakarta for financing, and hence much more vulnerable to manipulation from the center. The 1979 election of Idham was evidence of this trend, as to a lesser extent was the election of Ky. Ali Masyum in 1981, although the first case involved government interference and the second, orchestration from within the party itself. The key decisions were clearly being made in Jakarta, and dissatisfaction at the provincial level was muted.

The question of the candidate list highlighted these weaknesses of party leadership and the fissures within party ranks. The immediate public reaction of the NU leadership to the list presented by Naro in October 1981 was one of outrage, which took formal expression in a protest letter sent to the Election Board on November 6, following a full meeting of the NU officials (PBNU) at Ky. Masykur's house in Menteng on November 5. Even at this stage, many suspected Idham's complicity in the candidate list maneuvering. Not only was he known to have spoken with Naro and sent a list of his protégés to MI leaders before October 27, but the one thing that all of the dropped candidates had in common was their enmity toward Idham Chalid. Nevertheless Idham did sign the protest letter.

At the November 5 meeting, four options had been put forward and discussed by the party leadership. The first "minimalist" position was to have Idham

---

18. The same phenomenon had occurred in 1971 when Idham was elected *ketua umum* at the NU congress. See *Harian Abadi*, December 24 and 28, 1971; also *Harian Kami*, December 27, 1971.

and Ky. Masykur resign from their positions in PPP as a token protest; the second "minimalist plus" was to have them resign and, in addition, to require members of the government board of NU to choose between their NU positions and representing PPP; the third, "maximal minus" was to put pressure of an undisclosed nature directly on Naro; and the fourth "maximal" position was to withdraw from PPP entirely.

Option two was tentatively adopted, although no resignations were announced and no specific action taken. Over the next few months, as positions crystallized, four distinct groups emerged within NU. The first group included Idham Chalid and his associates. Probably involved in the original candidate list manipulation, Idham could gain nothing from resigning, nor from having NU withdraw from PPP in accordance with the second option. His position within the organization depended on his control of patronage from government sources, yet the flow of that patronage depended on his ability to "deliver" NU. Both he and the men around him--Nuddin Lubis, Chalid Mawardi, Zamroni, Ky. Anwar Musaddad, Ky. Ali Yafie, and others--survived because of their skill at maneuvering within the Jakarta elite, and none had large personal followings or geographically based constituencies. This group presented a threefold argument for remaining in PPP: first, without PPP, there would be no forum for channeling the political aspirations of the people; second, the party had always been involved in politics and did not have the experience or will to shift suddenly and devote itself wholly to social and educational activities; and, third, democracy would suffer a setback.

The second group were the "progressives"--Abdurrachman Wahid, Dr. Fahmi Saifuddin (a public health official and son of Saifuddin Zuhri), and Ky. Sahal Mahfudz and other kyai associated with a pesantren-based community development program run by a liberal Muslim social science research organization commonly referred to by its Indonesian acronym, LP3ES. Believing that traditional Islamic institutions were in danger of losing all relevance to modern Indonesia and that economic development was a widely accepted goal, founders of the LP3ES saw the pesantren as uniquely equipped to be the center of a community development effort because of the importance both of the kyai as a community leader and of the pesantren as an economic institution. They hoped to turn NU's rural base into a social movement resembling Muhammadiyah, and believed that, ultimately, it was more important for NU members to be managers of KUDs (rural cooperative societies) than representatives in Parliament. The "progressives," then, were on principle firmly committed to NU's withdrawal from politics and actually welcomed the Naro move as an excuse for getting out. They thought NU members should be released to choose whatever political party they wished, and, according to them, the only people who were determined to stay in PPP were those with formal positions in the government whose personal ambitions would be thwarted by an NU withdrawal. If such a withdrawal were actually to take place, the "progressives" argued, not only would the government cease to be suspicious of NU activities and NU civil servants, but the organization would most likely grow, just as it did when NU withdrew from Masjumi in 1952. Despite this determination to withdraw from PPP, however, the "progressives" tended to favor accommodation with the government, for they realized that government funds were ultimately the only available source for the kind of socioeconomic development program based on Islamic ideals which they espoused. Members of this group tended to be young and urban-based, also without any particular constituency.

Third were the leading kyai of the syuriyah, septo- and octogenarians, not particularly fond of Idham, but cautious of any major political move.

Their caution stemmed in part from age and experience, but also in part from the fact that, as important informal leaders in their home areas, they were beneficiaries, if not dispensers, of government patronage, and would be unwilling to jeopardize this status unless a clear emergency arose. They tended to counsel against withdrawing from PPP. "Withdrawal is an atom bomb," Ky. Machrus of Kediri noted, "and you don't use an atom bomb on a family squabble."[19] The caution expressed by these kyai was consistent with their acknowledged role as a brake on headstrong politicians. It also may have reflected their sensitivity to provincial politics, where signs of displeasure in Jakarta could easily turn into repressive actions by local officials anxious to earn the approval of their superiors.

The final group were the provincial politicians who looked toward such outspoken opposition leaders as Yusuf Hasyim. They at once had the most to lose by NU's withdrawal from PPP and the best means at their disposal for fighting back. In the provinces, elective office was the reward for service to the organization; membership in the Parliament was a source of patronage and prestige and an avenue of social mobility. It was one thing for a national figure like Yusuf Haysim or Saifuddin Zuhri to be dropped from Naro's list; they remained national figures, and they had other occupations to which they could return. But a local politician dropped from the list lost the high visibility and glamor associated with a position in the capital, and the only other alternative was a much less satisfying position in the provincial or kabupaten DPR. Furthermore, the provincial politicians too had personal constituencies and clients who looked to them for favors and assistance; their local patronage role would be eliminated without an elective position. Given the stakes involved in the Naro manipulations, the local politicians wanted fast and immediate retaliatory action, and they were much better equipped to take it, in part because of their control over the rank and file. Jakarta's actions were limited by the realities of what a huge mass organization could hope to achieve, as the four options outlined at the November 5 meeting indicated. The organization, as an organization, could certainly demand that its top two leaders resign and expect the demand to be obeyed. It was quite another thing to order all candidates to withdraw from active candidacy, knowing that many would put personal aspirations above party interests. An instruction from the center to local leaders had little chance of success unless it conformed with the latter's own inclinations.

The difference in center-periphery interpretations of events was a long-standing division in NU. It had been the *daerah* which protested most vociferously against the Jakarta leadership's acceptance of Sukarno's NASAKOM (nationalism/religion/communism) formulation in the 1960s and against the merger with PPP in 1973. And this time, it was most vocal in its calls for the NU to withdraw from PPP (*after* the elections), to boycott the elections, and for firm disciplinary action to be taken against Naro. But these provincial politicians shared no real common interests with the other group that advocated withdrawal, the "progressives." The "progressives" wanted to get out of politics on principle; the local politicians wanted greater political independence. For the "progressives" withdrawing from PPP was an end in itself; for the politicians, it was a way of retaliating against Naro and undermining his claims to leadership.

Thus there were a number of cross-cutting divisions. On the issue of whether or not to withdraw from PPP, there was a tactical alliance between

---

19. Interview, January 1982.

the "progressives" and the local politicians. On whether or not to get out of politics, the center and the local politicians had more in common--both being determined to stay involved in formal party politics--while the "progressives" and rural kyai would each have been happier to get out. With regard to the priorities of the organization as a whole, the natural alliance was, on the one hand, between the kyai and the local politicians, both of whom had clear personal and geographical constituencies, and, on the other, between the "progressives" and the collaborationists at the center, both of whom from their respective perspectives saw the need for interaction with the government.

Traditionally, these divisions were surmounted symbolically in the person of the rais aam, someone with sufficient authority to appeal to kyai, Jakarta political hacks, and local politicians at once. In this case, the rais aam proved the weak link in the NU chain, and Ky. Ali wavered back and forth between the "progressives" and the Idham faction, eventually ending up as titular head of the anti-Idham bloc. PPP remained intact through the 1982 elections, with a slight drop in percentage of the vote from 1977. NU did not fare as well.

Shortly after the elections, the leading kyai met in Jakarta and demanded Idham's resignation. He agreed, only to retract his statement several weeks later, when he set up an alternative NU leadership composed of like-minded accommodationists.

But the elections were over, and Golkar had achieved its usual margin of victory. PPP was in precisely the position the government wanted, with most of the real opposition out of Parliament, and the legitimacy of the party, either as the voice of a united "umat" or as an independent opposition, virtually destroyed. Suharto had made his point about the undesirability of independent political organizations; but now he was faced with a division in NU that pitted the old pro-Idham group against all of the influential kyai of East Java. The division was symbolized by the scheduling of two meetings--one of the ulama, to be held December 18-21 at Situbondi, near Malang at Ky. Asad's pesantren, and one of the Idham group to be held in Jakarta on December 7-8.

The sites chosen for the meetings were telling. The choice of a pesantren for the first underscored both the desire of the NU leadership to "return NU to the pesantren" and their commitment to the principle that authority rested with the ulama, not with the laymen. But that was in some ways the least of the symbolism. No national conference of ulama had been held in a pesantren since Indonesian independence, in part because of the jealously guarded individualism and autonomy of the kyai. To meet in one pesantren would be to acknowledge the superiority of one kyai over another, and for over thirty years this had been studiously avoided. The meeting in Situbondo was thus a clear acknowledgment of Ky. Asad's leadership, and a snub to the ostensible rais aam, Ky. Ali Masyum.

With two such clearly defined camps, the government seemed to have three options: to side with Idham, to side with Ky. Asad, or to remain neutral. That it ultimately chose a fourth option says much about the current state of the "umat." That option was to try to unite both factions, but to have the newly unified organization also accept the primacy of Pancasila and thus the legitimacy of the regime.

Without the kyai, Idham was clearly of no use to the government. Having no personal constituency, he was no longer in a position to play the intermediary role he had thrived on for so many years. This was not to be a repeat of the Parmusi coup in 1968 where the government backed Naro, the Idham Chalid of his party. With the PPP safely tamed, political leadership was not an issue. Idham could not claim to represent Islamic interests in any way, and it was Islamic support that Suharto was seeking.

At the same time, the link to PPP was important, if only to demonstrate to outsiders that organized Islam did indeed have representation in Jakarta. To have spurned the Jakarta politicians completely would have been to acknowledge the complete artificiality of the party and would have sanctified the separation of kyai from any government-orchestrated political processes. While Suharto, therefore, made clear his preference for the Asad faction by allowing the Situbondo meeting to take place and withholding a permit for the Jakarta meeting, the pressures to reconcile were apparent.

If the prime immediate issue at Situbondo was the fate of the party, and more particularly its leadership, the second most important issue to be discussed was *azas tunggal*, the recognition of Pancasila as the sole basis for all mass organizations, including those like NU, which had given Islam that honor in their charters.

The issue was a divisive one, with most conservative kyai and provincial politicians vociferously opposed to accepting azas tunggal, and the "progressives" in favor, presumably following the same principles that led them to support NU's withdrawal from PPP--that it was the only way to keep the organization above suspicion.

Ultimately, NU justified its acceptance of azas tunggal by the formula, as stated by Achmad Siddiq of Jember, that Pancasila was a *falsafah*, a philosophy created by human beings, whereas Islam was a revelation. There was therefore no question of the two competing with each other. But this was an interesting formulation, because to orthodox Muslims since the Mutazilite heresy of the ninth century, "falsafah" has always represented a threat to faith. In one of the many pamphlets he wrote for NU youth groups, Saifuddin Zuhri wrote that Bacon, Galileo, Descartes, Spinoza, Newton, Locke, Berkeley, Hume, Montesquieu, Rousseau, Kant, Hegel, Hamilton, Comte, Darwin, Spencer, Marx, Nietzche, and Einstein, who "called themselves progressive thinkers," were actually trying to use their philosophies to displace religion.[20] Calling Pancasila a philosophy may have been a calculated ploy to win over resistant kyai by ensuring that their formulation of acceptance could also be interpreted as contempt.

Whether or not the decision to accept azas tunggal turns out to have been a wise one, it does demonstrate the extent to which intellectuals (defined as anyone with a graduate degree--of whom there are a growing number) are influential in the organization. The respect accorded them has been clear since the 1950s, when, after a largely futile attempt to woo them into the organization, the NU tried to create its own intelligentsia through the IAIN, the state Islamic universities which until 1972 were controlled by NU. Thus far the influence of the intellectuals in NU has had mixed results. Ky. Ali Masyum's selection as rais aam clearly backfired, leading some to question the intellectuals' understanding of the rank and file. There is also some danger that under a more "modern," outward-looking leadership, there will be little to distinguish NU from other independent or state-sponsored Muslim organizations.

---

20. Saifuddin Zuhri, *Menghidupkan Nilai-nilai Ahlussunnah wal Jam'ah dalam Praktek* (Jakarta: Pucuk Pimpinan IPNU, 1976).

The Nahdatul Ulama in a Changing Community

One result of the combination of governmental manipulation and internal factionalism described above is that the political center of the Nahdatul Ulama has become divorced from its mass base, and this in turn has affected the organization's ability to define the limits of the "umat" for its members. The ability to provide that definition depended in part on the members' perception of NU as a national organization with a center in the capital, Jakarta. Indeed, one of the features of the aliran system, and one which made it particularly potent in the immediate postindependence period, was that Jakarta was the hub of each "stream," so that the terms of reference were the same for each and participation in the national political system an objective more or less shared by each. For the purposes of defining the "umat," that perceived role was crucial. Now with the Jakarta-based leadership in disarray and with no obvious overlap between the religious community and the most relevant political community, the nation, NU can no longer provide an all-encompassing framework within which members can order their lives. It cannot even represent all Javanese Muslims who follow the practices that have come to be associated with NU. The songs and chants of the various NU *ormas* or mass organizations today have a rather anachronistic ring--witness this example from the NU young women's association, Fatayat:

> Ahlussunnah is the group, the Quran and hadith the guides,
> Consensus (*ijma'*) and analogy (*qiyas*) together, these are the ways of the *madhab*,
> The friends Fatayat and Ansor, we are the leaders of the nation
> We must be forthright, modest, examples for the rest,
> We pray with the *ushalli*, read the *talqin* when we die,
> After death the *tahlil*, all this is put into practice,
> We open meetings with prayers, ask God for mercy,
> Also to the one who intercedes, he who leads the entire *umat*,
> The [NU] symbol is surrounded by a rope, nine stars shining,
> The leaders of Fatayat know they must do good and prevent evil,
> The stars of NU are four and five, the organization of NU is the fortress of the state,
> We submit to Allah, the all-powerful, he who guides mankind,
> Our lord, our God, love us and guide us,
> In our religion, our daily lives and in the next world.

The song implies that all those who read the ushalli and talqin[21] are members of NU, but this is clearly no longer true, and, as the ranks of those who may be "NU in their hearts" but Golkar in their jobs and on their ballots increase, many are looking for membership in an Islamic community that extends beyond the confines of the organization. As a result, the "umat" is once again expanding.

---

21. *Ushalli* is the "short declaration of intent pronounced audibly or mentally immediately prior to prescribed religious ritual in which the performer states his intent to perform the act"; *talqin* is a "term used to denote an instruction given by a religious teacher and generally denoting instruction given to the deceased at graveside at the close of the burial service." Both are considered heretical innovations (*bid'a*) by reformist Muslims. Howard Federspiel, *Persatuan Islam: Islamic Reformism in Twentieth Century Indonesia* (Ithaca: Cornell Modern Indonesia Project, 1970), pp. 206, 210.

The relationship between the Nahdatul Ulama and the state has also affected the NU's ability to define the limits of the "umat." The last thirteen years have witnessed a major shift in control of both Islamic education and the haj from NU, which controlled the Ministry of Religious Affairs until 1971, to the government. Curriculum in state and private Islamic schools is now regulated by three government ministries, Muslim teacher-training schools are run by the government, and transfer between the secular and Islamic school systems is possible through government equivalency exams. Scholarships to the Middle East, over which NU once had substantial influence, are now channeled through the Ministry of Religion. *Zakat fitrah*, which once went to private religious organizations including NU, is now collected by local councils set up by the Ministry, which also controls the haj, a major source of income. There is an increasing frequency of *haji dinas*, or pilgrims who made the haj at state expense, to reinforce Muslim credentials of key government officials, reward individuals for loyalty to the government, or even perhaps dilute the import of the title, "Haji" by enabling such peculiar pilgrims as Javanese *dalang* to acquire it.

Much of the state's ability to play a key role in Islamic affairs comes from its control over resources. But another major factor has been the growth of an international Islamic bureaucracy in which the state can only participate qua state: the Islamic Conference and the Islamic Foreign Ministers Conference are two examples. Through its importance as an international economic actor and the influence of Saudi Arabia within it, OPEC, though not an Islamic organization, made identification with the Islamic world a matter of political expediency for members and buyers of OPEC oil alike. The existence of such international organizations has meant that contact between Saudi Arabia and Indonesia increasingly takes place between government officials, not members of private organizations as before. (Such contact is also a logical consequence of Mecca being a Saudi city rather than an autonomous political unit with its own ruler.)

The role of the state in propagating "official Islam" is acceptable to what seems to be an increasing number of urban professionals who see no particular conflict between Islam and government, who are more comfortable in Golkar than in the old Muslim organizations, and who are content to be pious within authorized limits. Simultaneous with the government's increasing role in Islamic affairs has been the increasing pressure it brings to bear on Muslim organizations, to weaken them institutionally, cajole or coerce their members into becoming inactive, or strengthen accommodationist elements within them. The developments within NU are a case in point.

As government civil servants of "nominal" Muslim background become increasingly involved in Islamic affairs, and as more members of the Indonesian "umat" are coopted or coerced into Golkar, no longer can identity as a pious Muslim be determined primarily by organizational affiliation. Leading kyai, who by birth, education, past political involvement, and philosophy are Nahdatul Ulama archetypes, now officially belong to Golkar, while leading officials of the PPP seem more devoted to the pursuit of official approval than the defense and propagation of Islam.

As their decreasing political significance has hastened the decline of the old national Muslim organizations, so has demographic change. A whole generation has now grown up with no direct knowledge of the process by which their parents could say "I am a member of NU [or Muhammadiyah, or Masjumi]; therefore, I am a Muslim." They were not members of the Muslim militia during the Revolution, fighting a jihad against the Dutch; nor were they told by their kyai that it was forbidden (*haram*) to vote for anything but a Muslim party in a national election. The centers of Muslim thought in Indonesia today are not the organizations with a historical stake in the political process. They are small groups centered at schools, universities, and local mosques, often taking the form of Quranic study clubs. Precisely because they are not and cannot be mass organizations, their orientation is not limited by the geographic boundaries of the Indonesian state. Moreover, perhaps because organizational affiliation is no longer sufficient to establish Muslim identity, Indonesians are turning instead to external manifestations of personal piety--particularly, appropriate dress for women. Whether or not pious Muslim schoolgirls should be allowed to wear a headscarf as part of their school uniform, or to refuse to participate in sports where their arms and legs are revealed, are burning issues of debate in Jakarta. The "umat" is international for Indonesian Muslims today in a way it has not been for centuries. Ongoing processes--improvements in communication, migration to the Middle East, exchange visits of Iraqis and Bangladeshis, availability of Indonesian translations of the works of al-Maududi and Sayyid Qutub--have helped widen the "umat" that is most relevant to Javanese. There is a cross-fertilization currently taking place within Javanese Islam and between Javanese and their Muslim counterparts elsewhere. By focusing on the expansion and contraction of the community that gives meaning to Javanese Muslims, I have tried to break away from the image of Islam in Indonesia as something static. If a more dynamic view is taken, much of what appears to be the anomalies of Javanese Islam may turn out to have been only historical curiosities.

DEATH AND THE HISTORY OF ISLAM IN HIGHLAND ACEH

John R. Bowen

> "The trouble is that we talk of ritual very much as if it were a thing in itself.... In reality, the word merely describes chains of actions which ... are in a perpetual state of flux, so that, as we have seen, ritual may become the negation of ritual."
>
> —A. M. Hocart, "Ritual and Emotion"

Perhaps everywhere, death carries with it certain moral, aesthetic, and sociological imperatives: the soul must be cared for, the body must be buried, the social order must be reaffirmed.[1] Robert Hertz, in his essay on death of 1907, linked these three imperatives together in a strikingly effective model of death as passage, both spiritual and corporeal. Hertz drew primarily from Indonesian materials; Arnold Van Gennep, in an essay published two years later, incorporated Hertz' insights into a general theory of rites of passage.[2] Hertz' conception of death has been particularly fruitful for students of Indonesia and other, related societies, as illustrated by its central theoretical position in two recent studies of mortuary ritual.[3]

However, the form and meaning of mortuary rituals is not only a topic for anthropological analysis; it is also a subject for long-standing and hotly contested religious debates within Indonesia, between the proponents of Islamic modernism and those who would reaffirm the correctness of older, local ritual practices. My discussion will be of the susceptibility of death ritual to continuing reinterpretation by Indonesian Muslims, and the centrality of that

---

1. Earlier versions of this article were delivered at Cornell University on January 26, 1984, and Harvard University on March 20, 1984. I would like to thank those who attended the two seminars for their comments on the paper.

2. Robert Hertz, "A Contribution to the Study of the Collective Representation of Death," in *Death and the Right Hand*, trans. Rodney and Claudia Needham (Glencoe: The Free Press, 1960 [original in French, 1907]). Arnold Van Gennep, *The Rites of Passage* (Chicago: University of Chicago Press, 1960 [original in French, 1909]).

3. Maurice Bloch and Jonathan Parry, the editors of *Death and the Regeneration of Life* (Cambridge: Cambridge University Press, 1982), emphasize the recreation of society accomplished through mortuary ritual, while Richard Huntington and Peter Metcalf, in *Celebrations of Death* (Cambridge: Cambridge University Press, 1979), place more emphasis on the symbolics of the intermediary period and the reintegrating rituals. Both, however, make use of Hertz' analysis of mortuary ritual as a rite of passage.

reinterpretive activity to religious dialogue in twentieth-century Indonesia. In particular, I am interested in the nature of the reformist-modernist interpretive dialogue as it has taken place in the Gayo highlands of Aceh.[4] I will suggest, first, that the "traditional" form of Gayo death ritual is the outcome of an appropriation of Islamic signs in a local cultural framework, and, second, that modernist reinterpretations of ritual have been carried out in a similar way, by highlighting some, and downplaying other, elements of the ritual.

But there is a further question, to which I will return at the end of the paper. Is the Hertzian model of death as the soul's passage neutral to these interpretive debates? Are we analytically engaged in the local debate without knowing it? I will suggest that, in our theory if not in our ethnography, we have emphasized precisely those aspects of mortuary ritual which are highlighted by Islamic modernism, and that we have done so for reasons of our shared intellectual heritage.

Gayo Rituals of Death

There are about 200,000 Gayo now living in the homeland Gayo area, the high plateaus of three *kabupaten* in central Aceh. The largest town, Takengon, has a population of about 10,000, with another 30,000 Gayo in nearby villages. Those villagers who live near the town grow some wet rice and cash crops, primarily coffee and, very recently, the patchouli plant (Indonesian *nilam*) used for perfumes. Most Gayo, however, live in small villages of 300-1,000 inhabitants located in the valleys of the mountainous highlands, and cultivate a mixture of wet rice and small amounts of tobacco and coffee.

While the process of Islamization began on the north coast of Aceh in the late thirteenth century, the conversion of the Gayo probably took place between the fifteenth and seventeenth centuries.[5] I have suggested elsewhere that Sufi ideas of being and creation which were expounded in coastal Aceh in the sixteenth and seventeenth centuries have been preserved as the basis for speculative theology and ritual practice in the Gayo highlands.[6] Gayo religious teachers themselves studied either in traditional religious schools on the north coast or from Naqsyabandiah *tarekat* teachers near Meulaboh on the west coast. I have found no indication of reformist influences in Gayo Islam prior to the coming of modernism in the 1920s. Initial Dutch contacts, and the beginning of first-hand written accounts, date from 1900, and the area was brought under colonial rule by 1905. Over its long history in the region, Islam has played a major role in shaping Gayo political structure,

---

4. Fieldwork in the Gayo highlands was conducted between February 1978 and June 1980 with support from the Social Science Research Council, the National Science Foundation, and a Fulbright-Hays research grant, as well as administrative support from LIPI and sponsorship by the Universitas Syiah Kuala, Banda Aceh.

5. The only mention of the Gayo before the late nineteenth century is a short passage in the *Hikayat Raja-Raja Pasai* which states that the Gayo fled inland from the north coast in order to escape Islamization. I have examined the available early historical evidence in my Ph.D. dissertation, "The History and Structure of Gayo Society" (University of Chicago, 1984).

6. On this issue and the relation of the soul to the body, discussed below, see my "Islamic Transformations: From Sufi Poetry to Gayo Ritual," in *Religion in Indonesia*, ed. Rita Kipp and Susan Rodgers (forthcoming).

ritual form, and local history, and to be Gayo, as to be Malay or Acehnese, is to be Muslim.

Most Gayo villages have remained traditionalist or *kaum tue* (old group) over and against the modernists or *kaum mude* (young group). Gayo death ritual in these villages is intelligible in terms of both pan-Indonesian culture and Near Eastern Islam. I find that this intelligibility is most easily understood as a local historical process of selecting ritual elements from an Islamic repertoire which are compatible with Gayo ritual practice. The Gayo theory of the transformation of the soul at death, similar to ideas found elsewhere in Indonesia, is, today, signified with Islamic ritual signs.

Gayo speak of four souls which together account for different psychic states during life and death. Briefly, the *nyawa* secures life, and its departure at death is sudden and irreversible. Gayo conceive of death as occurring in the instant when the Angel of Death wrests the nyawa out of the body. After death it ceases to play a role in the individual's social being. The *semangat*, on the other hand, is a kind of passive transformer of external actions (particularly those of malevolent spirits) into states of well- (or ill-) being. It, too, only exists during life. The *ruh* roams in and out of the body during life, allowing the individual to dream of distant places. Some Gayo say that this soul becomes the fourth category, the *arwah*, at (or even forty days before) death; others say that the two souls are separate entities which can move about independently. In any case, it is the arwah alone which plays a role after the moment of death.[7]

Death as it is experienced in traditionalist Gayo villages establishes a new relationship of the invisible, inner, *batin* soul to its visible, outer, *lahir* counterpart. Whereas before the moment of death the soul was primarily associated with a human body, after death it becomes gradually associated with a gravesite, where it may be called upon to aid the descendants of the deceased or the community as a whole.[8] A series of mortuary rituals performed by the community serve to ease this process of transformation and to establish the new relationship between the living and the dead. Two key rituals in this series are the *telkin*, an instruction to the dead, and the *kenduri*, a series of ritual meals held at fixed intervals after death. Both are rites of communication with the soul of the deceased.

The Instruction to the Dead

All the souls leave the body at death, but the arwah hovers near the body as it is washed, wrapped in a white shroud, and carried to the place of burial. Burial takes place as soon as possible after death and is carried out by men

---

7. In Arabic, the word *arwah* is merely the plural of *ruh*. The notion that the two terms refer to separate classes of entities may have resulted from the use of the phrase "*alam arwah*," "world of the dead souls," or it may be part of the historical process of finding in Islam terms to correspond to pre-Islamic Gayo categories. In this case, the distinction between pre-mortem and post-mortem states of the soul has been mapped onto the grammatical distinction of singular and plural.

8. It is the gravesite and not the location of the buried body which marks the place of the post-mortem soul, since bodies of powerful individuals usually fly or walk away from their graves after death, leaving the soul behind, a point which I discussed in "Gayo Flying Graves," delivered to the Indonesian

for both men and women.[9] In the burial itself, as elsewhere in the Islamic world, the corpse is positioned on his or her right side and facing towards Mecca. A prayer is read aloud by the *imem*, and is joined in silently by all those present.

The primary concern after burial is to ease the "torment of the grave" (*sikse kubur*) experienced by the deceased's soul, to release it from early debts and spiritual sins, and deliver to it as much of the "pleasure of the grave" (*nikmat kubur*) as possible. The deceased is first reminded of the tenets of his religion. All those who witnessed the burial remain at the gravesite, while the imem takes hold of a stick inserted into the earth near the head of the grave and reads from a text called the telkin, from the Arabic *talqin*, "instruction."[10] As the imem reads the text, the arwah, which has remained near the head of body, listens, aided by the stick joining the imem to the grave. Near the beginning of the text is the passage "everything with a nyawa must die" which is read three times, slowly. Upon hearing these words, the arwah enters the body, allowing the person to awake from death and to feel the edge of his shroud, which, unlike all other clothes, has been left ragged. The deceased now realizes that he or she is dead.

The imem then continues, reading what one might call an Islamic catechism which reminds the deceased of the basic tenets of his religion: your God is Allah, your prophet is Muhammad, your book is the Qur'an, and so forth. This instruction is very useful to the deceased, as he will be visited momentarily by the two angels Mungkar and Nakir, who will pose these very questions to him, and beat him if he answers incorrectly.[11] The telkin is thus both a public demonstration of the continued sentient state of the dead person and a ritual of great instrumental importance in protecting him through his interrogations. As a sign of the possibility of communication with the deceased, the telkin acts as a ritual bridge to later exchanges and communications. As an instrumental ritual, it is seen by all those who are concerned about the deceased's welfare as a morally central part of the funeral.

Summer Studies Conference, Athens, Ohio, August 1983.

9. In a gender-based division of spiritual labor, the religious leadership of each village is invested in a single husband-wife pair, both referred to as the *imem* (although frequently reference to the wife is marked as imem banan, "female imem"). While the reading of prayer and performance of official public functions is the responsibility of the husband, the purifying and cooling of a bride and her mother, bathing of a newborn child, and the preparation of a female body for burial are responsibilities of the wife. Women never attend the burial.

10. The *telkin* is always in the form of an Arabic-language printed text, about three pages in length. Unlike all other important incantations or recitations it is never memorized, nor is it ever translated into Gayo as are most other lessons and instructions. It is thus as direct a conveying of the written word as is possible through speech, and serves as testimony to the power of written Arabic.

11. Similar *talqin* texts have been reported for elsewhere in the region. For a Malay text, see W. W. Skeat, *Malay Magic* (New York: Macmillan, 1900), pp. 406-7, and for Java, see Clifford Geertz, *The Religion of Java* (Glencoe: The Free Press, 1960), p. 71. Geertz reports that the text is sometimes read in Arabic and then in Javanese.

The practice of giving a preparatory instruction to the dead person appears in other parts of the Islamic world. Eduard Westermarck, whose description of Moroccan Islam is still probably the most compendious, remarks that, in parts of Morocco, Arabia, and Egypt, a slip of paper is put under the head of the deceased to remind him (or, I presume, although the matter is not clear, her) of the tenets of Islam, and that an oral instruction is frequently read after the burial as well.[12] But the practice is performed in a solitary fashion, and appears to be not very important. Indeed, whereas much of Westermarck's ethnography consists of the naming of customs, he fails to provide a name for the post-mortem instruction. Its importance in Gayo culture thus appears to be due to local, rather than pan-Islamic cultural imperatives.

Feasting and Intervals

Ritual meals (kenduri) are held on the first, third, seventh, and forty-fourth nights after the death.[13] These meals are put on by the immediate family of the deceased and often involve substantial expense. All men and women in the village of the deceased are invited to attend, and most women help in cooking, and men in chanting.

The primary materials of the kenduri consist of foods, of which the deceased will be sent the essence (*berkat*), and prayers, chanted by the assembled guests, of which the deceased will receive the merit (*pahala*). Always present at funeral meals are the small, round cakes called *apam*, made from rice flour, which have the inner property of holding off the clubs of the interrogating angels during the days of torment. The apam are also used for making requests to God. Two kinds of rice are served at the meals. While regular rice (*kro*) provides nourishment for the living, glutinous rice (*kunyit*) has the property of providing sustenance for the dead; in both cases sustenance comes from the spiritual property, or essence (berkat, from Arabic *baraka*, "blessing") of the food. Finally, benzoin incense (*kemenyen*) serves to carry words and berkat to God, Who is asked to pass them on to the soul of the deceased.

Words said at the kenduri generate merit and transmit it, through God, to the deceased. Texts are chosen which praise God and mention His name, thereby pleasing Him, and leading Him to reduce the suffering and excuse the sins of the dead. Thus, the Qur'anic verses, Al-Ikhlas, which contains the name of God, and Al-Fatihah, which contains the essence of the entire Qur'an (i.e., God's words), are very frequently recited at the meals. The form of the recitations is either as "Qur'anic reading" (*ngaji*), in which each man present takes a turn at reading a verse, or as *shamadiyah* (from Arabic *shamad*, "eternal"), in which all those present chant verses in unison, repeating the same verse over and over again. In both cases the recitation is under the leadership of a *tengku* (religiously learned person), through whom the merit of the verses is channeled to God. I was told that the merit is only sent if the correct intent (*niet*) is held by the tengku at the meal.

> If someone who is not a diligent Muslim, who never prayed, dies, a tengku will still come and pray and chant, but these prayers

---

12. Eduard A. Westermarck, *Ritual and Belief in Morocco*, 2 vols. (New Hyde Park, N.Y.: University Books, 1968 [original 1926]), 2: 464-65.

13. The word *kenduri* refers to any kind of formal meal, including those held for weddings, agricultural rituals, and healing. In fact, the word may be used as a refined way of referring to an ordinary meal.

> will be external only (lahir), so that the family will not be embarrassed. The prayers will not "hit the mark" because the tengku will think to himself: "He never prayed; how can we ask for his redemption." The result is *seriet berules, hakiket beropoh* [behavior in a ceremonial cloth; inner reality in a plain cloth]; just going through the motions.

In the case of the shamadiyah, the verses generate merit as the simple product of the number of repetitions and the number of chanters. In the sessions at which I was present, the chants were repeated twenty to thirty times; a repetition of 1,000 by a tengku (regardless of the number of others present) is said to redeem the sins of the deceased completely. In any case, all verses are said to be redemptions (*penebus*) for sins, and also to be the alms of the living (*sedekah*, from the Arabic *shadaqah*, "alms") given to the deceased by his "pious-performing children" (*anak amal saleh*).

The four funeral kenduri also demarcate stages in the transformation of the relationship of soul to body. I draw the following descriptions from funerals witnessed in Isak in 1979 and 1980. The first meal follows soon after burial.

> Preparations for the meal begin immediately after the body is made ready for burial. Large cooking pots are set up outside the house of the deceased, and women from throughout the village bring foodstuffs and help in the cooking. Most of the adult men of the village join in the ngaji session, and everyone takes a turn at reading a verse, and thus sending merit to the deceased, no matter how unsuited his voice may be to the task. Recitation continues until after midnight. Over the next three days, all cooking is done collectively in the large pots. No special prohibitions mark the behavior of close relatives during this period, and crying over the deceased is usually met with a remonstrance to the effect that to bewail the departed is to deny God His due.

During the three days after death the body is said to be intact, and the soul remains within it.

The ritual held on the third night is called the *nenggari*. The meal is less well attended, with perhaps a third as many men ngaji as on the first night. During the period following this meal, the body begins to decompose and the spirit moves restlessly in and out of it. The first seven days are days of torment for the soul, and the close relatives say an extra prayer at each of the five prayer times for its well-being. The widow, widower, or children of the deceased burn incense and put out apam cakes each day for the seven days, also with the purpose of reducing the torment. Rice and vegetables are put out each night for the soul, which is said to be both in and out of the house and near the body.

The seventh-day meal, *nujuh*, is the largest and most important of the series, and distant relatives will make a particular effort to attend. Many different kinds of cakes are made by women in the village for the meal, and everyone turns out. A shamadiyah chanting session is held, lasting about one hour. The climax of the ritual series comes on the following day, however (still part of the seventh day by Gayo time reckoning), when men and women visit the grave, and a daytime meal is held at which the closest relatives ask forgiveness. It is on the seventh day that arwah leaves the decomposed body. The grave, not the body, is now the home of the soul. The funeral of my closest informant's mother occurred when I was in the village, and on the seventh day:

> About a dozen of the closest relatives, both men and women, went to the grave, which had not been touched since burial, the men carrying stones, water, and uncooked rice, and the women carrying *mungkur* fruit [a ritually important citrus] and white cloth. Two men took two large, smooth stones and, putting a white cloth underneath each, placed them at the head and foot of the grave at the same moment, pronouncing the *tasbeh* [the expression of praise to God beginning "*Subhana'llah*"] as they did so. Then the women began to lay the smaller stones on the grave, saying the tasbeh to themselves as they did so. Then water was sprinkled on the grave, and everyone said the Al-Ikhlas (eleven times each, I was told later on) to himself before leaving. The tasbeh and the Al-Ikhlas are both in praise of God, and bring merit to the deceased. The stones will continue to say the tasbeh forever, on the deceased's behalf.

After visiting the grave, the family hold a kenduri at their house, with apam cakes and rice. The occasion is one of emotional climax, a release from the too-correct tension and stoic conduct of the first seven days.

> The main topic of conversation were the debts left by the mother. They must be settled quickly or she will feel torment [*sengsara*] in her grave. The son grew angry because there were debts which he had not known of, and the time needed to repay them would thus be longer. The Prophet said we should pay off all debts before the dead is buried, I was told, but during the seven days we may need to borrow more for the meals, so we only repay after the nujuh.
>
> But when he was finished, the son quickly leaned over to his father and crouched low to place his head in his father's hands [*semah*] and beg forgiveness for his mistakes. Then he did the same with everyone else, and so did the others who stood as children to the father. Everyone but the eldest son was crying, and one daughter started a long ritual cry. This moment was the first moment of release from the sadness and frustration of the previous week. Whereas crying at the moment of death was frowned on as defying God's will, crying now was over the event itself, the sadness they were all feeling. Even the suave imem from downstream [a "son" of the deceased] was crying.

This set of events on the seventh day constitutes the critical point of transformation. The soul is released from the body, the deceased is released from his worldly debts, and the live actors in the sequence released from their pent-up emotions. The period between death and the seventh day corresponds to what Hertz called the "intermediary period," which is represented in some Indonesian societies by the exposed corpse. Hertz' insight was that, in such societies, the exposed, decomposing body was the material basis for the theory of the soul's passage; Gayo also know of decomposition as a natural process, and similarly key ritual to it without exposing the corpse.[14]

---

14. Hertz, "Contribution to the Study," pp. 29-53.

During the period between the seventh and the forty-fourth day, the soul wanders in and out of its former house, remaining in or near the village. The debts which were figured out on the seventh day must be paid off during this period for the future peace of the soul. A small meal is held on the forty-fourth night, called the *nyawah lo*, "ending the days," at which apam cakes and glutinous rice are given to the arwah, and it leaves the house.

The spirit may return to the community at such times as it is called, or at certain fixed, propitious moments (e.g., the night before Friday prayers, or during the fasting month). But after the forty-fourth day the arwah is said to have left for the *awang-awang*, a place that lies somewhere between heaven and earth. The awang-awang is not a well-defined place, and the phrase is tantamount to saying, in our figurative sense, "up in the clouds." But, at the same time, the arwah is also spatially associated with the gravesite. Graves are visited frequently, cleaned, and sprinkled with water to "cool" the soul. A soul whose grave has been neglected may cause sharp, painful twinges in its descendants' stomachs as reminders that the grave needs to be visited.

All ancestors have healing powers, and any grave might be visited with a request to help cure an illness by interceding with God, since a deceased soul is closer to God than is a living person. The graves of prominent persons, particularly ancestors of important descent lines (*kuru*) are particular efficacious sources of healing power, and are visited by a wider range of people. The agricultural season is marked by kenduri at a third category of ancestors' graves, those of the founders of the community (*datu*) who are called on for permission to plant the land, for assistance in ridding the fields of pests, or who are given thanks for a good harvest.

The force of mortuary ritual is thus dual: it both eases the dead soul out of the community and locates it at a gravesite in the community. This "inherent bilocality of the dead," as Peter Metcalf has termed it, is in fact a transformation of the relationship between soul and body, from one of containment to one of mediation.[15] The power of the soul after death stems precisely from its role in overcoming the opposition between the community and the distant world of spiritual power. Power is drawn down to aid the community in its worldly needs.

This ritual pattern of easing out, and then communicating with, the soul appears to be present in non-Islamic societies in the Malayo-Indonesian world as well. For several Borneo peoples, for example, an initial period when the village is in danger and prohibitions are applied to a close relative of the deceased (often lasting seven days), is followed by a passage of the soul out of the community. However, the dead, from their graves in the land of the living, also continue to provide health and well-being to the community.[16]

---

15. Peter Metcalf, *A Borneo Journey into Death. Berawan Eschatology from Its Rituals* (Philadelphia: University of Pennsylvania Press, 1982), p. 235.

16. See ibid., pp. 109-10, 225-29, for the Berawan cosmology of the dead and the songs describing their journey. Alfred B. Hudson, "Death Ceremonies of the Ma'anyan Dayaks," *Sarawak Museum Journal* 13 (1966): 341-417, describes similar Ma'anyan rites. In Ngaju, seven days after the burial is the moment when a flame which has been lit at burial is snuffed out "so that it will accompany the deceased to the world of the spirits." See Sarwoto Kertodipoero, *Kaharingan: Religi dan Penghidupan* (Bandung: Sumur Bandung, 1963), pp. 60-63.

While we know nothing of the nature of Gayo death ritual before Islamization, Islam did make available certain signs which could have taken on local meanings, and thus religiously sanction pre-existing practices. The periods of three, seven, and forty or forty-four days after death appear in the Near Eastern Islamic world as common limits on mourning, taboos, and the moments for special meals. In parts of Morocco, cooking is prohibited for the first three days after death and a widow may not venture outside during that period. The first meal cooked at her home, and her first visit to the grave take place on the seventh day, and seven days is also the period of women's wailing in several parts of the Near East. Forty-four days frequently is the moment for a special meal on the grave of the deceased.[17]

The kenduri would have provided a new form in which communication with the dead could be carried out. Syafi'i law books which are used by Indonesian scholars equate the Persian term kenduri with the Arabic shadaqah, "alms," but as alms given by the host to his guests, rather than to the soul of the deceased.[18] I suggest that the kenduri and the talqin have become key funeral rituals for the Gayo because they were appropriate vehicles for Gayo ideas of the transformation of the soul at death, as both passage and continued speech, i.e., a form of passage which preserves ties of communication and transmission, or, thought of spatially, the "inherent bilocality" of the dead soul. Modernism, as we shall see below, has reinterpreted these signs in such a way as to downplay communication and emphasize passage, linearizing, in effect, the soul's progress.

Islamic Modernism and Religious Ritual

The history of Islam in Sumatra might be characterized as a series of reformisms, each one reinterpreting previous texts, institutions, and practices in a new light. Earlier reformisms include the orthodox reaction to Sufi ideas of being in seventeenth century Aceh, the rise of legalistic Islamic interpretations in eighteenth-century West Sumatra, and the socially purifying emphasis of the Padri movement in the same area.[19] In this century, modernist reformism in Sumatra and elsewhere in Indonesia has been dominated by the influence of the *Kaum Muda* (Young Group) movement, which received major contributions from the Sumatra Thawalib schools movement in West Sumatra, the Muhammadiyah, which began in Java but quickly spread to Sumatra and elsewhere, and the Persatuan Islam group led by Ahmad Hassan in Bandung. All three centers have influenced Gayo modernism.

Indonesian modernism was a combination of progressive Arabic thought in the Near East and a long-standing tradition of Indonesian (and particularly Sumatran) revivalism. Cairo was the center for a rethinking of the relationship

---

17. See Westermarck, *Ritual and Belief*, pp. 438-510, for descriptions of the funeral periods mentioned here.

18. Howard M. Federspiel, *Persatuan Islam: Islamic Reform in Twentieth Century Indonesia* (Ithaca: Cornell Modern Indonesia Project, 1970), p. 71.

19. See Christine Dobbin, *Islamic Revivalism in a Changing Peasant Economy: Central Sumatra, 1784-1847* (London and Malmo: Curzon Press, 1983), on the eighteenth century and the Padri movement, and Shekh Muhammad Naguid al-Attas, *The Mysticism of Hamzah Fansuri* (Kuala Lumpur: Oxford University Press, 1970), on the seventeenth-century religious debates in Aceh.

of the Islamic faith to the Western social and scientific world of the late nineteenth century. Jamaluddin al-Afghani and his student, Mohammed Abduh, wrote of the need to reinterpret Islamic rules and adapt them to a modern world.[20]

The most important direct link between the Cairo modernists and Indonesian scholars was, ironically, the Shafi'i *imam* at the Masjid al-Haram in Mecca.[21] Born in West Sumatra, Syekh Ahmad Chatib, a Minangkabau, came to Mecca to study, and became, not only the Shafi'i leader, but also the most important teacher of those Indonesians who were studying in Mecca in the 1890s. His influence is illustrative of the potential for reform within traditionalist frameworks. Although he upheld the teachings of the Shafi'i school against the direct reinterpretation of Scripture, he did not forbid his students from studying the writing of Mohammed Abduh and other modernists. Moreover, because he based his opinions strictly on an Islamic foundation, he was an outspoken opponent of Minangkabau matrilineal inheritance law and the joint lineage control of property, and of the several mystic orders (tarekat) that were prominent in Minangkabau society in this period.[22]

Students of Ahmad Chatib combined their teacher's criticisms of traditional society with the modernist teachings of Mohammed Abduh, and on their return to Indonesia in the early years of the twentieth century began to found modernist schools and movements in Indonesia. Kyai Haji Ahmad Dahlan, after his studies in Mecca in the 1890s, returned to Java where he founded, in 1912, the Muhammadiyah movement, while in 1919 others among Ahmad Chatib's students established the Sumatra Thawalib schools movement in Padang Panjang, West Sumatra.[23]

The Modernist View of Ritual

I now turn to the content of the dialogue that ensued between the Kaum Muda and the various groups and positions collectively referred to as the Kaum *Tua*, the "old group," which included traditional orthodox teachers (among them the Nahdlatul Ulama), but not the Javanese *abangan* syncretists, and only indirectly the spiritualist tarekat groups. This dialogue has continued to

---

20. On the influence of Abduh and al-Afghani, see Albert Hourani, *Arabic Thought in the Liberal Age, 1798-1939* (Oxford: Oxford University Press, 1962), pp. 103-60. The texts of the debate between al-Afghani and Ernest Renan on the relationship of Islam and science were secretly carried into Indonesia, and, to this day, a current of Islam-as-science thinking remains extremely popular in Takengon, including much speculation about the computerization of the Qur'an and the "prediction" of the atomic bomb in Scriptures.

21. Each of the four traditional schools was represented at the mosque by a leader or *imam*. The four schools were criticized by the modernists as perpetuating error; see below.

22. Deliar Noer, *The Modernist Muslim Movement in Indonesia, 1900-1942* (Kuala Lumpur: Oxford University Press, 1973), pp. 31-33.

23. On the growth of Muhammadiyah, see ibid., pp. 73-83, and Mitsuo Nakamura, *The Crescent Arises over the Banyan Tree: A Study of the Muhammadiyah Movement in a Central Javanese Town* (Yogyakarta: University of Gadjah Mada Press, 1984). On the Sumatra Thawalib, see Taufik Abdullah, *Schools and Politics: The Kaum Muda Movement in West Sumatra (1927-1933)* (Ithaca: Cornell Modern Indonesia Project, 1971).

constitute the primary field of discourse concerning Islam in Indonesia up to the present day.[24]

At the national level, this debate took place between (on the modernist side) novelists, journalists, and theologians who criticized, point by point, what they saw as un-Islamic practices, and (on the traditionalist side) long treatises summing up as many scriptural justifications for each such practice as could be found. The debates have largely avoided confrontations over broad social issues, but have remained focused on questions of strictly religious practice. Two specific lacunae in these debates are worth mentioning. First, traditionalists have not made reference to specific Indonesian cultural characteristics in defense of their interpretations of Islam, perhaps because of the cultural heterogeneity of Indonesia. Second, modernists have not, in these religious debates, made the question of allegiance to a non-Islamic state a central issue, probably because of the early alliances between modernists and the nationalist movement.

The position of the Young Group may be explained through their use of the two terms *ijtihad* (individual interpretation) and *bid'a* (innovation). The first is promoted and the second attacked. The fundamental truths, say the Kaum Muda, were set out in the Qur'an and hadith (traditions concerning the words and deeds of the Prophet), and in every age these two sources must be applied directly to current conditions through ijtihad, i.e., by examining Scriptures to determine the legal prescriptions or moral teachings contained therein, and then using reason to apply them to a contemporary situation. An attitude of unquestioning obedience (*taqlid*) to any one set of established interpretations is criticized, both because it stands in the way of modernity and progress, and because the interpretations of the four schools, one of which, the Shafi'i, is followed in Indonesia, may lead to heteropraxis.

These errors in the main turn on the second key concept, bid'a, or innovation. For the modernists, any change in a matter of worship (*ibadah*) is not permitted, since God himself ordained such matters and man cannot improve on them. Unless a practice can be justified by reference to clearly acceptable scriptures (and it is on the relative acceptability of various hadith that the argument often stands) it ought not to be followed.

On the other hand, continues the argument, one must strictly delimit matters of fixed ritual, the true domain of ibadah, from aspects of worship or religion in which the purpose is highlighted over the form. Thus, sermons and homilies which are delivered publicly, or individual prayers which are said silently, ought to be in the vernacular, rather than in Arabic, since these acts are primarily acts of communication and do not have a fixed ritual form. Similarly, some modernists consider the washing performed before the ritual prayer as primarily a cleansing act (highlighting purpose) rather than as a ritual act (highlighting form), and thus argue that it may be replaced by a good shower.

---

24. Among the texts used by Gayo in Takengon to support their positions on the following matters are, on the modernist side, Ahmad Hassan dkk. [et al.], *Soal-Jawab tentang berbagai masalah agama* (Bandung: Diponegoro, 1968), and the same author's *Pengajaran Shalat* (Bandung: Diponegoro, 1979 [original 1930]). The leading writer of Islamic texts in Aceh is T. M. Hasbi Ash-Shiddieqy, who takes a modernist position on the issues discussed here. See his *Al-Islam*, 2 vols. (Jakarta: Bulan Bintang, 1952), 2: 247-48. Prominent among Shafi'i traditionalist scholars is the *40 Masalah Agama* of K. H. Sirajuddin Abbas, 4 vols. (Jakarta: Pustaka Tarbiyah, 1976).

For the same reason, continue the modernists, the washing may not be performed in shorthand fashion, by wetting three hairs of the head, as is often done by traditionalists.[25]

While modernists emphasize strict delimitation, and the proscription of any worship-related practice not clearly prescribed by Scriptures, the traditionalists emphasize the power and goodness of many ritual practices, some of which are only recommended rather than required. Traditionalists base their arguments on the writings of famed older scholars and frequently mentioned practices or sayings of the Prophet. They thus accept a greater number of actions as having been sanctioned, in practice, by the Prophet. These actions range from the ritually incidental (the Prophet stood up when a funeral bier passed, so we should as well), to the instrumental (the Prophet was said to read a talqin to keep a dead man from torment, so we should as well), to the socially desirable (the Prophet spoke Arabic, and so, ideally, should we).[26]

Modernists refuse to use those traditions for which the chain of communication (*sanad* or *isnad*, lit. "support") is not composed of unimpeachable sources, primarily a matter of the moral character of those who transmitted the tradition. Modernists also frequently reason from analogy and employ arguments of the form "if we were to accept this, then. . . ."

Proper conduct of funerals has been a salient issue in the debates between modernists and traditionalists throughout Indonesia, although in some areas it has been eclipsed by other social issues (e.g., inheritance law in West Sumatra). I will suggest that the prominence of mortuary ritual in the debates is due to the adoption of Islamic signs to support what is seen by modernists as a pre-Islamic system of communication.

Nationally, the most vocal debates on the issue of the talqin were carried out in the 1930s between Ahmad Hassan, the strictest constructionist of modernism, and various exponents of the Shafi'i position. Hassan's view, and that of the modernists generally, was based both on a strict examination of the isnad of those traditions claimed as supporting the practice (each was found to be weak), quotations from the Qur'an, and what was offered as simple good sense: how could the dead possibly hear the instruction? Among those verses cited in opposition to the instruction to the dead was *An-Naml* (The Ant) 27:80, which reads: "You cannot make the dead hear, nor make the deaf hear the call when they have turned to flee." Thus, conclude the modernists, the practice is useless, as the Qur'an itself states, and "is the work of fools." What is worse, since it is not a prescribed part of the funeral ritual, and since the funeral is part of ibadah, the instruction to the dead is an illegitimate innovation (bid'a) and thus must not be carried out.[27]

The modernist objections to post-mortem kenduri were on similar grounds. All traditions which claimed that the Prophet had attended such meals were stated to be weak. Special objections were made to those meals (such as the Gayo kenduri of the third and seventh days after death) which have as their

---

25. See Ahmad Hassan, *Pengajaran Shalat*, p. 202.

26. I know of several Gayo families who moved to the Pekalongan area of Java, one with a large number of people of Arab descent, and adopted Arabic as their language of the home.

27. Ahmad Hassan, *Soal-Jawab*, 1: 210-14, and *Pengajaran Shalat*, pp. 365-67. See also Ash-Shiddieqy, *Al-Islam*, 2: 247-48.

purpose the generation of merit on behalf of the deceased. If it were possible to transmit merit to someone else by our actions, objected the modernists, then why would we ever need to worship? Surely it would be easier to ask someone else to pray for us. But clearly we do have a duty to worship, so merit must not be transferable.[28]

The response of the traditionalist text writers on these issues was to amass traditions and authorities speaking for the practice. Such writers as Sirajuddin Abbas (one of the most widely read) insisted on the correctness of using hadith that have weak histories if they concern matters of optional worship and not the central pillars of Islam.[29]

Gayo Modernists and the Nature of Death

Modernist ideology came to Takengon in the late 1920s, when Minangkabau traders brought an attractive combination of trading skills, modern forms of education, and what seemed to some to be a more rational form of Islam. These reformers-cum-peddlers quickly sought protection from Raja Bukit, the native ruler (*Zelfbestuurder*) in Takengon, in order to avoid being branded as Communists by the Dutch.[30] The traders, members of Muhammadiyah, built a mosque in the center of town at which services were conducted in the modernist manner.[31] Many Gayo traders became adherents of Muhammadiyah, and several Gayo left for schooling in modernist schools in West Sumatra and Java in the 1930s, and returned several years later to build the indigenous modernist movement.

Three social features of the movement determined its overall character in Takengon. First, modernism grew out of cross-ethnic social relations, led by newcomers to the region. It brought the expansion of trade outside the Gayo region, new forms of education, and an emphasis on the Indonesian language. The focus of the movement was on problems of religion in general, rather than on the particular institutions of Gayo society (as was not the case in West Sumatra, where reformists were of local origin, and had been taught by Syekh Chatib to oppose matrilineal institutions). Second, the movement enjoyed strong support from a powerful traditional ruler. This support provided an additional factor diverting Gayo modernism from the kind of direct attack on traditional social and political structures that was carried out in Minangkabau and Acehnese societies. Third, modernism has benefited from the powerful political position of the *ulama* (religious leaders) in postindependence Aceh as a whole.[32] Modernism thus established itself as a supraethnic, town-based movement with strong local and regional political support.

---

28. Ahmad Hassan, *Soal-Jawab*, 1: 216-19, and Federspiel, *Persatuan Islam*, pp. 70-74.

29. Abbas's defense of the talqin is in Abbas, *40 Masalah*, 4: 78-126.

30. By that time, the Sumatra Thawalib school in West Sumatra had developed an "ilmu kominih" (Communist branch of knowledge) (Abdullah, *Schools and Politics*, p. 41.

31. The mosque is still commonly referred to as the *mersah Padang* (after the capital of West Sumatra).

32. A series of violent confrontations between the *ulama* and the traditional rulers in coastal Pidie shortly after Independence firmly established the

The institutional base of modernism in Takengon was in the Muhammadiyah schools. In 1934 a five-year Muhammadiyah school was erected in Takengon and taught a broad range of subjects, including some Dutch language instruction. The Raja Bukit signaled his support for the movement by laying the corner stone for the school, which was the first alternative in Takengon to the three-year Dutch *volksschool*. In 1938 a second modernist-minded five-year school was opened, the Pendidikan Islam (Islamic Education), which taught mathematics and geography as well as religious subjects.

Until independence in 1945 the only traditionalist alternatives in Takengon to these two schools were the *pondok* schools of Qur'an recitation; children from traditionalist families thus had to seek further study in coastal Aceh. In 1957, however, a branch of the Medan-based al-Washliyah movement was opened in Takengon. This was a moderate traditionalist movement designed to support traditional Shafi'i religious views without rejecting the possibility of alternative positions. From 1970 to 1975 this group operated a university in Takengon, which produced nineteen nationally recognized BA graduates and had a total enrollment of 300 students. Arabic language learning and religious subjects were emphasized.

Gayo modernism has remained centered on the town of Takengon, but it began to make its influence felt in a number of villages in the 1930s, when divisions occurred over the issue of proper Frday prayer procedure, and groups of Kaum Muda adherents moved out to set up their own reformed communities. A number of villages near Takengon remain divided between modernists and traditionalists, with each keeping to its own mosque and prayer house (*mersah*). More isolated villages are virtually all traditionalist. Perhaps 85-90 percent of Gayo remain traditionalist by their own admission.

The emphasis of Gayo modernist reformism has been on three areas of Gayo culture: technical issues regarding the forms of ritual worship (*shalat*), the status of bridewealth and inheritance, and the propriety of mortuary rites. While the first two issues, shalat and property transfers, have given rise to extended debate within the Gayo community, they are both seen as technical matters, where each individual ought to choose to follow either a traditional set of practices or a modernist one, without a socially necessary uniformity of religious practice.

In both the administration of the *shari'a* (Islamic law) and communal worship, a high degree of contextual segregation between kaum mude and kaum tue is possible. In the Islamic court (*Mahkamah Shari'a*), Islamic law must take precedence over local precedent if an inheritance question comes to a formal decision, but the judges of the Takengon Court prefer that families reach informal settlements among themselves rather than be made subject to the imposition of shari'a. Traditional inheritance rules involve a division of property among those children who remain in the lineage after marriage, but there is not the salience of a non-Islamic inheritance rule such as characterizes Minangkabau society; the issue is thus relatively low-key within the culture as a whole. Similarly, rather than quarreling over forms of the shalat, modernists and traditionalists tend to build separate mosques in the community and to carry out their respective services in their own ways.

---

former as the political elite of Aceh. See Anthony Reid, *The Blood of the People: Revolution and the End of Traditional Rule in Northern Sumatra* (Kuala Lumpur: Oxford University Press, 1979), pp. 185-217.

The Religious Centrality of the Funeral

It is the third issue, the proper conduct regarding the dead, that has become the primary, salient, and unavoidable religious diacritic in Gayo society, the issue around which Gayo must publicly sort themselves into kaum tue (or Shafi'i) and kaum mude (or Muhammadiyah).

While national-level debates on the legitimacy of funeral rituals have centered on the acceptability of particular hadith, the discourse within Gayo society has focused on the possibilities of communication between the living and the dead. Modernists reinterpret death ritual by highlighting one aspect of the soul's transformation, namely, its passage out from the body of the deceased and the community of the survivors. While the traditionalist's means of guaranteeing health and prosperity are predicated on communicating with the dead, it is precisely this possibility of communication that is radically undercut by modernists, who see it as illegitimate innovation in what is essentially a religious matter.

For the modernists in Takengon and the villages near the town, the moment of death itself breaks the ties between the deceased and the community at large. Once the nyawa has left the body, the person can no longer hear instructions read to him, and his fate in the grave can no longer be altered nor his merit increased, by the performance of feasts or by providing apam cakes. "For the dead," say the modernists, "good deeds (*'amala*) no longer help you, except for three: children who do good works (*anak amal saleh*), alms given while alive (*sedekah jariah*), and useful knowledge taught to others (*ilmu manfa'at*)."

This text is a hadith from Abu Daud, and quoted by modernists and traditionalists alike, but from opposed interpretive perspectives.[33] For the traditionalist, the tie of the deceased to his anak amal saleh is interpreted to imply the duty of his "children" in the widest sense to organize large and effective ritual meals and chanting sessions, in order to generate merit for the deceased. For the modernist, however, the passage is read as strictly limiting those who are capable of improving the lot of the deceased to his "real" children, and even then only in their prayers to God.[34] To do otherwise, to engage in telkin or kenduri, is to carry out an illegitimate innovation (*bid'a*) or addition to what may properly be done at a funeral. Moreover, appeals to the deceased for assistance in life are viewed as setting up alternatives to God (*nduei Tuhen*, "duplicating God"), and thus constitute the sin of polytheism (*syirk* [Gayo *musrik*]).

Instead of the telkin, modernists remind the person near death of the tenets of his religion, and urge him to die with the words *la ilaha ilallah* (there is no God but Allah) on his lips. The "torment of the grave" is equally important to modernist notions, but it is a torment the outcome of which is entirely dependent on the preparation of the deceased for death during his life, and there is nothing we can do to intervene directly, except offer our prayers to God to treat his soul with compassion. The soul is already beyond the reach of the community. Modernist Gayo funerals involve a burial, with a short prayer but no telkin, and a short gathering at the home of the deceased

---

33. It is cited in Ahmad Hassan, *Soal-Jawab*, 1: 218.

34. An ethnobiological view of kinship runs throughout much modernist discourse, some of it based on a tendency within Islamic law to favor real over adoptive children in matters of inheritance.

without a meal. Sometimes guests might bring food for the family of the deceased, but they would not partake of it themselves.

The textual methods of modernism thus involve emhasizing a definitive transition from sentience to nonsentience as the essence of death. In this view, the crucial break between the body and soul occurs on the first day after death, rather than with the release of the arwah from the body on the seventh day. Death, for the modernist, is primarily passage from this world to the next. After death, the living have very little to do with the dead.

The modernist view thus denies the living their accustomed avenues of recourse in the case of illness or poor crops, or merely when they wish to ensure prosperity. The gravesites, which for the living serve as markers of Gayo history, are deprived of their power as executors of fortune over the land and its inhabitants. Moreover, the deceased is no longer to be treated as one of the community. As one friend of mine put it: "You cannot treat a person like a chicken, just throw him away when he dies."

Villagers see the issue as a general conflict over the possibility of communication between living persons and other beings. A traditionalist village leader gave me the following answer when I asked him about the differences between modernists and traditionalists:

> Another difference [he said, after talking about prayer] is with the shamadiyah. There, we have a meal and we chant to reach the dead person. The Kaum Muda says that the chant could not reach him because he is already dead. But that is like saying that when we go by a grave and say "How are you doing in there, in the grave?" that he cannot hear us. But of course he can, only we cannot hear his answer--he does answer, though.
>
> It is like the Prophet Suleiman: in his time, people could talk with the plants and the animals, and the dead could answer our questions. But since then it has been forbidden. But trees, for instance, have souls--you know because they have green leaves that they must. We were taught by our teacher that if you must cut down a tree you have to say "bismillah irahman irahim" first, to the tree. That was Teungku Bit, a Sufi teacher.

Disagreement over religious ritual form is thus perceived as implicating the general relationship between the living and all other elements in the world, including dead souls, plants, and spirits. The debate is thus one on which, at least for the traditionalists, the prosperity of the community rests.

While in the majority of Gayo villages the population is entirely kaum tue, and thus traditional ritual form and function is preserved, in the villages near Takengon and in the town itself the population is mixed. Here, the issue of proper funeral form serves as an unavoidable test of one's stand on the traditionalist/modernist issue generally. The salience of funerals is due to three characteristics of the ritual: the mortuary rituals are *public*, involving performance of chants and prayers and attendance at ritual meals; *socially obligatory* for all kin, neighbors and nearby acquaintances of the deceased; and *religious*, in that their content clearly has to do with God, spirits, and human communication with both. Modernists are unable to explain away mortuary rituals as "culture" (*kebudayaan*) or "tradition" (*adat*), and therefore they are forced to take a religious stand on the propriety of the rituals. Modernists cannot refuse to stay away from traditionalists' funerals, because doing so would violate rules of social etiquette. Moreover, one's mere attendance at a funeral ritual signals a level of acceptance of the entire proceedings. The result is to place modernists in a double bind, where one cannot attend (for religious reasons) and also cannot not attend (for equally compelling, or nearly so, social ones). It is the unavoidable signaling of religious commitment that takes place in attending a funeral that has made these rituals central arenas in the modernist/traditionalist debate.

When I attended funeral meals, I frequently saw uncomfortable modernists for whom even the taking of a glass of water represented a religious deviation, but for whom the cultural prescriptions of feast attendance still weighed heavily. The only funeral during the period of my fieldwork at which successful spatial segregation of modernists and traditionalists occurred was at the death of the brother of the Bupati of Central Aceh. Because the Bupati's house is a uniquely large and multiroomed structure, it is subject to different symbolic valuations than is an ordinary house: rather than a basic front room for male guests and a back room for close friends and female guests, the Bupati's state house has several, well-separated front rooms, an arrangement which allowed him to escape choosing between religious feast styles by holding two ceremonies at once after his brother's death. At one ceremony were the traditionalist villagers, largely on his father's side, who ate splendidly on that and the succeeding nights; at the other were the modernist town folk, largely on his mother's side, who were not even served tea, but prayed briefly and left.

Models and Modernism

Modernism had acted, I have argued, by reinterpreting texts and ritual forms already in place, highlighting the elements of passage contained in Gayo funerals and denying the elements of communication which are also contained therein. Modernism has thus proceeded in a fashion analogous to a model of early Islamization proposed here, by adopting certain Islamic texts as guides to the evaluation of earlier cultural forms, and transforming them in a way that remains recognizable to members of the society.

The advent of modernism in Gayo society, and, *mutatis mutandis*, elsewhere in Sumatra, has brought about the confrontation of two radically different ideas of ritual. One is the "life-giving" ritual of the village traditionalists, which is concerned with the well-being of the dead and the health, fertility, and prosperity of the living community. Mortuary ritual underscores the continuity of communication between the living and the dead and the possibility of mutual assistance; from the living to the dead during the mortuary ritual series, and vice-versa thereafter. This sort of ritual is Hocart's "ritual of life" based on a conception of "life, fertility, prosperity, vitality."[35]

The opposing idea of death ritual sees it as primarily or even uniquely, a passage out of this world into another, emphasizing the rupture between the living and the dead at the moment of death, and the eventual judgment

---

35. A. M. Hocart, *Kings and Councillors* (Chicago: University of Chicago Press, 1970 [original 1936]), pp. 32-33. James Boon suggested the fruitfulness of Hocart to this analysis. On Balinese parallels to the contrast I draw below, see James Boon, *Other Tribes, Other Scribes* (Cambridge: Cambridge University Press, 1982), pp. 200-204.

of the dead at the end of the world. Reintegration, in this conception, must await Judgment.

In this conflict of local interpretations, our use of the Hertz-Van Gennep model of death as a rite of passage favors the second, linear, modernist idea, rendering elements of communication secondary to the main lines of the ritual as a whole. Hertz himself pointed to the fact that, in some Indonesian societies, the soul continues to carry on "regular relations" with the living after death. This observation, however, was a minor addendum to his general model in which a return to the living occurs only after a journey to a distant, separate, world of the dead, a final resting place for the soul. The world of the dead serves to provide a "realm of the ideal" for the living.[36]

For Hertz, the Olo Ngaju presage another, more elaborated model of passage and eventual return which is to be found in Christianity. The idea of "the resurrection and the life" guaranteed by the Church appears at the end of Hertz' analysis as a "rejuvenated form" of secondary burial, a *passage et retour* which completes earlier forms of the religious life (and death).[37]

Modernist Islam, in its return to Scriptures for its revisions of local practice, shares a Judaeo-Christian-Islamic eschatology with Hertz, so that parallels between Hertz' analytic emphasis on passage and the similar interventions of the modernists are not fortuitous. In both, the radical separation of the dead from the living converts death from a transformation of the soul which underwrites Life into a prelude to an eventual moral Judgment. An emphasis on sequence in itself, one could argue, casts continuity in a background role, and makes communication and protection dubious characteristics of the dead. If not the negation of ritual, a single model of the general form of mortuary ritual may be an analytic party to its radical revision.

---

36. See Hertz, "Contribution to the Study," pp. 61, 59 ff., 79, respectively, for the passages cited above.

37. Ibid., pp. 77-79.

REPRESSION AND REGROUPMENT: RELIGIOUS AND NATIONALIST ORGANIZATIONS IN WEST SUMATRA IN THE 1930s*

Audrey R. Kahin

Repression

In March 1937 West Sumatra's political landscape appeared calm, with no sign of agitation or disturbance.[1] Looking back from that tranquil viewpoint to the turbulent events of a few years earlier, A. I. Spits, the Dutch resident soon to become governor of Sumatra, drew a vivid picture of the situation that had precipitated his government's repression of local political activity:

> The whole of Sumatra's West Coast was then in a state of political turmoil; the ideas of independence were being propagated by young and old in the various organizations of the Permi, PSII, PNI, and PI; "Indonesia free, now or within a few years" was sung in all keys, not only in the larger population centers, but also in the countryside. The Minangkabau politicians did not limit their activities to the West Coast, but sent their propaganda over all Sumatra. Police measures were inadequate to contain this, the government lowered its guard [het gezag nam zienderoogen af]; there was a threatened split among the Volkshoofden; duties towards the government were being carried out badly, further deterioration could only be checked by extraordinary means. Characteristic of the mentality of the Minangkabauer is the fact that by then the bloody lesson provided by the suppression of the disturbances at the beginning of 1927 seemed already to have been forgotten, or better perhaps, the facts had not been forgotten, that could not yet be, but the large majority had not drawn the correct lesson from them. The ideal of freedom put forward by reckless popular leaders still seemed to possess such a great attraction that the people let themselves be pushed on to a road that could lead to repetition of the occurrences of 1927.[2]

In response to these developments, in the summer of 1933 the colonial regime

---

* Research for this article was carried out in 1981-82 under a postdoctoral grant from the Committee on Southeast Asia of the Social Science Research Council. I would like to thank the council for their support.

1. H. Bouman, *Enige Beschouwingen over de Ontwikkeling van het Indonesisch Nationalisme op Sumatra's Westkust* (Groningen/Jakarta: Wolters, 1938), p. 87.

2. Koloniën Memories van Overgave [henceforth MvO] van den aftredenden Resident van Sumatra's Westkust, A. I. Spits, *Mailrapport* [henceforth *Mr.*] 504/1937, p. 45. (Unless otherwise stated all documents cited are in the Algemeen Rijksarchief [henceforth ARA], The Hague).

had acted against the two most radical religious parties, the Permi (Persatuan Muslim Indonesia, Association of Indonesian Muslims) and PSII (Partai Sarekat Islam Indonesia, Indonesian Islamic Union Party). It forbade meetings of these organizations,[3] arrested and exiled their top leaders, and restricted the rights of lower-ranking members. After a transitional period, Resident Spits was able to conclude in 1937 that these measures had proved "completely effective."

By this date there had indeed been a fundamental change in the nature of political activity in West Sumatra. This article will examine the process by which the inability of the religious political parties to provide an effective vehicle for the nationalist movement led to the emergence of a more diffuse political constellation, wherein the anti-Dutch struggle was waged in a less openly confrontational manner. It will argue that, although the colonial authorities were successful in destroying the strongest nationalist religious party in the region, the goal of the nationalists did not change—only their strategy.

To understand the nature of the changes and the resulting regroupment of political forces, it is necessary first, however, to focus on events of the early 1930s and the character of the threat posed by the religious/political parties to Dutch administration. At that time, four religious organizations were dominant in the region. Two of them, Permi and PSII, were strongly political and would become major Dutch targets. The other two were the social and educational organizations, Perti (Persatuan Tarbiah Islamiyah, Islamic Educational Association) and Muhammadiyah.

Muhammadiyah

Founded in Yogyakarta in 1912, the Muhammadiyah spread to many parts of the Indies over the subsequent decade, but did not exert much appeal in West Sumatra until 1925. In that year, H. Abd. Karim Amrullah (Haji Rasul)[4] who was one of the leading Minangkabau modernist ulama and a co-founder of the Sumatra Thawalib schools, introduced the Muhammadiyah into the region. He saw its philosophy and aims as consistent with those of his generation of modernist religious teachers, and with their determination to confine their activities to the religious, social, and educational spheres, eschewing involvement in political affairs. Shortly after he established the Muhammadiyah, however, it became a haven for many of the former students from whom he had become alienated in the early 1920s as they had turned for leadership to radical Islamic/Communist teachers. With the Communist uprising of January 1927 and its suppression by the Dutch, these young activists fled the nationalist and Communist organizations they had joined, and sought protection within the apolitical Muhammadiyah. Thus, the Muhammadiyah's West Sumatra branch grew in size and energy, spearheading protests and demonstrations in 1928 against the government's proposal to extend the "guru ordinance" (a restriction on private schools) to West Sumatra.[5]

---

3. See "Memorandum" signed by Resident van Heuven, "Ten Uitvoerlegging vergaderverbod," dated August 5, 1933, and "Toepassing vergaderverbod," dated August 24, 1933, attached to *Mr.* 1249/33 (August 1933).

4. The fullest biography of Haji Rasul is Hamka [Haji Abd. Malik Karim Amrullah], *Ajahku* [*My father*] (Jakarta: Djajamurni, 1967).

5. The guru ordinance actually stipulated that: "Anyone wishing to give instruction on the Mohammedan religion to persons other than his immediate family

Alarmed at these developments, Dutch authorities warned the Muhammadiyah's executive board on Java of the dangerous course its Minangkabau branch was pursuing. Efforts by the central leadership to moderate these local activities then caused many of the Muhammadiyah's new activist members to break away to form another association tied to the Thawalib schools.[6]

Thus, after being established in 1925 as a purely social and educational body patterned on the Java Muhammadiyah, the West Sumatra Muhammadiyah enjoyed a brief period of political activity which came to an abrupt end in 1929. In response to Dutch pressure, the central leadership of the association on Java now condemned any political actions by its members, and under A. R. Sutan [St.] Mansur, who was to head its Sumatra consulate from 1931 to 1944, activists within the Minangkabau branch were demoted and the organization "cleansed."[7]

Permi

Permi was a direct descendant of the student organizations of the Sumatra Thawalib schools,[8] many of whose members participated in the Communist-led activities of the early 1920s that culminated in the January 1927 uprisings. Suppression of the revolt shattered the radical student associations within the schools. Although scattered and subdued for a while, the young religious activists, as noted above, reunited in the Muhammadiyah with their moderate elders in opposition to the guru ordinance, and after a brief period of cooperation broke off to form the Sumatra Thawalib Union at the end of 1928. At its third conference in May 1930, the Union was transformed into the Persatuan Muslim Indonesia--known first as PMI and later as Permi. From its inception the Permi aroused Dutch suspicions, Resident Gonggrijp characterizing it as made up of those "religious intellectuals and small traders most receptive to Communist preaching."[9]

Over the next two years the Permi's influence expanded rapidly. Djalaluddin Thaib, a graduate of the Thawalib schools, was joined in its leadership by two dynamic returnees from Al-Azhar in Cairo, Iljas Jacoub and Muchtar Luthfi.[10]

---

should inform the regent, or patih, in Java or the district chief in the Outer Regions," and should get a letter of registration from the district office. See Taufik Abdullah, *Schools and Politics: The Kaum Muda Movement in West Sumatra 1927-1933* (Ithaca: Cornell Modern Indonesia Project, 1971), p. 112. On the development of the Muhammadiyah in West Sumatra, see ibid., pp. 70-97; Hamka, *Ajahku*, pp. 163-70; Deliar Noer, *The Modernist Muslim Movement in Indonesia 1900-1942* (Singapore: Oxford University Press, 1973), pp. 73-78; and MvO G. F. E. Gonggrijp, *Mr.* 360/32, pp. 3-6.

6. MvO Gonggrijp, p. 5. See also Abdullah, *Schools and Politics*, pp. 91-92.

7. MvO Gonggrijp, pp. 6-7. A. R. St. Mansur (b. 1895) had been educated in government schools and in the Sumatra Thawalib, where he was a disciple of H. Rasul, marrying his eldest daughter in 1917. For a biography, see Hamka, *Ajahku*, pp. 257-60.

8. The authoritative study on the West Sumatra schools and the growth of the Permi is Abdullah, *Schools and Politics*. See also Noer, *Modernist Muslim Movement*, pp. 46-56.

9. MvO Gonggrijp, p. 5.

10. For biographies of Djalaluddin Thaib, see Abdullah, *Schools and Politics*,

Retrospectively, Resident van Hoeven in 1934 was to portray these three men, together with businessman and trader, Abdullah gelar [glr.] Basa Bandaro,[11] as the core leadership of the Permi, with other central board members acting principally as their spokesmen.[12] By December 1932, when the party had to begin moves to evade growing government surveillance, it had about 160 groups throughout West Sumatra, with about 4,700 male, and 3,000 female members,[13] a total which reportedly reached 10,000 in the following months. Its activities spread to Bengkulu, South Sumatra, Aceh, East Sumatra, and Tapanuli.[14] With headquarters in Padang, it was particularly active in schools, educational associations, affiliated youth groups, and in publishing newspapers and pamphlets. It was also associated with trade unions, religious organizations, and merchants' associations.[15]

The party was distinguished from most other nationalist organizations by the equal importance it accorded to the roles of Islam and nationalism in opposing the Dutch and by its refusal to deemphasize one in favor of the other. This orientation was in tune with a widely held view among West Sumatran Muslims that much of the dissonance in the Indonesian nationalist movement sprang from its leaders' reluctance to recognize Islam as the strongest unifying factor for their struggle. According to this view, Indonesian nationalists were making a basic error in taking as their model the Indian nationalist movement, where indeed the major line of tension ran along the Hindu-Muslim rift. In Indonesia, however, where 90 percent of the people were Muslims, to be afraid of using Islam as a basis for the nationalist movement was like "a tiger fearing to flee to the jungle or water fearing to flow to the sea."[16] The religious disputes between Muslims and Hindus which threatened the unity of the Indian nationalist movement had been transformed in Indonesia to secular/religious disputes which sapped the strength of Indonesian nationalism.[17]

In so viewing the nationalist movement, Permi clashed not only with non-political religious associations, but also with other nationalist political parties. Despite their differences, however, a rapprochement was reached with Sukarno's Partindo in the first half of 1932, largely through the efforts

---

pp. 64-65; Iljas Jacoub, see ibid., pp. 139-40 and *Haluan* [Padang], August 12, 1976; Muchtar Luthfi, Abdullah, *Schools and Politics*, pp. 145-46; and Hamka, *Ajahku*, pp. 133, 262-63.

11. One of the most important merchants in the Pasar Gadang of Padang, Basa Bandaro promoted ties between Permi and the Himpunan Saudagar Indonesia, a trading association which provided considerable funding to the Permi. He became treasurer of the party, and was described by Resident Gonggrijp as being behind all political activity in Padang. MvO Gonggrijp, p. 9. See also Mardjani Martamin, Ishaq Thaher, Amir B. Mahyuddin, *Sejarah Kebangkitan Nasional Sumatera Barat* (n.p.: Proyek Penelitian dan Pencatatan Kebudayaan Daerah, 1977/78), pp. 77.

12. *Mr.* 254/35 (MvO B. H. F. van Heuven [December 31, 1934]), pp. 26-27.

13. *Mr.* 357/33 (January 1933), p. 17.

14. MvO van Heuven, pp. 25, 28.

15. MvO Gonggrijp.

16. *Soeara Islam* [Bukittinggi], November 1, 1931.

17. Ibid.

of Basa Bandaro. The two parties agreed not to compete, and Partindo leaders, Muhammad Yamin and Gatot Mangkupradja attended a special Permi conference in July of that year at which the agreement was approved.[18]

Permi spokesmen voiced their nationalist and religious aims candidly, proclaiming in their speeches their opposition to colonial rule. Police agents, attending the party's public and private meetings, frequently halted the proceedings as Permi leaders, notably the party's most effective orator, Muchtar Luthfi, inflamed their audiences with attacks on Dutch colonialism. Equally outspoken was the party's outstanding woman leader, Rasuna Said, as can be seen from a report of her address to a public meeting of Permi in Payakumbuh in November 1932:

> So long as Indonesia is still not free, Islam can not be exalted [hoog]; Indonesia can not be prosperous, the will of the Qur'an can not be fulfilled; the society can enjoy no peace, so long as Indonesia is still "colonized."
>
> Imperialism is the enemy of the P.M.I. [Permi].
>
> Everything that is ugly belongs to Indonesia, everything that is beautiful in our land, that is, the beautiful buildings and the asphalt roads, belong to "Hindia Belanda."
>
> To die in damnation (the current situation) is like dying in wantonness, therefore you must free yourself from the bonds of colonialism. . . .
>
> Though I am but a woman, I work and offer myself for the people, religion, and the fatherland; I will scorn the man who does less than I.
>
> In our political struggle two fates are possible for us: should we fail we will have our later happiness in heaven; should we be successful, we will gain freedom.[19]

It is not altogether surprising that she was arrested the next month by the Dutch, together with a woman colleague, Rasimah Ismail, the first two members of the party to be sentenced to long jail terms.[20]

Although Permi continued to expand over the first half of 1933, its meetings became less frequent because of the increased government surveillance.[21] In July the crushing blows began, with travel restrictions imposed on many of the party's leaders. On July 11, the authorities arrested Muchtar Luthfi, and the following month imposed the ban on assembly (vergaderverbod) on Permi and the PSII and their affiliated youth organizations. To circumvent these restrictions, the party started to send out written courses; the authorities confiscated them, and in early September arrested their author, Iljas Jacoub, and publisher, Djalaluddin Thaib.[22] All three leaders were exiled to Boven

---

18. MvO van Heuven, pp. 23-24, and Mr. 590 (February 1933), p. 15.

19. Mr. 115/33 (November 1932), pp. 9-10.

20. Rasuna Said was imprisoned for fifteen months (Mr. 227/33 [December 1932], pp. 10-11); Rasimah Ismail was sentenced to nine months in jail for a speech she had made in October (Mr. 590/33 [February 1933], p. 17).

21. Mr. 813/33 (April 1933).

22. Mr. 1187/33 (July 1933); Mr. 1249/33 (August 1933); Mr. 1367/33 (September 1933).

Digul at the end of 1934. With its organization decapitated, the Permi had to struggle to maintain skeletal communication among its members in the face of the continued ban on its meetings, publications, and travel, and its fear that government spies had infiltrated its ranks.[23]

PSII

The Minangkabau branch of the Sarekat Islam was never very strong during the organization's early heyday in the 1910s. In part this was because in West Sumatra it split into different factions, supported by traditional and modernist ulama.[24] Also its foremost modernist adherent, Syekh Abdullah Ahmad, refrained from politics and concentrated on educational activities, founding the Adabiah school in Padang in 1908 and accepting Dutch support and advice in running it.[25] It was only at the end of 1928 that the PSII became active politically, when two *penghulu* (traditional village leaders) from Maninjau set up a section of the party there, and the fiery speeches of one of them, Hasanoeddin glr. Datuk [Dt.] Singo Mangkuto, brought the Dutch to arrest him at the end of July 1929 and sentence him to two years in jail. Largely inactive during his detention, the PSII revived after Dt. Singo Mangkuto's release, when he, together with H. Uddin Rahmany and Sabilal Rasjad glr. Dt. Bandaro, began to expand PSII influence beyond its Maninjau base.[26] Described by the Dutch resident in 1932 as "a noncooperative political organization which sees its goal as the full independence of 'Indonesia' within the shortest possible period, based on Islam, which as a truly democratic system must provide the foundation for the free 'Indonesian' state,"[27] PSII political goals were similar to those of the Permi. The local PSII leaders, however, were conscious of, and took pride in, the Indies-wide character and history of their party; in addition within West Sumatra they drew more support from the penghulu than did the Permi. These differences precluded any chance that the two organizations might merge.[28]

In April 1932 the PSII held a provincial congress in Padang Panjang--the first congress of a political party after the 1927 uprising to espouse a platform of non-cooperation with the Netherlands Indies government.[29] The PSII's head office on Java later disavowed various decisions of the congress, but these continued to govern the party's actions not only locally but also in Tapanuli and the East Coast, where PSII branches had close ties with those in West

---

23. *Mr.* 2/34 (October and November 1933).

24. On the early years of the Sarekat Islam in West Sumatra, see Abdullah, *Schools and Politics*, pp. 24-31.

25. See Hamka, *Ajahku*, pp. 234-36.

26. MvO Gonggrijp (*Mr.* 360/32), pp. 13-14. It had sections in Bukittinggi, Guguk, Suliki, and Padang Panjang.

27. Ibid., p. 14.

28. The Dutch in fact reported PSII attacks on Luthfi's espousal of Islam and nationalism, though such a position seems to have been close to their own. (*Mr.* 590/33, February 1933, p. 9.)

29. MvO van Heuven (*Mr.* 254/35), p. 32. At the congress, it protested the agricultural laws, letting of lands to large industry, heerendiensten, and various taxes.

Sumatra.[30] Although the party's membership numbered only about 2,800 before the mid-1933 crackdown, its influence was considerable in several districts of the Minangkabau heartland, particularly in the rural areas, with Padang Panjang its only important urban stronghold.[31]

The parent organization on Java denied its more radical West Sumatran offspring permission to set up an autonomous "West Sumatra section," although it did accept Dt. Singo Mangkuto as the party's local head.[32] The Minangkabau branch had an added incentive to assert its autonomy, for the PSII leadership on Java was adopting policies that were generally critical of the adat, while much of the party's rural support in West Sumatra came from traditional leaders in the villages.[33]

The government moved against the PSII and the Permi at the same time, viewing them as "the two most militant associations in this region." Permi "being purely Minangkabau, had a larger membership, yet in its fierceness of action the PSII held its own."[34] In August 1933, Batavia applied the ban on assembly to the PSII, and on September 2 Uddin Rahmany and Sabilal Rasjad were accused of violating the ban and arrested,[35] ultimately being exiled to Digul with the Permi leaders in December 1934.[36]

Perti

As with Permi and Muhammadiyah, the Perti too grew from an educational association, this time one of the traditionalist Kaum Tua (Old Group) who relied on the Shafi'i madzab and saw themselves as its defenders in the region. To an even greater extent than in the modernist schools and surau, ulama in the traditionalist schools exerted a powerful influence over their students and the education they received. Syekh Abbas of Padang Lawas was the leading figure in bringing traditional ulama together to combat the modernist ideas penetrating the region via the Sumatra Thawalib schools. As early as 1918, while still providing traditional religious education in his school he had begun to introduce modern teaching methods. And in May 1928 Syekh Abbas sponsored

---

30. Ibid., p. 33.

31. According to this report, Dt. Singo Mangkuto tried to establish the center of his personal support in Padang Panjang, but was pushed aside by a "fanatical local leader" Marzoeki Oesman. The centers of the party's rural strength were in the subdistricts of Empat Angkat, Kamang, Guguk, and Maninjau. Ibid., pp. 34-35.

32. *Mr.* 227/33 (December 1932), p. 2.

33. The anti-adat stance of the PSII was made explicit later at its congress in Banjarnegara in June 1934, where it passed a motion against adat and adat law, citing in particular (possibly at the instigation of H. Agus Salim) the matrilineal social order in Minangkabau. *Mr.* 877/34 (June 1934), p. 8.

34. MvO Spits (*Mr.* 507/37), p. 47.

35. Hasanuddin Dt. Singo Mangkuto was visiting Java at the time and was not arrested. *Mr.* 1249/33 (August 1933), p. 6; *Mr.* 2/34 (October 1933), p. 6.

36. A third PSII leader, Ahmad Chatib glr. Dt. Singo Maradjo, who had been arrested in June 1934 for introducing political courses in PSII schools, was exiled to Digul along with his colleagues. See *Mr.* 877/34 (June 1934), pp. 9-10; *Mr.* 139/35 (December 1934), p. 6.

a meeting with other leading traditionalists (Syekh Sulaiman ar Rasuli of Candung and Syekh Muhammad Djamil Djaho of Padang Panjang) to unite their schools in an association called the Madrasah Tarbiah Islamiyah. Two years later, they again met to form a social organization, Persatuan Tarbiah Islamiyah (PTI or Perti), which they described as "the single defensive barrier" protecting the Shafi'i tarekat of Sunni Islam in the region.[37] The Perti soon spread outside the Minangkabau. It claimed to have branches in Indragiri, Tapanuli, Palembang, Bengkulen, East Sumatra, and Aceh, and even in West Sumatra itself had reached a membership of about 4,000 by 1932.[38] In its opposition to modernist Islamic teaching it cooperated with Minangkabau adat leaders.[39] Although the Dutch hoped that the Perti would act as a counterbalance to the more aggressive nationalist Muslim associations, seeing its leaders as loyal to the colonial government, they recognized that its conservative teachings were unlikely to attract a wide following among the younger generation.[40]

* * *

It was not only Islamic organizations that were active politically in West Sumatra in the early 1930s. Although specifically Communist associations had been outlawed in the mid-1920s, there were branches of most other Jakarta-based nationalist parties in the region. The most influential was the Pendidikan Nasional Indonesia (PNI-Baru) headed at the national level by Mohammad Hatta and Sutan Sjahrir. Mohammad Hatta formally introduced the party into West Sumatra on a visit home in November 1932, shortly after his return from the Netherlands, and he appointed a local youth leader, Chatib Suleiman, to lead it. The PNI-Baru attracted support mainly from among religious nationalists, particularly students and teachers, in Padang Panjang, youth leaders, and Muhammadiyah members. Its strategy, both nationally and locally, was to emphasize cadre building rather than agitation, a policy which its national leaders believed would yield more enduring results, although a smaller following. PNI-Baru membership had only reached about 250 at the time the government clamped down on party activity in the region.[41]

As the Dutch administration tightened its restrictions, leaders of the political parties initially tried all avenues to avoid abandoning their nationalist activities. They substituted written courses for public meetings, reformed the parties' executive boards to bring more moderate leaders to the fore, and loosened their bonds with affiliated schools, youth organizations, and publications. Nevertheless, the authorities continued to harass all attempts

---

37. *Kepartaian dan Parlementaria Indonesia* (Jakarta: Kementerian Penerangan, 1954), p. 431; *Riwayat Hidup dan Perjuangan 20 Ulama Besar Sumatera Barat* (Padang[?]: Islamic Centre Sumatera Barat, 1981), pp. 67-69; 78-80; see also Noer, *Modernist Muslim Movement*, p. 221, and Abdullah, *Schools and Politics*, pp. 135-36.

38. According to Perti's own account, it had a membership of 350,000 by the time of the Japanese occupation. *Kepartaian*, pp. 430-31.

39. The Perti flag was a sun on a black background. According to one of its leaders, the sun represented the Perti and the black background symbolized the adat. *Mr.* 505/40 (January 1940).

40. MvO Gonggrijp (*Mr.* 360/32), p. 19.

41. MvO van Heuven (*Mr.* 254/35), pp. 37-39.

at political activity. This harassment was certainly aimed most directly against the Permi and PSII, but the PNI-Baru was also targeted. In Jakarta, Hatta and Sjahrir were arrested and exiled in late 1933. Party leaders in West Sumatra were not initially subject to such extreme measures, but the local authorities restricted the meetings of the PNI-Baru, forbade travel by some of its members, and greatly curtailed the party's activities. When they attempted to defy these orders, several PNI-Baru leaders in West Sumatra too were jailed.[42]

Of all the parties, however, Permi was the hardest hit. Its members left in increasing numbers as it became clear that political actions were impossible within it. By 1937, at the time of Resident Spits' report, activity within the Permi had reached its nadir. Mohammad Sjafei, the sole remaining active member of its executive board, formally dissolved the party on October 18, 1937, but by then its dissolution apparently did not even spark political comment in the local press.[43]

Regroupment

Anticolonial nationalists in West Sumatra, then, had tried the road of open revolt in 1927 and that of nonviolent political party activity in 1929-33. Both methods had failed, and the Dutch had effectively blocked both avenues of activity. This did not necessarily mean, however, that the regime was successful in blunting opposition to colonial rule, nor did the character of the nationalist movement in West Sumatra change to one of cooperation during these final prewar years.

Demands coming from those nationalist leaders who had not been exiled were certainly moderated and their activities became more accommodating. This was evident in the enthusiasm with which many of them responded to the establishment in 1938 of a Dutch-sponsored, purely advisory semi-representative body, the Minangkabauraad, and the number of former activists, including Permi members, who attempted to gain membership in it.[44]

There is also no doubt that the Dutch succeeded in crushing the Permi, which never again emerged as a political force in its own right. Activist Islamic nationalist organizations with the philosophy of the Permi never again wielded major political power in West Sumatra. Nevertheless, as they sought

---

42. In early 1935, one of the party's leaders, Mohammad Noer Arief, was exiled to Digul; and the following year two others, Leon Salim and Tamimi Usman, were jailed (the first for a year, and second for only 20 days). See *Mr. 510/35* (March 1935); *Mr.* 212/36 (January 1936); *Mr.* 967/36 (August 1936).

43. *Mr.* 6/38 (November 1937).

44. Among those seeking representation to the Minangkabauraad were candidates from noncooperative parties such as Permi, PNI-Baru, and PSII, including Mohammad Sjafei and Fachroeddin H.S., and Soeleman Paris glr. Dt. Maharadjo Diradjo from Permi; Chatib Suleiman from PNI-Baru; and Hasanuddin glr. Dt. Singo Mangkuto from PSII (*Mr.* 470/38 [April 1938]). See also *Persoverzicht* for August 1938 [attached to *Mr.* 958] which has an article from *Persamaan* of August 11, where Darwis Thaib (a former member of the PNI-Baru and Permi) comments on Spits' view that now the situation in West Sumatra has indeed changed through establishment of the Minangkabauraad.

ways to minimize the effects of their party's destruction, the Permi leaders did enable its youth organizations and educational institutions to survive by severing the party's ties with them. The Islamic nationalist ideas of the Permi were then kept alive in the religious schools by teachers trained particularly in the Islamic College in Padang and the newly opened (February 1935) Islamic Training College in Payakumbuh, headed again by former Cairo graduates.[45] A Malay who spent most of the 1930s as a student and teacher in these schools and colleges gave some indication of the atmosphere there and the type of education offered:

> When the teachers taught history they would use Dutch books, but teach them in Indonesian and give them a different slant; for example, the first Governor-General was described as the first Dutch pirate who came to Indonesia. The teachers went to jail, perhaps for a week or two, then they came back. Someone else would take their place teaching school. Then they would be arrested. If the schools were shut down, another school would open. . . .
>
> The curriculum was the same in all the Thawalib schools, even the books, although there was no central committee for the schools. Every one was organized separately, but you could recognize the similarities. The leaders came from the same background and all had the same ideas. The organizers were all political people. Two or three or four of the top leaders really knew about Permi and also about modern education. They would pick cadres in the kampung. Would explain to them what their stand was, and the cadre would have this in common . . . no overall organization bound them, but they understood each other and established organizations just like the others.[46]

The other major haven for the Islamic nationalists was again the Muhammadiyah. As government persecution intensified, many Permi members fled to the apolitical association, and its accommodationist leadership was unable to bar their entry. Even after the Muhammadiyah's earlier "cleansing" several of its local leaders maintained their active anticolonialism, most notably S. J. St. Mangkuto who continued to hold high positions on the board despite his activism. The Muhammadiyah's Java board and its Sumatra consul, A. R. St. Mansur, still frowned on any politicization, but "not only did [St. Mansur] acknowledge the presence of leftist elements in his organization, but above all [recognized] his *impotence* to retain control over them."[47] In May 1936, the Dutch again reported that St. Mansur was aware of the dangerous influence of former Permi members on the Muhammadiyah, but when he investigated this danger, "he encounters difficulties from local leaders who will not always give information on their members."[48] In the late 1930s up to half of the officials in some of the Muhammadiyah's local branches were former Permi members.[49] This does not necessarily mean

---

45. These were Nazaruddin Thaha, H. Iljas Mohamad Ali, and H. Zainuddin (*Mr.* 384/35 [February 1935]; and interview with Nazaruddin Thaha, Padang, October 1976).

46. Interview with Kamaluddin Muhamed (Krismas), Petaling Jaya, December 21, 1981.

47. *Mr.* 607/35 (April 1935), emphasis in the original.

48. *Mr.* 616/36 (May 1936).

49. For example, *Mr.* 117/39 (November 1938) in noting the large number of

that the Muhammadiyah as an association thereby became more radical, for, despite Dutch suspicions, most of these new members probably viewed it mainly as a refuge from reprisal and did not use its willingness to harbor them as an opportunity to radicalize it. Nevertheless, it was never to become the purely social/educational association its parent was on Java.[50]

The apparent Dutch success in defusing the "dangerous" situation in West Sumatra did not lead government authorities to soften their own attitudes towards political activity, for they now, for example, assigned the Muhammadiyah to the same radical place on the political spectrum previously occupied by the Permi. In arguing for continued vigilance, and against lifting restrictions on the local PSII, Resident Spits contended that the "extremist" nationalism of the Minangkabau still lay just below the surface, ready to reemerge as soon as the repressive measures were relaxed: "The earlier party spirit is still latent in political circles, the various occasions on which people forget themselves testify to this. Political catchwords and slogans are not yet forgotten and would quickly push the current expressions of loyalty aside [if the measures against the political parties were relaxed]."[51]

In this, I think, Resident Spits was correct. Notwithstanding the lack of open opposition to the Dutch authorities, the mainstream of the local nationalist movement remained noncooperative throughout the closing years of colonial rule. What did change in the wake of the intensified Dutch repression of 1933-36 was the role the political parties had previously played as the major vehicle for anticolonial nationalism. In their place there developed much more diffuse and fluid alliances, created ad hoc in response to openings offered by the Dutch. From 1937 on it is interesting to note how each clumsy step taken by the authorities, and each sensitive issue they bungled, was immediately seized on and shaped into a fulcrum for reviving political activity, with organizations that sprang up capitalizing in particular on Dutch mishandling of religious and/or traditional issues.

The first such step was the Dutch attempt to introduce a Marriage Registration Bill into West Sumatra in mid-1937. Believing that this bill conflicted with Islamic law, ulama from throughout the region, alongside former Permi members and Muhammadiyah organizations, set up protest committees.[52] Within a month traditional (Kaum Tua) and reformist (Kaum Muda) ulama cooperated to form a "Majlis ulama" demanding withdrawal of the bill.[53] Less immediate though

---

Permi adherents who were now executive committee members of Muhammadiyah, cites one district of the Maninjau region where six former Permi members who sat on its eleven-man executive committee included the chairman, vice chairman, treasurer, and commissioners.

50. This was certainly the charge of Resident Spits: "Indeed it has repeatedly appeared that branches of Java associations assume a completely individual character here. When in 1928 the Muhammadiyah took off here in a big way, within a brief period it changed into an extremist political association. . . . And even now it still repeatedly appears that the Muhammadiyah groups are under the influence of former Communists and similar elements." MvO Spits, Mr. 504/37, p. 13.

51. Ibid., p. 45.

52. *Mr.* 845/37 (August 1937), p. 11.

53. *Mr.* 921/37 (September 1937), p. 12.

no less important was the reaction of adat groups. Two penghulu who led Muhammadiyah organizations in Batu Sangkar, Dt. Boengsoe and Dt. Simaradjo, formed a discussion committee at the end of October, and three months later were able to muster 360 penghulu to attend a meeting in Padang Panjang, where a new adat organization MTKAAM (Majelis Tinggi Kerapatan Adat Alam Minangkabau, High Consultative Council of the Adat of the Minangkabau World) was formally established. For the first time in recent history there was now a Minangkabau adat association that was not essentially conservative and cooperative. All five of its committee leaders had been members of the Muhammadiyah, with one of them having also belonged to the Permi.[54] As the organization spread and developed, the Dutch viewed it with growing suspicion, seeing its membership as largely "made up of discontented, troublesome elements among the penghulus."[55] Conservative penghulu officials in the Dutch administration, notably their long-time adviser Dt. Toemenggoeng, tried to exert a moderating influence, but they were rejected by the membership as a whole,[56] and by June 1939 "more and more people of dubious reputation" were joining the MTKAAM.[57] Despite Dutch suspicions, however, the MTKAAM acted within the political guidelines laid down by the government and did not emerge as an openly nationalistic organization until after the Japanese invasion.

In the specifically religious field, the Dutch authorities provided their opposition with a potent issue when it was reported that Law 177IS, a statute that limited Christian missionary activity in mainly Islamic areas, might be repealed.[58] Resistance to this proposal brought together a kaleidoscope of local personalities representing nationalist, political, adat, and religious ideas from across the spectrum. The two major organizations established in August 1939 to combat the proposed repeal (the Majlis Pertahanan Islam [Council for the Defense of Islam] in Padang and the Badan Permusyawaratan Islam Minangkabau [Minangkabau Islamic Discussion Body, BPIM] in Padang Panjang) included among their leaders members of Permi, PSII, Muhammadiyah, and PNI-Baru, together with educators and businessmen.[59] It was with this issue too that the former leader of the PNI-Baru, Chatib Suleiman, "moved more and more to the foreground of the corporate political life of this residency,"[60] where he was to remain throughout the Japanese occupation and revolution until killed by the Dutch in 1949. In his pamphlet entitled, "Sikap Moeslimin Indonesia: Artikel 177 IS akan ditjaboet [Attitude of Indonesian Muslims: Article 177 IS is to be repealed]" and in his speeches as vice chairman of the BPIM he revived the Permi theme of the early 1930s that Islamic and nationalist forces should combine.[61]

---

54. *Mr.* 187/38 (January 1938), pp. 14-17.

55. *Mr.* 244/39 (December 1938).

56. "C.M.T.K.A.A.M.-congres van 15-19 Maart 1939 te Fort de Kock," in *Mr.* 535/39 (March 1939).

57. *Mr.* 885/39 (June 1939).

58. *Mr.* 1230/39 (August 1939).

59. Mahmoed Joenoes was chairman of the Padang committee, with Moechtar Jahja as vice chairman; A. R. St. Mansur was chairman of the Padang Panjang committee with Chatib Suleiman as vice chairman. For the full membership of the committees, see ibid.

60. *Mr.* 178/40 (November 1939), p. 2.

61. *Mr.* 1406/39 (September 1939).

The son of a trader who had gone bankrupt at the end of World War I,[62] Chatib Suleiman had been educated up to the level of junior high school (MULO), with assistance from the Padang businessman and political activist Abdullah Basa Bandaro. After first earning a living playing the viola and piano in the movie theater in Padang, he became an active youth organizer in Padang Panjang and taught at the Muhammadiyah HIS and the religious Madrasah Irsyadinnas (MIN) run by maverick ulama Adam B.B.[63] In 1932, together with Leon Salim, he founded and led the West Sumatra branch of the PNI-Baru, but gradually withdrew from active participation in the party as it became clear that Dutch repression was eviscerating it. He then turned his major attention to education and business. He established his own Merapi Institute in Padang Panjang in 1935, and with Leon Salim published a magazine, *Pemberi Sinar*, focusing on economic affairs. In the Padang business community, he was still close to his benefactor, Basa Bandaro, the former treasurer of Permi, and he had close ties with Anwar St. Saidi, an important merchant in Bukittinggi, who founded the "Bank Nasional" in 1930. With Anwar and other friends, he established a trading association, "Bumi Putera" and the import company, "Inkorba" (Inkoops Organisatie Batik) in 1938.[64] His economic activities and backing from Anwar's National Bank gave him a financial base from which to carry on political and educational activities.

Assuming a role similar to the one he was to play throughout the subsequent decade, Chatib Suleiman now began to introduce a strategy for bringing together previously dissenting elements into broader, more amorphous associations, based on principles to which they could all agree. The cooperation of all religious groups in opposing the proposed repeal of 177 IS was the first of these, and the Indonesia Berparlemen movement became another--one that appealed to an even broader spectrum of Minangkabau opinion, bringing together the adat and religious leaders, as well as the traditionalist and reformist ulama.[65] As keynote speaker at the first public meeting of the Indonesia Berparlemen movement on December 17, 1939, Chatib Suleiman pursued an interesting line, as recorded by a government observer:

> Chatib Soeleiman chose as his theme "Indonesia demands Parliament." He asserted that the words "Indonesia Berparlemen" could leave no single Indonesian still less any "foreigner" unmoved. A full-

---

62. Apart from material in the Dutch mailrapporten, most of the information on Chatib Suleiman is drawn from the following sources: Rifai Abu and Abdullah Suhadi, *Chatib Suleman* [sic] (Jakarta: Departemen P & K, 1976); M. Raid Malik, et al., *Riwayat Hidup dan Perjuangan Almarhum Chatib Suleiman* (Padang Panjang: n.p., 1973); interviews with Leon Salim, Jakarta, October 1976.

63. Adam B.B. had studied and taught at Haji Rasul's school, but when the Sumatra Thawalib was established, he left to found his own school in Padang Panjang, where there could be a more direct relationship between teacher and pupil and greater authority lodged in the teacher than in the Thawalib schools. Hamka, *Ajahku*, pp. 124-25, 181, 264.

64. The other founders were Marzuki Yatim and Mr. Nasrun. See Abu and Suhadi, *Chatib Suleman*, p. 14; see also *Mr.* 378/38 (March 1938), which notes that Anwar was the principal promoter.

65. About 2,000 people attended the organization's public meeting on December 17, with representatives from such political and religious organizations as the PSII, Muhammadiyah, MTKAAM, and Perti.

fledged parliament in this land would first forge a stronger tie between the Netherlands and Indonesia. Chatib Soeleiman then brought the parliamentary history of other lands into his argument. He cited the French revolution, the driving away of the emperor, and the takeover of power by the people. Here, the speaker got his first warning from the Assistant Wedana. He received his second warning when, via the Sarekat Islam, he came to the Partai Kominis Indonesia as an expression of the people's desire to take their fate into their own hands.[66]

In contrast to the themes of this speech, those of the other speakers were entrenched deeply in local traditional and religious arguments. The chairman of the MTKAAM, Dt. Simarajo, claimed that the people in the Minangkabau could trace the parliamentary system back to their *balai* adat, the traditional meeting hall in the Minangkabau village, while H. Sirajuddin Abbas, who now headed the conservative religious Perti, "repeated the 38th ayat of the Qur'an as showing that a parliament is in line with Mohammedanism. Where 85 percent of Indonesians are Islamic it is only right that a full-fledged parliament should come to Indonesia."[67]

It seems that in organizing the meeting, its leaders were very conscious of the dangers of alarming the Dutch over renewed political or religious radicalism in the region. Their strategy to avoid this was revealed in the proposal by Anwar St. Saidi, vice chairman of the Indonesia Berparlemen committee,[68] that these two leaders, Dt. Simarajo and H. Sirajuddin Abbas, as spokesmen of an adat and a conservative religious party, should be the Minangkabau representatives to the Indonesia Raya Congress in Batavia.[69]

It was on December 28, 1939, only a week after this meeting that Muhammad Yamin, elected by the Minangkabauraad as its representative on the Volksraad, visited West Sumatra. This visit undoubtedly formed the basis for his opinion that the situation in West Sumatra "is healthy," with "Kaeoem Adat and Kaeoem Agama now able to cooperate with each other."[70]

* * *

Thus by the end of the 1930s the Minangkabau nationalists appear to have absorbed the lessons from their earlier defeats at the hands of the Dutch colonial government. In so doing they had had to change many of the methods they used for working towards their ultimate goal of independence. Not all of these, however, were altered; the Muhammadiyah, for example, was still playing essentially the same role in the later 1930s as it had in the aftermath of the 1927 uprising, providing the "apolitical" haven to which religious activists could retreat; and parallel to it in the adat sphere there had now emerged a "nonpolitical" but also nonconservative adat organization, the MTKAAM,

---

66. *Mr.* 323/40 (December 1939), pp. 4-5.

67. Ibid.

68. Abdoel Rivai, a local private doctor, was its chairman. Ibid.

69. Ibid. Soeleman Paris glr. Dt. Maharadjo Diradjo, ex-Permi council member, member of the Minangkabauraad, and secretary of the MTKAAM executive board was also scheduled to attend at his own expense. (*Mr.* 178/40 [November 1939].)

70. Quoted in Bouman, *Enige Beschouwingen*, p. 88.

which could play the same role for those penghulu who were not in accord with Dutch colonial rule. The principal lessons that had been learned were not just that the Dutch would not permit open political party opposition to their government, but that, in order to be effective, it was necessary for the various streams in Minangkabau society, that had previously worked in opposition to one another as well as to the Dutch, now to cooperate among themselves. This they were willing to do, spurred by pragmatic leaders, particularly those who had some economic role in the society, such as Chatib Suleiman, Basa Bandaro, and Anwar St. Saidi.

In other parts of Indonesia, oppositionist and cooperative nationalists came together in such organizations as Parindra and Gerindo. But neither of these gained strength in West Sumatra. As a former Permi member wrote in the newspaper, *Persamaan*:

> The Parindra and Gerindo have less chance of succeeding in this residency, because in their Indonesianism they are indifferent to or opposed to Islam. The Minangkabauers always demand a religious foundation for their political lives . . . they must be established in the spirit of the Permi "Persatoean Moeslim Indonesia" incorporating within themselves the special qualities and insights of the above named party.[71]

It was this spirit that was to characterize the political life of the region to some extent during the Japanese occupation and more notably after 1945, when the local Republican leaders largely succeeded in building their opposition to the Dutch return on a fusion of religion and nationalism, and at the same time were able to operate in conjunction with the adat MTKAAM.

By 1940, then, the various streams in West Sumatran society had begun to converge in preparation for carrying their struggle to a further stage. They adopted policies not of cooperation with the Dutch but of constructive obstructionism and the forging of informal ties that could subsequently be strengthened in attaining the objective of independence. What marked the closing years of colonial rule off from the early 1930s was not the goal sought but the tactics employed. No longer was open confrontation--either physical or political--a viable option, so alternative methods were tried. But although in this period, the nationalists avoided confrontation, their militancy, as Resident Spits was aware, nevertheless remained latent, just below the surface and ready to assert itself whenever conditions were propitious.

This opportunity finally came in March 1942 at the time of the Japanese invasion of Indonesia. On Java the Dutch Governor-General had surrendered on March 9, but A. I. Spits, now Governor of Sumatra, expressed his determination to continue resistance there.[72] Opposed to the "scorched-earth" policy proclaimed by the Dutch, Chatib Suleiman and his associates began organizing demonstrations to be held throughout West Sumatra, demanding that the Dutch transfer their administration to Indonesian hands, so that Indonesians could be the ones

---

71. *Mr.* 1089/38 (September 1938); quoting *Persamaan*, September 27, 1938, with article by Darwis Thaib Dt. Marah Indo.

72. The Dutch forces on Sumatra actually lost contact with the Chief of the General Staff on Java on the evening of March 7. For the Dutch account of their actions in Central Sumatra after the fall of Java, see *Nederlands-Indië contra Japan*, vol. 6, *De Strijd op Ambon, Timor en Sumatra* (The Hague: Staatsdrukkerij, 1959), pp. 94-110.

to negotiate Sumatra's surrender with the invading forces, rather than merely being transferred as "articles in the inventory" from the Dutch to the Japanese. On March 12, the Dutch authorities in Padang Panjang arrested Chatib Suleiman, together with Leon Salim and four other leaders of the projected demonstrations, charging them with attempting to undermine the Netherlands Indies government. So concerned were the Dutch at their defiance that they took these prisoners with them when Netherlands Indies forces retreated to their final stronghold at Kota Cane on Aceh's southern borders, and the six Minangkabau nationalists only regained their freedom on March 29, 1942 when the Japanese stormed the jail where they were imprisoned.[73]

---

73. A full account of these events appears in "Tawanan Kutatjane," by Leon Salim (typescript, 1953) in my possession.

THE POLITICAL AND SOCIAL LANGUAGE OF INDONESIAN MUSLIMS: THE CASE OF *AL-MUSLIMUN*

Howard M. Federspiel

I. Introduction

There is a stereotype long held in the West and in the Arabic world that Islam in Southeast Asia is lacking in depth and commitment to general principles of Islamic belief and practice. Western scholarly and nonscholarly writings about Southeast Asia over the past century have usually spoken of Islam's accommodation as it encountered peoples influenced by animism, Hinduism, and Buddhism.[1] Most studies that appeared up until the 1940s, while not denying the significant impact of Islam and the existence of some pious Muslims in the region, presented Islam in Southeast Asia as hopelessly mixed with local cultural practices and out of step with more purist forms in the Middle East. The trend was reinforced by certain Indonesian nationalists in the second quarter of the twentieth century who were persuaded that Islam's dominance in the sixteenth and seventeenth centuries had harmed native political strength and created conditions favorable to the establishment of European colonialism.[2] In general this perception of a syncretic Islam prevailed among scholars East and West until the 1970s.

There were notable exceptions to such a perception, however. The work of Anthony Johns,[3] Hamka,[4] and Aboebakar Atjeh,[5] *inter alia*, argued that while many Muslims did accommodate their religion to the cultures of the region, a strain of purist Islam has maintained itself for several centuries. In

---

1. C. Snouck Hurgronje, *Nederland en de Islam* (Leiden: Brill, 1911), esp. pp. 23-25; Ph. S. Van Ronkel, "Islam," in *Encyclopaedie van Nederlandsch-Indië*, vol. 3 (Leiden: Brill, 1918), esp. pp. 171-72; R. O. Winstedt, *The Malay Magician* (London: Routledge, 1961), esp. pp. 81-102; Richard J. Wilkinson, *The Peninsular Malays*, vol. 1 (Leiden: Brill, 1906), pp. 1-81.

2. Bernhard Dahm, *Sukarno and the Struggle for Indonesian Independence* (Ithaca: Cornell University Press, 1969), p. 338.

3. A. H. Johns, "Aspects of Sufi Thought in India and Indonesia in the First Half of the Seventeenth Century," *Journal of the Royal Asiatic Society Malayan Branch* [henceforth *JRASMB*], 28, 1 (1955): 70-77, and "Malay Sufism as Illustrated in an Anonymous Collection of Seventeenth Century Tracts," *JRASMB*, 30, 2 (1957): 5-111.

4. Hamka [H. Abd. Malik Karim Amrullah], *Ajahku* (Jakarta: Widjaya, 1958).

5. Hadji Aboebakar Atjeh, *Sedjarah Hidup K.H.A. Wahid Hasjim dan karangan tersiarnja* (Jakarta: Panitya, 1957), and "Pengantar," *Sedjarah Sufi dan Tasawwuf* (Bandung: Tjerdas, 1962).

fact, the rise of modernist Islam throughout the region in the first quarter of the twentieth century resulted from the efforts of individuals and organizations associated with that purist outlook.[6] That outlook remains politically and socially important in Southeast Asia today.

It is with the purist strain of Islam that I am concerned here, and, accordingly, criteria for determining its characteristics will be outlined and tested. This study contends that these criteria will serve as a valid measure to determine the identification with Islam of individuals and associations through their statements, writings, and practices. By identifying the attitudes of those who are closely connected with their religion, we can begin to understand better the diversity of belief in Southeast Asia and study it beyond the realm of stereotype.

The criteria put forth here are not to determine who is a Muslim and who is not. That is a matter for the community of Muslims to establish itself, in the context of its own tradition. Rather, what is attempted is to study those staunch Muslims in Southeast Asia who are deeply concerned about commitment to their faith and to examine the attributes that identify many of them.

The study postulates four thesis statements about Muslim attributes in Southeast Asia. They are:

1. Enunciation of Islamic principles as elaborated in standard Islamic sources of Qur'an and Traditions (Ar: ḥadīth),[7] and expanded by important theologians, mystics, and legalists associated with the religion. Generally, Muslims maintain that God (Ar: Allāh) is the Creator, that he has sent prophets, including Muhammad, and his Word (Ar: Qur'ān) to mankind for guidance. Belief and practice are necessary to fulfill God's direction. For the purposes of this study Islamic principles are those outlined in several standard studies of Islam: notably Fazlurrahman's *Islam*, and Gibb's, *Mohammedanism*.[8]

2. Heavy use of Arabic to express religious values, including names, terms, terminologies, and scriptural quotations. Muslims are committed

---

6. See in particular, G. F. Pijper, "Het Reformisme in de Indonesische Islam," in *Studien over de geschiedenis van de Islam in Indonesia, 1900-1950* (Leiden: Brill, 1977), pp. 97-145, and William R. Roff, *The Origins of Malay Nationalism* (New Haven: Yale University Press, 1967).

7. Foreign words in parentheses are Indonesian unless preceded by "Ar:" indicating they are Arabic terms transliterated into Roman script. Qur'an and Allah, as words commonly used in English, are used in the text with these spellings and are not otherwise marked. The spelling of Indonesian words throughout is that used in the 1950s.

8. Fazlurrahman, *Islam* (New York: Holt, Rinehart, 1966), and H. A. R. Gibb, *Mohammedanism* (London: Oxford University Press, 1953). References cited in this section on methodology are to standard works known internationally and held in high regard by Islamicists, whether Muslim or not. The principles of Islam outlined in these works are distilled from books on specific subjects by the theologians, jurists, and other Muslim writers working on Islamic belief and practice. The specific studies use specialized language, often are not available except in Arabic, and are not generally available in most university libraries in the West. Hence, standard works are used in this study.

to the use of Arabic: 1) as an absolute requirement for the preservation and use of religious sources (i.e., Qur'an and Tradition of the Prophet); 2) as a carrier of the exposition of Islam in numerous books on law, philosophy, and mystical practice; 3) in terms used in description of religious thought and practice; and 4) in the recitation of prayer. These terms are further identified in Padwick, *Muslim Devotions* and Hughes, *Dictionary of Islam.*[9]

3. Attempts to put the Islamic principles into everyday use, particularly 1) those concerned with the importance of worship and religious obligation; and 2) in cases when other actions are not contrary to or outlawed by Islam sources. This is specifically reflected in the concept of divine law (Ar: *sharī'a*). This concept demands the application of the principles of justice derived from sources that establish God's law among men. Worship ranks high on both scores. This definition rests on the fuller elaboration given in Juynboll, *Handleiding tot de kennis van de Mohammedaansche wet* and Khadduri and Liebesny, *Law in the Middle East.*[10]

4. Nonrecognition or condemnation of other viewpoints that challenge Islam's importance in society or state or otherwise detract from the importance of Islam. The concept of the community of believers (Ar: *umma*) is at work here. It is important to promote a unity of believers to close ranks against outsiders whose beliefs, practices, and values challenge those of Islam. Consequently, there is a refusal to recognize the validity of other viewpoints except as they conform to the general Islamic perception of how things should be. Accommodation with outsiders is limited in time and extent. This statement rests on the fuller explanation of attitudes clarified by Smith, *Islam in the Modern World* and Haykal, *The Life of Muhammad.*[11]

This article will examine material contained in the periodical *Al-Muslimun* between 1955 and 1959 to illustrate the foregoing assumptions. We already know from previous studies that the Persatuan Islam, the publisher of *Al-Muslimun*, is an Islamic society, acknowledged as firmly Islamic by members and critics alike and, as such, a study of its contents could be expected to deal directly with Muslim attitudes and would constitute a test of the validity of the indicators outlined above. Our examination can be expected to yield very positive results.

II. Description of Al-Muslimun

The magazine *Al-Muslimun* was published in Bangil, East Java between 1954 and 1960. During the first three and a half years issues appeared monthly, and over the next two and a half years numbers appeared irregularly. It had a total run of forty-five issues before it ceased publication.

---

9. Constance E. Padwick, *Muslim Devotions* (London: SPCK, 1961), and Thomas P. Hughes, *A Dictionary of Islam* (Labore: Premier, 1964).

10. Th. W. Juynboll, *Handleiding tot de kennis van de Mohammedaansche Wet* (Leiden: Brill, 1930), and Mejid Khadduri and Herbert Liebesny, *Muslim Law in the Middle East* (Washington: Middle East Institute, 1955).

11. Wilfred C. Smith, *Islam in Modern History* (Princeton: Princeton University Press, 1957), esp. Chapter 1, and Muhammad Husein Haykal, *The Life of Muhammad* (Cairo: Shorouk International, 1983).

Al-Muslimun was the voice of one center of an Islamic association, named the Persatuan Islam, which had been in existence since 1923 and had played an important, but never dominant, role in Indonesian political activity in the two decades prior to World War II and in the parliamentary period of independent Indonesia (1950 to 1957).[12] The Persatuan Islam was not fully reflective of the wider Indonesian community that regarded Islam as important. Two differences are apparent. First was its association with Pan-Islamism and the corresponding deemphasis of Indonesian nationalism. Arguing that Muslims should concentrate on the unity and prosperity of all Muslims in whatever lands they were located, leaders of Persatuan Islam were prone to argue for promotion of Islamic values in Indonesia in accord with the wider Muslim world. In the prewar years this stance was expressed as antinationalism, but in the 1950s Persatuan Islam accepted Indonesia as a political reality and emphasized guiding the nation toward being fully Islamic. This stress on Islam was more marked than among other Muslim associations in Indonesia, most of which were more favorably disposed towards nationalism. A second characteristic of Persatuan Islam was the dominance of Ahmad Hassan, a Tamil from Singapore who had immigrated as an adult to Indonesia in the 1920s. Learned in Islamic lore and concerned, like others around him, about colonialism, he justified his own participation in anticolonial activity on the basis of Islam rather than nationalism. His influence was still strong in the 1950s and, significantly, his son, Abdulkadir Hassan, who was an editor of Al-Muslimun and was rising in prominence in the Persatuan Islam at this time, held similar views to those of his father.[13]

In a tradition of widely distributed and controversial publications issued by the Persatuan Islam, the form of Al-Muslimun most reflected Pembela Islam,[14] except that its stress on holy law was perhaps more pronounced. Al-Muslimun included articles, presented in serial form, that outlined the traditional sciences of religious investigation and knowledge; articles on the vitality of Islam in contemporary times; an editorial column that spoke to issues of politics, social conflict, and threat to the community; and a column called Sual-Djawab (question-response) that answered readers' questions about appropriate conduct in religious affairs and everyday life. It is the last item that we will return to as the chief point of investigation.

Materials for Al-Muslimun came from a variety of sources. Some sections were reprints of previously published pieces, usually from elsewhere in the Muslim world.[15] The sections on Islamic sciences, the editorials, and the answers to readers' questions were produced by the editorial staff or someone else connected with the Persatuan Islam. In particular, Abdulkadir Hassan and Abdul Musa, the editor, seem to have prepared much of the material, including

---

12. Pijper, "Reformisme," pp. 122-24; H. M. Federspiel, The Persatuan Islam (Ithaca: Cornell University Modern Indonesia Project, 1970).

13. For a view of accommodation with non-Muslim principles, see Ruth T. McVey, "Faith as an Outsider: Islam in Indonesian Politics," in Islam in the Political Process, ed. James P. Piscatori (London: Cambridge University Press, 1983), pp. 199-221. For further information on Ahmad Hassan, see Howard M. Federspiel, "Islam and Nationalism," Indonesia 24 (October 1977): 39-47.

14. Pembela Islam (Bandung: Persatuan Islam, 1929-35).

15. Examples are articles by Sa'īd Ramadhān of the World Muslim Congress, Muhammad Asād, the prominent Indian Muslim writer, and Nasīruddīn Al-Albānī, a Syrian Muslim scholar.

responses to readers' questions. Other Muslim contributors assisted from time to time.

The magazine was published monthly and probably had a circulation of several hundred copies. Advertisements indicate that it was sold at bookstores in various places on Java, Sumatra, Kalimantan, and Sulawesi, and in Singapore. A few copies apprently were sent to Syria, Pakistan, and Malaysia, as the masthead cited association with people in those countries. Although written in Bahasa Indonesia, the magazine made heavy use of terms from Arabic, a trend in keeping with Indonesian works on Islam, but less in line with the general development of Bahasa Indonesia at that time when the infusion of Javanese, Sanskrit, and Western terms was much more pronounced.[16] Quotes in Arabic when citing Islam scripture were consistent with standard writings on Islamic sciences and used extensively in every issue.

1. The Sual-Djawab Section: General Overview

The Sual-Djawab section is especially relevant to this study because it reflects readers' concerns about the relationship of religion to their lives. Further, the answers indicate how the Persatuan Islam attempted to lay out a guide for concerned Muslims reflecting the association's understanding of the application of Muslim values to contemporary Indonesian society. Over the five years of publication 378 cases were printed, many dealing with multiple questions. About ten questions were answered in each issue, with the average response taking up less than a page, or about 100 to 200 words, although some covered several pages. Apparently readers liked the columns, for, in the second year of publication, an editor's note stated that "not less than 500 questions" had been received and that every effort would be made to respond to them.[17]

In dealing with questions from readers, the reader's request was summarized in a short essential question (or questions) and then answered precisely and directly. Use of this "question-response" technique was not unique. It had been employed extensively and successfully by Ahmad Hassan, and, in fact, was his common method of dealing with questions concerning Islam. Throughout the period from 1925 to 1960, in the magazines *Pembela Islam* and *Al-Lisaan*, his books on religious issues, and in some of his interviews, he used "question-response" as he addressed issues confronting Muslims.[18] His son, Abdulkadir Hassan, was now attempting in this set of cases to address problems facing Muslims, in keeping with the work of the father. The method of presentation undoubtedly seemed appropriate.

The answers to questions varied. In some cases technical answers were given. In others, however, matters were elaborated and traditional Muslim views were challenged. A good example is provided by case 155 concerning the use of a special prayer before Friday worship service.

(155) Meritorious prayer before Friday Communal Worship

Question: Is prayer meritorious before the Friday communal worship?

Response: The meritorious prayer which people often perform before

---

16. Khaidar Anwar, *Indonesian: The Development and Use of a National Language* (Yogjakarta: Bulaksumar, 1980).

17. *Al-Muslimun* 2, 3 (March 1955): 11.

18. Federspiel, *Persatuan Islam*, pp. 21-24.

the Friday communal prayer is the performance of two prayer sets after the first call to prayer. . . .

This sort of worship never existed in [early] Islam; neither the Prophet [Mohammed]--peace be on him and blessing--nor his Companions performed it or approved it.

People who maintain the existence of meritorious Friday prayer obviously have several justifications but none of these justifications are acceptable in the light of examination of firm religious sources.

Let [those who advocate this prayer] show if there is a firm basis for [this practice] from Religion [itself].[19]

This case speaks, of course, to the importance of preciseness in religious practice. Here the Persatuan Islam, in keeping with the traditional Islamic science of legal inquiry, holds that only practices clearly prescribed in religious sources are permitted. All other practices are innovation and an abomination to proper worship. A second case deals with a more complicated matter and a more elaborate response was given.

(136) The Call to Prayer using the Local Language

Question: Can the summoner to Friday communal prayer change the call from Arabic to the local language, because, according to our viewpoint, the *bilal* [summoner] is the leader of the congregation?

Response: [With the term] bilal, the petitioner certainly means *adhan* and *iqama* [i.e., the first and second calls to prayer].

[The person who] calls to prayer is not the same as the leader of a congregation, either in form or purpose, for several reasons, among them:
  I. The call to prayer has a text defined for all time, while the [role of the] leader of a congregation is a temporal matter.
  II. The call to prayer has a text defined for all time, while the congregational leader does not [have such a text], rather, it changes according to his need.
  III. The call to prayer is a matter for which an [eternal] reward is given to the person performing it, while the leader of the congregation has a temporal function . . . which has no relationship with the rewards of the Hereafter.

From the standpoint of religious teaching we are taught the call to prayer and commanded to utter it with the precise pronunciation which we have been taught. Such a matter is called a "religious matter," a matter of the "hereafter" or "worship." . . .

Praying or worship is the province of Allah and His Prophet. Indeed it is [from these sources] that Religion receives its precise form and its characteristics.

As followers of the Islamic Religion, we are prone to fall short, exceed or alter matters of worship set by God and the Prophet. . . .

The basis for the preciseness [in this case] is the [tradition of the] Prophet [which states]:

> "Anyone performing an act which is not commanded of him, is rejected."

Certainly the call to prayer is such an action.

---

19. *Al-Muslimun* 2, 6 (September 1955): 10.

> Therefore the call to prayer which was taught by the Prophet
> ... cannot be changed to the local language.
> This also applies in several other cases as well. ...[20]

The differentiation made in this case between matters of worship (*'ibadat*) and temporal matters (*perbuatan keduniaan*) is unusual. As part of a worship ceremony it would seem to follow that it too is a matter of worship but the writer holds that its purpose actually is temporal since its contents are not prescribed or limited to matters of worship.

2. Sual-Djawab: General Content

The 378 cases cross a wide spectrum of subjects but there are perceptible trends in the material. For purposes of our investigation three general categories have been applied: religious belief, religious obligation and practice, and political and social matters. The summary of that categorization is found in Table 1.

Table 1. General Subjects Covered in the Sual-Djawab Section[21]
by Year

	1954-55	1955-56	1956-57	1957-60	Total
Religious Belief	17	24	12	13	66
Religious Obligation and Practice	27	62	56	34	179
Social and Political Matters	46	37	29	21	133
Total	90	123	97	68	378

Cases of religious belief consisted of matters of general information, questions of proper investigation into religious sources, application of belief to the Indonesian context, and compatibility of religious tenets to scientific and technological developments of the current age. The cases of religious obligation and practice dealt with ritual cleanliness, death and funerals, the poor tax, proper observance of prayer, fasting, and the pilgrimage to Mecca. The cases on social and political matters dealt with marriage and divorce, dietary issues, status of men and women, tolerance of non-Muslims, national law, and the national state. These categories, of course, are arbitrary, but do relate to the terminology used in the cases themselves. While many readers, particularly those in the West, might regard marriage and divorce, dietary issues, status of men and women, and tolerance of non-Muslims as religious, they are not regarded as such by the writers of *Al-Muslimun*. Rather, the writers see these categories as matters of social intercourse, in which Muslims are free to establish their own practices, except where God has set some limitations. The discussion under *bid'a*, below, where religious and nonreligious practice is defined, elaborates this point further.

The greatest number of cases fall in the area of religious obligation and practice, indicating a great deal of concern with proper observance of prayer and worship and general religious requirements. Even in the category of social and political matters, nearly half of the cases deal with traditional Muslim concerns regarding dietary regulations, and marriage and divorce matters.

---

20. Ibid. 2, 5 (August 1955): 6-7.

21. Sources, ibid. 1-5 (1954-60).

On the other hand, twelve cases deal with science, medical practice, and technology, a comparatively small number considering that the issue of modernization was being nationally debated in Indonesia at this time. Political matters, particularly the role of Islam in the national state and national law, received considerable coverage in the early period--some eight cases in the first year--but this particular issue was not directly addressed in the last two years. Undoubtedly the advent of Guided Democracy made discussion of it a moot point and a political dangerous venture.

3. *Content of the Cases: Concepts and Specialized Language*

One way of examining the contents of the cases is to isolate key terms and analyze their meaning to Muslims as expressed through their use in the cases. The concepts selected for this study deal with three different, but interrelated matters: 1) terms used in applying religious principles to human behavior; 2) terms used in defining social relationships; and 3) terms used in defining political relationship. In the first category the concept "change" or "accretion" (bid'a) and five related terms of religious acceptability-- "necessary" (*wadjib*); "meritorious" (*hasan*); "allowed" (*halal*); "reproachful" (*makruh*); and "forbidden" (*haram*) have been selected. These terms, common to Muslim jurisprudence and Muslim codes of behavior are used as a means of applying religious principles to human behavior.[22] In social matters a set of five terms has been selected to show social distance between Muslims and other groups. The terms are "community of believers" (*ummah*), monotheists (*ahli kitab*), non-Muslims (*orang jang bukan Islam*), "unbeliever" (*kafir*), and "heathen" (*musjrik*). The third category deals with political matters, and, as such, contrasts "divine law" (*shari'a*) with "man-made law" (*undang-undang*).

a. *Terms used in applying religious standards.* Perhaps the key term for the writers of *Al-Muslimun* in responding to the questions of the readers is bid'a, a religious term of Arabic derivation. In a case entitled "Definition of bid'a," the writer states that bid'a in general . . . means: "Something that is new, creating something . . . such as electricity, radio and so forth, which had not existed previously."[23] It can have a neutral or even a beneficial meaning, but in religious matters the definition is negative. In matters of worship, bid'a is an action which adds to the principles of religion. When the new action (bid'a) is first undertaken, those who perform it believe that the action is properly part of religion, even though, in reality it is not. The writer further notes that such pseudo-religious practices were installed by religious authorities in the past to introduce into religion many special elements which they believed were beneficial and meritorious.[24] The viewpoint of the author is that such change is not to be countenanced in religious matters. The measure for determining whether behavior is actually part of religion or an accretion is whether it was commanded by God in the Qur'an or practiced

---

22. These six terms, given here with their Indonesian equivalents, have approximately the same meaning as the Arabic words despite the different script. The same is true for "unbeliever" and "heathen" later in the paragraph. The Arabic equivalents are not given, as they would be repetitious of the Indonesian words.

23. Ibid. 2, 3 (June 1955): 7.

24. Ibid.: 6-7.

by the Prophet as recorded in the Traditions. If it fails this two-way test, it is bid'a, an unacceptable accretion. The basis for this view is a tradition of the Prophet in which he states that "bid'a is error and belongs in the fire."[25] Consequently it can be said that bid'a, well intentioned or not, has no place in religious matters. In secular or temporal matters, however, change is acceptable unless religious sources specifically reject such change. The discovery of technical instruments and medicines, which have been beneficial and are not at odds with religious principles, are cited as examples. On this basis, in many cases the writers repeat the principle that action regarding religious activity is permitted only when expressly commanded by the key religious sources and that, in matters of nonreligious earthly behavior, all actions are permitted except those expressly forbidden by religious authority.

It remains, then, only to decide whether or not a matter concerns religion. At this point, several key categories appear. Included in religion are all matters connected directly with worship. The language of worship, except the Friday sermon, must be in Arabic. The call to worship may not be altered to suit local custom. Adding extra phrases to prayers as a sign of piety is not permitted.[26]

The principle of religion extends to the funeral and particularly to the gravesite, where behavior is seen as involving worship. Consequently, extra activities often prescribed in the Muslim books of jurisprudence (Ar: *fiqh*) are regarded as unacceptable accretions. Specifically addressed are the last prompting (*talqin*) in which the deceased is given instruction to help him answer the questions of belief that the angels of the grave will ask him to determine whether he is truly a believer. Another case expresses the view that common Islamic recitation formulas--the *dhikr* and *tasbih*--and any special readings from scripture, such as the *Surah Jasin*, also cannot be justified, in that they are not commanded.[27]

The area of rival religious values also is viewed as involving worship. The use of amulets and charms is not permissible, not because they are *ipso facto* wrong, but because the Qur'an and Traditions do not enjoin their use. In the matter of holding a *slametan* (ritual meal) during an eclipse of the moon, the writers find that, since there is a worship ceremony for such an occasion, to add a slametan would be to add uncommanded behavior to a religious ceremony. On this point, however, the question specifically addresses the situation in which the ritual meal is added to the prayer. The issue of a slametan by itself is not addressed. In another case a reader asks about cutting the hair of an infant and having a *kenduri* (ritual meal) as part of the proceedings. The reply: "As for holding a kenduri religious observance . . . [it has] no basis in religion."[28] The writers turn aside the practice of consulting a soothsayer (*dukun*), stating that belief in mystical matters does not have a basis in religion and cannot be used by Muslims.[29] On such matters, where the force of custom or the popularity of the action contribute to its use, the author states forcefully: "Religion does not look to the great

---

25. Ibid.: 7.

26. Ibid. 2, 12 (March 1956): 6-7; 2, 5 (August 1955): 7.

27. Ibid. 2, 7 (October 1955): 9-10; 2, 2 (May 1955): 4.

28. Ibid. 3, 1 (April 1956): 210, 214-15.

29. Ibid. 3, 30 (August 1957): 10-11.

majority of people or to religious authorities ... but to the principles from God and His Prophet."[30]

In areas of behavior regarded by the writers of *Al-Muslimun* as temporal affairs there is a complex group of prohibitions and commands. The writers note that food and eating belong to this category and that pork may not be eaten, as it is forbidden by religious sources, but that dog may be eaten because it is not expressly prohibited. They note that all sports are permitted and that music as well fits in this nonreligious category. Tattooing is forbidden, while nearly all matters of commerce and trade are permitted. As noted above, even the Friday sermon, as distinct from the worship service itself, is seen as a temporal matter. The sermon is prescribed by religion but the contents are not regulated and may deal with whatever matters the speaker to the congregation wishes.[31]

The second concept in this category is a set of terms defining behavior by Muslims in particular situations. Here the five-fold category common to Muslim schools of law is used--"necessary," "meritorious," "permitted," "reproachful," and "forbidden."[32] Usually the matters fall into necessary, permitted, or forbidden, and it is seldom that meritorious and reproachful are used. As we have seen in the section on bid'a, matters of religious performance which are necessary (wadjib), include prescribed prayer, giving the alms tax, and fasting during Ramadan. Likewise some actions, usually in nonreligious matters, are forbidden (haram), such as drinking alcohol. A large number of matters are permitted (halal), such as working with a non-Muslim, undertaking business activities, and participating in sports. The category of "meritorious" (hasan) is more circumscribed, but some actions are listed, such as praying at night. The category of "reproachful" (makruh) is similarly circumscribed, including only one immediate example when certain categories of meat are discussed, such as "wild animals, snakes and tigers."[33] Readers are admonished that analogy should not be used to make "reproachful" into "forbidden" matters, such as, "one may not eat dogmeat because it equates to pork," or making meritorious into "necessary" matters because they seem good, such as extra recitations of *Surah Jasin* (102).[34] Categories exist as God sets them, not as mankind would like to have them.

b. *Social concepts.* Any discussion of social vocabulary must start with the concept of community of believers. Once this has been elaborated, Muslim perceptions of other groups in society then become clear, being placed in an understandable context. In this elaboration, then, an examination will be made of the social distance between Muslims and four other identified groups: other monotheists (ahli kitab), non-Muslims (*orang jang bukan Islam*), nonbelievers (kafir), and heathens (musjrik). The cases deal extensively with these various groups and Muslims' relations with them.

The community of believers (ummat) receives no special attention as a concept and in no case is a precise definition given. The term is used occasionally

---

30. Ibid. 2, 2 (May 1955): 4.

31. Ibid. 1, 8 (November 1954): 5-6; 1, 10 (January 1955): 9; 2, 9 (December 1955): 11; 2, 2 (June 1955): 5-6; and 3, 29 (August 1956): 5.

32. See above p. 62. Case 70 in *Al-Muslimun* 1, 10 (January 1954): 7-8, outlines these classifications.

33. Ibid. 1, 10 (January 1954): 6-7.

34. Ibid. 2, 2 (May 1955): 4.

by both petitioners and writers and seems to possess known implications for both sides. The term is used to fit with general Islamic thinking, wherein those who confess Islam and identify with the religion are regarded as belonging to the community. There is no attempt to differentiate the general follower (Ar: Muslim) from the true believer (Ar: *mu'min*), so the community includes both the casual and dedicated follower.

But if a definition is not given, the principle of responsibility for community action and behavior is both implied and carefully elaborated in a number of cases. This is clear in Case 11 when the writer advises that anything that relates to mystical practice or forms a kind of worship "may never be practiced by the community of Islam," unless there is a clear command of God and His Prophet to do so.[35]

Another case deals with specific instances. Case 22, concerning the alms tax incumbent on all Muslims, outlines some of the basic obligations that seem to be covered by the term "in the way of God" and for which alms may be given. Since many of these obligations cannot be undertaken by individuals, there is an implication that they are the community's responsibility. These include "the study of knowledge, undertaking the pilgrimage, shrouding the dead, constructing bridges, building fortifications, enriching mosques, developing foodstuffs and water in the countryside, building health facilities, establishing hospitals, sending out Islamic missionaries, covering the operating expenses of mosques and their teachers, and various other matters of benefit and public importance which are acknowledged by God."[36]

In Case 70, titled "respecting religion," the writer warns Muslims not to depart from their religious obligations for other enticements or even other obligations, such as momentary feeling, psychological justifications, conformity with custom (*adat*), political position, circumstance or situation, or family obligations, except when permitted to do so under conditions of danger, where survival is threatened. The case concludes with some direct warnings about the plight of the Muslim community in Indonesia and offers advice on what Muslims must and cannot do. Pointedly the author states that it is obviously rather difficult to define the means for influencing the public so that religion is respected, especially in a country like Indonesia where Islam is not a popular religion (*dimana Islam tidak mendjadi Agama Ra'jat*), a situation made worse by the antireligious efforts of those who want to divide the unity of Islam. "But if, among us, the majority want to persuade people to accept Islam so that it has no rivals, want to preach everywhere, want to teach the genuine picture of religion, want to increase the number of religious books in circulation, educate people not to imitate blindly," then they will make an impression on the general populace. But, if on the other hand, Muslims remains ignorant and adopt passive attitudes, then the greatness of the Islamic community will be lost.[37]

In Islamic history a great deal of stress has been placed on Islam's relationship with other believers of monotheism, the so-called "People of the Book (ahli kitab), a term generally applied to Christians and Jews. Writers of *Al-Muslimun* reflect that position, and in three cases they spell out a relationship of general tolerance and acceptance. In Cases 146 and 271, marriage

---

35. Ibid. 1, 2 (May 1954): 9-10.

36. Ibid. 1, 4 (July 1954): 8-12.

37. Ibid. 1, 10 (January 1954): 8.

between a Muslim male and a Jewish or Christian woman is permitted, and it is explicitly stated that conversion of the woman to Islam is not a precondition.[38] The basis for the view is the record of behavior of the Companions of Mohammed, some of whom married Christian and Jewish women. In a third case, dealing with a Muslim working in a church, the response noted that a Muslim taking part in a worship service of the church would be considered an unbeliever, but that general work there is not forbidden. The writer questioned, however, the appropriateness of a Muslim choosing to work in such a situation, even though it is not forbidden.[39]

Only one case specifically concerns dealings with non-Muslims. In Case 230 it is stated that a Muslim may undertake a business venture with a non-Muslim. The Muslim's portion of the business would be subject to the Muslim's alms-tax while the part belonging to the nonbeliever would not.[40] On the other hand, the terms "unbeliever" and "heathen" are often referred to in the cases and a very negative view emerges. The cases on heathens generally identify Chinese as belonging to that group, while Communists and some nationalists are identified as unbelievers.

In Cases 9 and 85 a definition is given of an unbeliever (kafir). The writer explains that the term denotes a person who does not believe in Allah and the other things that Islam commands to be believed, "such as the existence of God or ... the Justice of God." The case notes that there are various kinds of unbelievers. "There are those who do not want to accept or believe, such as Marx, Lenin, Stalin and [other] Communists." A second group, named hypocrites (*munafiq*), hide their disbelief and profess belief. They make a pretense of confessing Islam, but their intention is to confuse Muslims, "as the P.K.I. [Indonesian Communist Party] does." A third type of unbeliever is one who truly knows the truth of Islam but does not want to recognize it, "such as Mr. Hardi" (at the time, leader of the Indonesian Nationalist Party). The last variety is based on adamant denial, such as Satan (*Iblis*) himself, who knows of the existence of God but refused to say so openly. The case ends with the admonition that the ultimate fate of all unbelievers is in the fires of hell.[41]

The view that some unbelievers, especially Communists, are deceitful is further elaborated in Case 92, which deals with the question of whether a person confessing to be a Muslim should be taken at his word. The petitioner specifically questioned the validity of a marriage, performed by a Muslim mosque official, wherein the groom was a member of the Communist Party and the bride was a Muslim. In this particular case the mosque official (*pengulu*) asked the prospective groom to recite the Islamic confession (*sjahadat*), which he did, and, on that basis of identification with Islam, the official undertook the Islamic marriage ceremony. The response notes that belonging to the Communist Party and being a Muslim are incompatible, since the Communist Party is dedicated to principles that are antireligious and against Islam. Anyone associating with the Party aids its disbelief and is an unbeliever. Only by leaving the Party can this association be voided, and it is only when this has been done that the former member should be married in a Muslim ceremony. The writer

---

38. Ibid. 1, 5 (August 1954): 4; 3, 33 (November-December 1957): 5-6.

39. Ibid. 1, 10 (January 1954): 5.

40. Ibid. 3, 27 (June 1956): 7.

41. Ibid. 1, 2 (May 1954): 6-7; and 1, 12 (March 1956): 7-8.

concludes that mosque officials should rigidly question those suspected of belonging to the PKI and perform marriage ceremonies for them only if they have left the Party.[42]

In a third case dealing with communism, the writer responds to a petitioner who asked whether a particular verse from the Qur'an was fitting to be used as a basis for combatting communism. In stating that Muslims are free to reply to PKI distortions concerning Islam, the response draws on a wide range of Qur'anic verses which invoke the use of spiritual effort (Ar: *jihād*). The term for actual fighting, as in armed conflict, is to be employed when an enemy attacks Islam and the defense is to be undertaken by a Muslim army, not by individual groups of Muslims.[43] In this sense the writer recognizes some limits on a Muslim's conduct towards his political enemies.

Association and dealings with heathen (musjrik) are described in less hostile tones than those with unbelievers. In Case 217 the writer notes that some Muslims do not want to have much to do with the Chinese, because they eat pork and are described as "doing evil and pernicious things." He rejects this view, saying that normal business relationships between Muslims and Chinese are quite acceptable. However, close social relations should be avoided and Chinese contributions to a mosque would not be proper.[44] In Case 283 the writer expresses the opinion that meat slaughtered by Chinese is unacceptable for use by Muslims because Traditions note that slaughtering for Muslim use must be done by either a Muslim or a monotheist who pronounced "in the name of God" (*bismillah*) as the slaughter takes place.[45] While in expressing this view the writer denies holding any animosity towards the Chinese, certainly the refusal to consider using meat or accepting contributions from them indicates that it is preferable to maintain a distance from the Chinese.

c. *Political concepts.* Political thinking in the cases is conveyed through the concept of law expressed in the terms shari'a and undang. The definitions, use of the terms, and the range of situations covered deal precisely with the differences in Muslims' obligations towards their religion and towards the Indonesian political state. Without doubt the two loyalties are difficult to reconcile, even though the writers of *Al-Muslimun* attempt to do so. Their conclusion that religious must be above state law was at odds with the government claim regarding the supremacy of national law.

The term shari'a is used sparingly, but, when employed, it is with the understanding that it is a basic principle that needs no great explanation. In Case 59 on surrogate mothers and Case 95 on polygamy, the term shari'a is used in this sense. Shari'a is seen in the first case as the "exact" or "firm" law (*hukum jang tegas*).[46] A fuller explanation is offered in the second case in answer to the question of whether, because of changed conditions, the law of polygamy in Islam might change also. In his explanation the author notes that, to answer the question, he must outline the difference between the shari'a and laws which are instituted by man. "Laws (undang-undang) are made by man; the shari'a is from God." Since man is weak and deficient, then the laws

---

42. Ibid. 2, 1 (April 1955): 5-6.

43. Ibid. 1, 10 (January 1955): 4.

44. Ibid. 3, 25 (April 1956): 10-11.

45. Ibid. 3, 34 (January 1958): 8-10.

46. Ibid. 1, 9 (December 1954): 10; 2, 1, (April 1955): 7-8.

he institutes will be weak and deficient and, accordingly, his laws will need changing. This is not the case with the shari'a, for one of the attributes of God is "complete knowledge of whatever will ever exist." Accordingly, his shari'a is applicable to all time. "The shari'a of God is permanent and non-changing."[47]

These explanations indicate that the term shari'a is used in a classical Islamic sense as the holy law with its exact form known only to God, and it thus can only be approximated by mankind. The basic principles are known to man, as revealed by God through prophets, and mankind must seek to put those principles into effect so that the community can strive to conform with this holy order.

The translation of the shari'a to man-made law is addressed in several cases. First, in line with the modernist Muslim position, the claim of the classical Muslim schools of law to have incorporated the shari'a in their law codes is rejected on the basis that no command in scripture points to the schools of law as the repository of divine law. In a rather lengthy series of arguments, not germane to this particular presentation, the writer rejects the various arguments for following the codes of jurisprudence put forth by those schools.[48] At the same time, the writers of *Al-Muslimun* use the science of examining scripture employed by the founders of the schools of jurisprudence, and that science--*Uṣūl al fiqh*--is outlined in a special series of articles in *Al-Muslimun* alongside the Sual-Djawab section.[49]

The case for Islamic principles, rather than jurisprudence, is outlined succinctly in an unnumbered entry (between 120 and 122) titled "The Matter of Responsibility." The writer notes that responses to questions from readers are derived from the "verses of the Qur'an, the Traditions, the stories (of the companions)," and other sources. In context, however, it is apparent that matters of principle draw only on the first two sources and the other sources have validity in amplifying the Qur'an and Traditions, but are almost never original sources in their own right. The case also acknowledges "independent investigation" (ijtihad) as a valid tool for locating religious principles and applying them to contemporary issues.[50] The editors view the application of such principles as consistent with their attempts to approximate the shari'a.

Independent investigation has been widely heralded, by Muslims and observers of Islam alike, as the tool for liberating Muslim scholars from the fetters of stagnant thinking. As indicated by the writers of *Al-Muslimun*, however, independent investigation does not change any of the rules for examining and using religious sources, but merely allows the investigator to ignore the previous interpretations in formulating a new one based on his own investigation. Previous interpretations, particularly those of the highly heralded jurists of the classical period, may be used for guidance. While ijtihad has been a useful tool for changing attitudes in some areas, such as health and medicine, and somewhat in banking, it has often imposed even further restrictions, particularly in funeral practice and conformity with a region's cultural mores. This is

---

47. Ibid. 2, 1 (April 1955): 7-8.

48. Ibid. 1, 9 (December 1954): 4-9.

49. Abdulkadir Hassan, *Ushul-Fiqh* (Bangil: Persatuan Islam, 1956), as serialized in *Al-Muslimun* 1, 1 (April 1954) - 5, 45 (December 1960).

50. Ibid. 2, 4 (July 1955): 4-5.

also the case with *Al-Muslimun*'s writers. They do review all the sources anew--and seem to be very thorough. The result is frequently, however, an insistence on more restrictions on Muslim conduct than observed by those holding to the old interpretations and rejecting ijtihad as heresy. The writers of *Al-Muslimun*, of course, see this as evidence that the new interpretation is needed as a means of fortifying religion and bringing practice into closer conformity with the ideals of Islam.[51]

The second concept, undang-undang, denotes law made by human society. Case 87 "According to National Law" (*Menurut Undang-Undang Negara*) addresses this directly in the question: "Every nation dispenses justice according to its various laws: What is the ruling?" The response notes that Islam recognizes laws dealing both with worship and with temporal matters. Muslims cannot avoid the necessity of obeying the laws of their religion since these are obligatory not optional. National laws which do not have an Islamic form may be observed by Muslims if they do not conflict with the commands or requirements of Islam. The response concludes that, if these laws conflict with the tenets of Islam, it is forbidden to obey them. The view is based on a Tradition of the Prophet that states that "We may not obey man in rebelliousness to God; only in obeying what exists in goodness."[52]

A great deal of attention is given in the early cases--those between 1955 and 1957 when the issue was being debated nationally--to the importance of making national law compatible with the shari'a. As if to leave no doubt in the minds of the readers of *Al-Muslimun* about the editors' view on the matter, the very first case deals specifically with this issue. It bears the title, "Joining Parties other than Islamic Parties." The opening statement of the response pointedly notes that "in several verses of the Qur'an God commands [Muslims to] follow God's laws alone, whether in everyday life or in regard to the state." A person who does not want to follow the laws of God or does not want the institution of the laws of Allah ... is called a sinner (*fasiq*), a wrongdoer (*zhalim*), and an unbeliever (*kafir*). *Al-Maidah* 2 is used as the justification of this position.[53]

Two other cases further explain the use of law in a nation. In Case 45, dealing with capital punishment, the writer notes that Muslims must distinguish between laws based on Islamic principles and those based on other criteria. When a government uses punishments identical to those propounded by Islam without intending to do so, this is not the same as following the laws of God, it merely conforms to those laws. The writer notes that intention is important. "We, the Community of Islam, are never satisfied with laws that accidentally fit with the laws of our religion."TR In Case 202 a petitioner asks about a specific case where a person who killed someone was sentenced to prison, presumably by an Indonesian court. The response is that the sentence was not consistent with Islam, since a verse of the Qur'an (*Al-Baqarah* 178) commands that those who kill be killed in turn. The writer notes that a lighter sentence may not be imposed since the sentence is clearly stated in the Traditions

---

51. For a discussion of ijtihad in contemporary times elsewhere in the Muslim world, see John Obert Voll, *Islam: Continuity and Change in the Modern World* (Boulder: Westview Press, 1982), pp. 83-86, 224-25, and 251-52.

52. *Al-Muslimun* 1, 12 (March 1955): 9.

53. Ibid. 1, 1 (April 1954): 4.

54. Ibid. 1, 7 (October 1954): 8.

of the Prophet. He warns that not to follow God's command constitutes sin (*dosa*).[55] While not criticizing the government directly, the case makes it clear that the author finds Indonesian national law inconsistent with his concept of a divine law. In a final case, however, the writer warns that Muslims are not themselves free to inflict the punishments ordered by God for certain crimes. In Case 60 he specifically states that "in an Islamic state, as well as in other states, it is not right for the people to become judges themselves," but, rather, it is the responsibility of specifed organs of the national state.[56]

This discussion clearly contends that Muslims have an obligation to use Islamic principles and laws in the governing of a state. If the laws are not in place Muslims are not, under normal circumstances, to take it upon themselves to apply the punishments prescribed by the shari'a when the state fails to do so. Muslims certainly must regard non-Islamic laws and decisions as wrong and recognize that they should be replaced by Muslim laws and decisions when Muslims, exerting their best efforts, are able to do so.[57] There is no argument for immediacy, as was the case with the Darul Islam in 1948, when one stated reason for its attempt to establish an Islamic State of Indonesia was to apply religious law. The position of *Al-Muslimun*, then, was consistent with that of other Muslim organizations, such as the Muhammadijah and the Nahdatul Ulama, which also worked for the eventual establishment of Islamic law, but who were willing to settle for less temporarily.[58]

4. *Sual-Djawab: Religious Authority*

The sources of religious authority the writers use in responding to the cases are consistent with the call to employ principles from Muslim scriptures. Table 2 outlines these sources. Each year between 25 percent and 41 percent of the cases contain references to the Qur'an, and well over half the cases cite Traditions. Actually, over 80 percent of all cases for the entire period use references to Qur'an and Traditions. This approach is consistent with the modernist, fundamentalist position of the Persatuan Islam which emphasized those two sources as the primary repository of Islamic principles. Moreover, the writers demonstrate a rich knowledge of those sources, particularly when they draw on the traditions, where over twelve separate collections are employed in 600 references.[59] While some readers might quarrel with the selection of a particular verse in a given case, the scriptural quote is always germane

---

55. Ibid. 2, 12 (March 1956): 8.

56. Ibid. 1, 9 (December 1954): 10-11.

57. Ibid.

58. On the Darul Islam's pronounced views, see Karl D. Jackson, *Traditional Authority, Islam, and Rebellion* (Berkeley: University of California Press, 1980), pp. 84-86. A full study of the views of Darul Islam villagers toward religious values is given on pp. 98-128.

59. The compilers, with frequency of use in parentheses, are: Muslim (131), Bukhārī (101), Aḥmad (81), Abū Dāwūd (70), Nasāʾī (41), Ibn Ḥadjar (35), Tirmidhī (32), Salāmallah (24), Ibn Qudāmah (23), Ḥākim (22), Ibn Madjāh and Baihaqī (20). A discussion of the compilers is found in H. A. R. Gibb and J. H. Kramers, *Shorter Encyclopedia of Islam* (Leiden and London: Brill and Luzac, 1961), pp. 116-20.

to the issue under discussion. Moreover, the scripture is nearly always quoted first in Arabic, followed by an Indonesian translation. This approach is consistent with the orthodox Sunni Muslim position that in matters of doctrine the Arabic text of the scripture should always be used. Supplying the translation is consistent with the modernist Muslim position that even Muslims who are ignorant of Arabic should have an opportunity to understand in their own language the general meaning of any Islamic text.

Table 2. Percentage of Various Sources Used in Cases[60]

	1954-55	1955-56	1956-57	1957-60	Average
Qur'an	41.5%	32.1%	20.4%	25.0%	29.4%
Traditions	53.9	65.1	57.1	57.3	58.0
Islamic Religious Sources	12.4	16.0	11.2	16.1	13.6
Previous Entries	4.5	14.2	5.1	2.9	7.2
Authors of Persatuan Islam	3.8	.8	1.0	11.7	3.4
General Islam	5.6	2.6	5.1	2.9	4.0
No reference	7.8	6.2	17.3	16.1	11.2

(N = 388 cases with several different sources used in many cases.)

Other sources are used as well. About twenty-five cases employ classical and modern sources on Islamic jurisprudence, ranging from the highly respected classical legal theorist al-Nawāwī to the modernist Syrian commentator Rashīd Riḍā'. In about twelve cases this set of sources is supplemented by reference to works by members of the Persatuan Islam. In contrast to the scriptural references, however, these sources are used to support interpretation of scripture or as references for further information. By using these contemporary writings, the authors set themselves apart from those who follow the schools of jurisprudence, since traditional Muslims would rely heavily on previous interpretations to provide the correct answer to the issue under discussion.

A small number of cases use the general term "Islamic principles" without elaboration of just what those principles are, or listing a scriptural text. No source is used in 11 percent of the cases, where further elaboration seems unnecessary because of the nature of the answer.

Striking is the lack of other Indonesian sources, particularly from the Indonesian Muslim community, on the same subject. Undoubtedly this emphasis reflects a view that Islamic scriptures are timeless and that current literature would not add significantly to any discussion at hand. The editor verifies this position in an editorial note where he states that scripture must be the source of the responses and that the use of other views is to be avoided.[61]

The pattern on the use of sources is extremely narrow and reflects a cultural bias against those in Indonesian. Undoubtedly this reluctance to use other Indonesian sources is explained in part by doctrine and is not necessarily an evidence of cultural bias. The writers are interested in basic religious sources which, in their view and that of nearly all modernist Muslims elsewhere in the Muslim world, must be used in the original Arabic for accuracy. Consequently Indonesian writings on these subjects would not be usable. However, a cultural bias toward Arabic writings does seem apparent in some texts used

---

60. Sources, *Al-Muslimun*, 1-5 (1954-60).

61. *Al-Muslimun* 2, 5 (August 1955): 4.

to elaborate principles. Here, Arabic sources are almost always relied on, while the elaborations of Indonesian Muslims on the same subjects are ignored. There was no absence of Indonesian sources at the time on any of these matters, and a series of writings had dealt with significant issues over the previous fifty years which certainly were known to the editors of *Al-Muslimun*. Hasbi Ash-Shiddieqy's elaboration on the acceptability to Islam of blood transfusions and Agus Salim's justification of socialism are two significant examples.[62] Even the pioneer work of Ahmad Hassan, the most respected writer in the Persatuan Islam, is largely ignored in this context. The primary cause of these omissions seems to have been a confusion between primary sources and elaboration, and the result was to ignore a rich tradition in Indonesian that could have been drawn on for comparison.

III. Conclusions

In reviewing the hypotheses presented in the introduction, our examination shows that *Al-Muslimun* is closely associated with Islamic values generally found in Middle Eastern Islam.

1. *"Enunciation of Islamic Principles...."* The examination shows that the principles of Islam as expressed in the standard books on Islam are reflected in the responses given to the questions presented by readers. The cases are replete with references to God and his word, the Qur'an, to the Prophet Mohammed and the record of his words and acts (Traditions), and to the standard articles of faith and obligations for all Muslims. Much of the material speaks to the Indonesian context, and every attempt is made to apply Muslim standards to the Indonesian environment.

2. *"Use of Arabic...."* Arabic expressions, names, and scriptural quotations are used extensively in the cases. In particular there is a heavy use of Arabic religious terms and frequent quotation of religious sources to support the positions taken in responding to concerns of readers.

3. *"Attempts to place Islamic principles into everyday life...."* There is a heavy emphasis on the importance of Islam in everyday life. Indeed the purpose of presenting the cases is to accomplish that goal. Religious activity, or at least concern with religion in the performance of all activity, is seen as the proper concern for Muslims. Worship in all its aspects is regarded as a necessary emphasis in life, while all other behavior is to be kept consistent with religious principles and should never transgress the limits set by religion.

4. *"Non-recognition or condemnation of other viewpoints...."* Attitudes towards political enemies and certain non-Muslims are expressed sharply. The Communists and nationalists are regarded as, at worst, enemies of God and, at best, sinful, while the Chinese are viewed as heathen and beyond the pale of spiritual salvation. Distance from such creatures is recommended.

---

62. K. H. Moehammad Hasbi Ash-Shiddieqy, *Pemindahan darah dipandjang dari sudut hukum agama Islam* (Jakarta: Bulan Bintang, 1954); Hadji Agus Salim, "Kemadjuan Perkara harta," in *Djedjak Langkah Hadji A. Salim* (Jakarta: Tintamas, 1954), pp. 19-22.

It is apparent from the foregoing study that *Al-Muslimun* can act as one model for measuring conformity with Middle Eastern perceptions of Islam and can be used as a marker in that regard. Obviously other valid models exist, some perhaps more cognizant of the Southeast Asian environment, that would challenge *Al-Muslimun*'s views within a Muslim context. Nevertheless, *Al-Muslimun*'s identification with Islam can be seen as intimate and genuine.

PANCASILA AS THE SOLE FOUNDATION

Sjafruddin Prawiranegara

Editors' Introduction

The debate in Indonesian religious circles regarding "Pancasila as the *azas tunggal* [sole foundation or principle]" came to the fore in August 1982 when President Suharto stated that "all social-political forces, particularly the political parties, should accept the state ideology as their azas tunggal." He reassured religious organizations two months later, however, that they would continue to enjoy "rights and an honorable place in the Pancasila-based state," and that Pancasila was neither a religion nor a substitute for religion.

A major item on the agenda for the March 1983 general session of the People's Consultative Assembly (MPR) was the drafting of national policy guidelines (GBHN--Garis-Garis Besar Haluan Negara). Incorporated in these guidelines was an MPR resolution that the two political parties and Golkar now adopt Pancasila as their sole foundation.* All the MPR explicitly declared with regard to social organizations (*ormas, organisasi masyarakat*), however, was that a law concerning them must be promulgated.

This, then, became a major matter of debate. One of the most thoughtful statements against the adoption by religious organizations of Pancasila as their sole basis came in an open letter to the President from Sjafruddin Prawiranegara SH, dated July 17, 1983, which presents in detail many of the arguments put forward by those organizations.

In the early years of independence, Sjafruddin had been a member of the progressive wing of the Masjumi Party and served as the Republic's minister of finance (1946-47) and minister of welfare (1948). He became president and acting prime minister of the Republic's Emergency Government formed on Sumatra after the Dutch captured Yogyakarta in December 1948. In 1950 he was again appointed minister of finance, but later, increasingly opposed to Sukarno's policies, he joined the PRRI rebellion in 1958 and was prime minister of the rebel government. He surrendered in 1961 and was kept in close confinement until 1966. He has been an outspoken critic of the Suharto government in behalf of Muslim interests.

The following translation of Sjafruddin's letter is based on the version appearing in a collection of reactions from religious and other organizations concerning the proposed law.** (The footnotes incorporated in the translation appeared in the original.)

---

* Ketetapan MPR No. II/1983 tentang GBHN Bab IV.

** *Perihal: Pancasila Sebagai Azas Tunggal* (Jakarta: DDII, Jl. Kramat Raya no. 45, n.d. [1983?]), pp. 3-14.

His Excellency
The President of the Republic
of Indonesia

26 Ramadhan 1403H
Jakarta, July 7, 1983M

With all respect

Assalamu'alaikum w.w.

In connection with the efforts of the Government of the Republic of Indonesia--after the MPR/DPR [People's Consultative Congress and the House of Representatives] proclaimed that the Pancasila was to become the *azas tunggal*, the sole foundation for all political parties, including the Golkar--to extend enforcement of this principle to all types of social organizations in Indonesia, and also in view of the anxiety and unrest thereby aroused among the majority of the Muslim community, I feel compelled, in order to maintain a feeling of unity and justice in the Indonesian nation, to convey my opinion on the question of this "sole foundation" to you, in the sincere hope that you will be willing to order the cessation of these efforts to enforce the Pancasila as the sole foundation of all social organizations.

In order to render this "sole foundation" issue quite clear for us all, we may start by asking a question which at first sight does not need to be put because the answer is quite clear. However, precisely because, in my opinion, those who wish to enforce the Pancasila as the sole foundation do not properly understand what the real meaning of the Pancasila is, it is necessary for us to study this issue first.

I. *What Is the Pancasila?*

The answer usually given is: The Pancasila is the State Philosophy, the philosophy that is the basis of the 1945 Constitution, that constitutes the basis of law for the Republic of Indonesia.[1]

But, if we look for further information on the Pancasila in the 1945 Constitution, either in its body or in the explanatory commentary, we do not even once encounter the word "pancasila" let alone an elucidation of it. Yet what is actually binding on us as citizens, whether as ordinary people, or as civil servants, or as civilian or military officers of the state not in the civil

---

1. See for example, the special Publication of the Ministry of Information of the RI, dated February 19, 1959, entitled "Kembali Kepada Undang-Undang Dasar 1945" [Return to the 1945 Constitution].

service, is the Constitution and all laws and ordinances based on this Constitution, such that they should not contain any provisions in contravention of the Constitution.

So where can we find an elucidation of this Pancasila, which is said to be the basis of the 1945 Constitution?

As we all know, elucidations of the Pancasila can be found only in the speeches that preceded the establishment of the 1945 Constitution, specifically in the speech of Bung Karno closing a session of the "Body to Investigate Efforts for Preparing [Indonesian] Independence" the BPUPKI (in Japanese, the "Dokuritsu Zyunbi Tyoosakai") on June 1, 1945, which subsequently has usually been referred to as "The Birth of Pancasila Address." Bung Karno's address of June 1, 1945 was then reformulated by a Committee of Nine on June 22, 1945, and ratified in subsequent sessions of the BPUPKI.

Soekarno himself emphatically rejected the belief that he was the "creator" of the Pancasila. In his inaugural address when he accepted the honorary degree of Doctor Honoris Causa from Gajah Mada University, he stated: "Do not say that I am the formulator of the Pancasila teaching. I am only the discoverer [excavator] of the Pancasila teaching."[2]

But nevertheless, that closing address, which summarized all the speeches preceding it at the BPUPKI sessions held from May 29 through June 1, 1945, is the most important source for understanding the Pancasila philosophy.[3]

According to Bung Karno the Pancasila is the *"philosofische grondslag"* of Indonesian Independence. This philosofische grondslag means foundation, philosophy, the most profound thought, the spirit, and the deepest desire, upon which to build the eternal, indestructible mansion of Independent Indonesia.

> "What is our 'Weltanschauung' for building the Independent Indonesian state? Is it national-socialism? Is it historical materialism? Is it the San Min Cu I, as stated by Dr. Sun Yat Sen?
>
> "Brothers, we have had sessions for three days, many ideas have been presented--all kinds--but how true are the words of Dr. Soekiman, of Ki Bagoes Hadikoesoemo, that we must seek agreement, seek a consensus of our opinions. We are together seeking unity of "philosofische grondslag," we are seeking a single 'Weltanschauung" on which we all agree. I say again "agree." Something to which Brother Yamin agrees, to which Ki Bagoes agrees, to which Ki Hadjar agrees, to which Brother Sanoesi agrees, to which Brother Abikoesno agrees, to which Brother Liem Koen Hian agrees, in short: to which we all agree.
>
> "For the Muslim group, this is the best place to protect religion. We all, I too, are Muslims--pardon, a thousand pardons, my Islam is far from perfect--but if you were to open my breast and look into my heart you would surely find that it is no other than a true Islamic heart. And Bung Karno's Islamic heart wishes to defend Islam through consensus, through a meeting of minds. By

---

2. See H. Endang Saifuddin Anshari, "Piagam Jakarta 22 Juni 1945 [The Jakarta Charter of June 22, 1945], under paragraph 1: The Shaping of Soekarno's Pancasila," p. 21.

3. Moh. Roem: "Tiga Peristiwa Bersejarah" [Three Historic Events], pp. 30-31.

the way of consensus we improve everything including the welfare of religion, that is by discussions and consultations in a People's Repesentative Assembly.

"Whatever is not yet satisfactory, we will discuss further in consultation. The Representative Body, that is the place for us to present Islamic demands. It is there that we should propose to the people's leaders whatever we think is needed for improvement. If we are indeed a Muslim people, let us work as hard as we can. So that the majority of seats in the People's Representative Body that we are establishing are held by Muslim representatives. If indeed Muslims form a majority of the Indonesian people, and if indeed Islam is truly alive in the ranks of the people, let us leaders mobilize the entire population to send as many Muslim representatives as possible to this representative council.

"In the representative council, let our Muslim brothers and our Christian brothers work as hard as possible. If, for example, Christians wish every single letter in the ordinances of the Indonesian state to conform with the Bible, let them do their utmost to ensure that a majority of the delegates entering the Indonesian representative council are Christians. That is just--[that is] "fair play."

Bung Karno's explanation concerning the basis of the "Weltanschauung" or the "philosofische grondslag," that was to become the foundation of Independent Indonesia (meaning the basis for the Constitution of the Indonesian Republic) was summarized in the following words:

"Brothers! The 'Foundations of the State' I have already proposed. They are five in number. Are they the Panca Dharma? No! The term Panca Dharma would not be appropriate here. Dharma means Duty, whereas we are speaking of *foundation*. . . .

"Its name should not be Panca Dharma, but--I name it on the advice of a friend who is a linguist--rather *Pancasila*. Sila means *basis* or *foundation*, and on this five-fold foundation we will build the Indonesian State, everlasting and eternal." (Loud applause.)[4]

In Bung Karno's speech, the five principles were named in the following order:

1. Indonesian Nationalism
2. Internationalism or humanitarianism
3. Consultation--or democracy
4. Social welfare
5. Belief in God

As we all know, in the preamble to the Constitution which was subsequently drawn up, the Pancasila--*without its name being mentioned*--was formulated as follows:

Formulation June 22, 1945
- Belief in God, with the obligation for its adherents of abiding by the *shari'a* [laws] of Islam
- Humanitarianism, righteous and civilized

---

4. Bung Karno's speech of June 1, 1945, appears inter alia in "20 Tahun Merdeka" [Twenty Years of Independence] R.I. Department of Information edition, 1965.

- Unity of Indonesia
- Democracy [*kerakyataan*] guided by wisdom in the consultations of [the people's] representatives
- Social Justice for all the people of Indonesia

Formulation of August 18, 1945
- Belief in One Almighty God
- Humanitarianism, righteous and civilized
- Unity of Indonesia, and
- Democracy guided by wisdom in the consultations of representatives, together with realization of
- Social justice for all the people of Indonesia

II. *Pancasila was not intended to become the foundation of citizens' organizations, whether of a political character, or of a social or other character*

From the excerpts I have taken from Bung Karno's address, it is clear that the Pancasila was intended to be the Foundation of the State, and the basis for the *Constitution*. This means that the Pancasila principles have been incorporated [*verwerkt*] in, have been realized through, the articles of the 1945 Constitution. Anybody who agrees with the 1945 Constitution--and everybody who regards himself as a citizen of the Republic of Indonesia must agree with the 1945 Constitution--implicitly and automatically recognizes and is committed to the Pancasila. This means that whichever religion, belief, or ideology an individual or group of citizens espouses, that person [or group] is committed to live and work in a harmonious and peaceful manner within and outside the Republic of Indonesia. Or, to borrow Bung Karno's worlds: "The Indonesian state that we are founding must be a 'gotong-royong' [mutual assistance] state."

This idea of gotong-royong implies that each person joining in this gotong-royong preserves his own identity and personality. The Muslims remain Muslim, the Christians remain Christian, the Buddhists remain Buddhist, the Hindus remain Hindu, and so on.

But if Christians are no longer permitted to form organizations based on Christian principles, whether Protestant or Catholic, and if Muslims cannot establish organizations based upon Islamic principles, and the same is the case for other citizens espousing other religions or ideologies, who are forbidden to found organizations based upon their respective faiths or ideologies, but all citizens are allowed only to have organizations based upon the Pancasila, then Indonesia, this fertile and prosperous country, with its many hills and valleys, must, as it were, be transformed into a barren Sahara desert, consisting of only stones and undifferentiated particles of sand [*yang zatnya sama*].

From a Pancasila State as conceived by the "Founding Fathers" of our beloved Republic of Indonesia, a democratic Republic--Indonesia will become a national-socialist i.e. fascist state just as bad and brutal as a communist state.

If Pancasila, rather than being the foundation of the state has to be turned into the basis of human life, then this means that the religions revealed by Almighty God (or so perceived) have to be exchanged for an ideology, which does not call itself a religion, but in its behavior seems to wish to replace existing religions.

Just consider: formerly there was no "Pancasila Morality" because problems of morality were left up to the individual religions. Then a committee was established consisting of people regarded as "smart"--not a single ulama of good standing in the Muslim community was included--and this committee of smart people drafted a kind of holy writ filled with moral prescriptions that had to be studied and practiced by all our citizens, yet not all these prescriptions could be swallowed by the Muslims, for many of them contained tenets in conflict with Islamic teachings.

Now that a "Pancasila Morality" has been drawn up, there is certain to appear "Pancasila Law," "Pancasila Economy," etc.

Indeed, as you yourself, Mr. President, have pointed out in your address on the occasion of the "Nuzulul Qur'an" commemoration on Monday June 27 last, the Pancasila is not a religion and cannot ever replace religion. This is certainly true. However, even if the Pancasila is not a religion, with the power that lies in your hands and with the support of the People's Representative Council--which more reflects the sovereignty of the President than that of the people--the Pancasila is de facto put into effect and is being enforced as a comprehensive religion, that touches on all aspects of the lives of those human beings who are Indonesian citizens.

In this connection I may be permitted to refer to the editorial in KOMPAS of July 4, 1983, which appeared under the heading, "Penggarapan Undang-Undang Keormasan" [The Implementation of the Law on Social Organizations] and reads:

> "If the issue is viewed solely from the standpoint of practical politics, the government, with the support of majorities in the representative bodies and the surfeit of power it possesses, can as it were enforce anything it pleases, and the community will acquiesce, at least formally, and for so long as the power structure supporting it remains effective.
>
> "Still, because what is to be achieved and preserved is essentially a political infrastructure and political culture which is to unify the nation and the state, mere formal acquiescence, without the process of dialogue, cannot suffice.
>
> "A statesmanlike political approach will at the same time strive for implanting strong roots and building a firm structure, so that not mere formal acquiescence and enforcement are achieved but rather a form of dialogue that is nationally oriented, so that, even though it may take some time, a national consensus will ultimately be attained."

There is a Dutch proverb, that says "Beter ten Halve gekeerd dan ten hele gedwaald" which can be translated as "It is better to turn back halfway than to err the whole way."

In your address celebrating the Nuzulul Qur'an commemoration, to which I referred earlier, Mr. President, you yourself pointed out: "Pancasila and religion are not in opposition to each other and must not be made to oppose each other."

If this were true, why must the Islamic basis of the one remaining Islamic political party, the Partai Persatuan Pembangunan be replaced by the Pancasila? And why does Minister of Youth and Sports Abdul Ghafur try with all his might to replace the Islamic basis of the Islamic Students League (HMI) by the Pancasila? After all, the Islamic basis of the Islamic political parties and social organizations has long existed and been recognized as not in conflict, but rather in accord, with the 1945 Constitution. Why only now has the Islamic foundation to be replaced by the Pancasila? What crime has the Partai Persatuan Pembangunan (PPP), or the HMI, or any other Muslim organization committed?

Because the HMI in its recent Medan congress refused to change its foundation, arguing that no Law on Social Organizations yet exists mandating such a change, the Government has now begun to draw up such a law. And because the People's Representative Council more often expresses "His Master's Voice" [sic] than giving voice to its own feelings, it will not be difficult to produce the law described by the government.

But actually it is not just the HMI, but the Indonesian Muslim community in general (which still loves its faith, although the majority are not yet brave enough to express their true feelings) that rejects replacing the Islamic foundation by the Pancasila foundation, not only because this would be contrary to Islamic teachings, but also because it would be contrary to the 1945 Constitution. They are afraid to express their true opinions for fear that they will lose their positions, their offices, or their funding, or are afraid to be considered "confrontational dissidents"--feelings similar to the misgivings expressed recently by Abdurrachman Wahid in KOMPAS--with all the related risks: interrogation, detention, and suchlike by various civilian and military instruments of the state.

If I have steeled myself to write this letter, it is not with the intention of seeking a confrontation with you, the President, but only to exercise my rights and duties, as laid down in Article 27, paragraph (1) of our Constitution.

Replacing an Islamic foundation by a Pancasila foundation conflicts with a Constitution which is based upon the Pancasila, and thus is in contravention with the Pancasila itself. That is, the original Pancasila, which formed the basis of the 1945 Constitution. What is plain is that to exchange this basis contravenes the freedom of religion and worship guaranteed by Article 29, paragraph (2) of the Constitution. Because, according to Islamic teachings, the establishment of an Islamic association whose membership consists of Muslims who want to practice Islamic teachings together--that is an association which is based upon Islam--is in itself an act of worship which is blessed by Allah. For, according to the teachings of Allah, all Believers are brothers. And therefore it is very good for them to establish organizations consisting of Muslims, in whatever field.

This does not mean that Muslims are not allowed to become members of, or to found, organizations whose membership is not exclusively Islamic. Nor does it imply that Muslim associations cannot admit non-Muslims as extraordinary members, as long as they accept its Islamic foundation, though such cases will necessarily be very rare.

If Muslims are no longer allowed to establish Islamic associations--whether political organizations or social organizations--then Islam will come to be regarded as a private matter, which is completely contrary to Islamic teachings. The Islamic religion is not merely a private matter, but is also, and primarily, a matter of the "Ummat" [Community]. The "sholat" [act of worship], for example, may be performed individually, but communal prayers are mandatory, i.e., where a number of Muslims wish to perform the required prayers, namely the five daily prayers. Also payment of the "zakat" [religious tax] also indicates the existence of a community, with the purpose of bridging the gap between the rich and the poor, although those receiving the zakat do not have to be Muslims, but can be any poor person in need of help.

To put it briefly, if the Indonesian Muslim community is to be prohibited from establishing and maintaining Islamic associations, whether in the political field or in other social fields, this is not only in contravention of the 1945 Constitution--and thus in contravention of the Pancasila itself, but, in practice means an attempt to kill Islam--through the Pancasila! For the Pancasila, being a creation of men, can be interpreted and applied according to the wishes and thoughts of men, namely those men who hold power, the power-holders controlling the Armed Forces! And in the long run, the teachings of religion--particularly the Islamic religion will--so I fear, and tens of millions of Indonesian Muslims share my fear--be suffocated by Pancasila Morality, Pancasila Economy, Pancasila Law, and all other such Pancasila offspring, the results of which we can already observe: alcoholism and narcotics, promiscuous sex and the resulting proliferation of venereal disease in society, particularly among teenagers, rampant criminality and corruption, alongside measures to combat them, which on the one hand are completely ineffective, and on the other hand show symptoms of no longer being under the control of [the] law.

And it is very sad that Islam, up to now, has been able to do little or nothing to help improve the situation, because those Muslim leaders who still want to carry out the order of Allah, "amal ma'ruf, nahi mungkar," urging people to act well and behave correctly, and forbidding them from doing wrong and acting evilly, are continually mistrusted and prevented from proselytizing.

And the condition of society will become even worse if the Government succeeds, formally at least, in enforcing the imposition of the Pancasila as the sole foundation for all social organizations.

If this matter of the sole foundation is also to apply to all social organizations, the situation for the Christians, Protestant and Catholic, will not be as bad as for the Muslims. Because they have their priests and clergymen, who are the leaders of the organization of the Christians known as the "Church." The mosque is not the same as the Church. A mosque is a place of worship, managed by a committee, whose members are not sacral officials such as priests or clergymen. But a Church is an organization whose members consist of people who share a belief in the Christian religion, and it is led by priests or clergymen within a hierarchy. Every Church has at least one, but usually several, even possibly thousands of churches spread throughout the world, as for instance the Roman Catholic Church. Thus their "Church" is a fortress for the followers of a specific Christian denomination.

If the Muslim social organizations are banned, then the Mosques constitute a very fragile fortress, because their committees can be captured by Golkar minions who profess to be Muslims but are more obedient to the President and to other superiors than they are to Allah, His Prophet, and His Holy Scriptures.

I cannot assess the position of the Buddhist and Hindu communities, but they also have their religious leaders, similar to the Christian priests and clergymen, and they too cannot easily be interfered with by the Pancasila. The weakness, but also the strength of Islam, lies in the fact that its Ulama and Kyai are not like Christian priests and clergymen. Because of this it appears that Islam can easily be subdued and dominated by temporal rulers. But make no mistake! Islam ultimately is protected by the True God.

Because of that, rather than fighting Islam, distrusting and interfering with the ulama and the da'i [preachers] who remain faithful to Allah, His

Prophet, and His Holy Scriptures, it would be better to treat them as friendly allies in the development efforts.

If Allah so wishes, we will be able, together with the ulama and da'i, to combat alcoholism and narcotics, and all the vices besetting our society. They do not seek rank or payment from the authorities. They hope only that justice be upheld and that they receive the blessing of Allah, and, ultimately a place at His side when they have to leave this mortal world at His ordaining.

If earlier Indonesia could only achieve independence thanks to the Grace of Allah and the Muslims, now too Indonesia can only be saved with the help of Allah and of devout Muslims. Making Pancasila the sole foundation for all social organizations may at first glance appear to be the way to bring about national unity and social improvement. But believe me, you will only achieve the opposite.

I hope that you, Mr. President, are aware of the dangers threatening our country and people, if the Sole Foundation plan should be implemented.

And I hope that, after you have read this letter of mine, you will agree at the very least to halt the enforcement of Pancasila as the "sole foundation," in accordance with the recommendation offered by Mr. Hardi in KOMPAS of last July 4 [reproduced on pp. 19-23 of the pamphlet].

But it would be still better if the application of the Sole Foundation idea was also to be revoked for the political parties, particularly the PPP, and that all citizens be allowed to establish any organizations whatsoever, so long as the aim of these organizations is to work for the benefit of Indonesian society, and in pursuit of their objectives they refrain from all illegal actions, specifically the use of force. This would be in accordance with Article 28 of the Constitution which guarantees the principles of freedom of association and assembly and of the expression of opinion in speech and writing, as was laid out by Bung Karno in his address at the end of the BPUPKI's session on June 1, 1945, and also in accordance with the promises of the New Order at the beginning of its career--namely your promises to implement the 1945 Constitution in a pure and principled manner.

May Allah show you and your assistants the true path, and at the same time, in the hope that Allah will accept our fasting and our other good deeds and worship, I wish a Happy Idulfitri in this year of 1403 H for you and your family, and please forgive me if this letter of mine contains any words that do not please you. My aim is none other than to point out what is just and fair according to my own convictions.

Wabillahi taufiq wal hidayah
Wassalam

Sjafruddin Prawiranegara.

copies being sent to:

1. The Vice President of the Republic of Indonesia
2. All Ministers of the Fourth Development Cabinet
3. The President, the Vice President and member Justices of the Supreme Court
4. The President, Vice President and members of the Supreme Advisory Council
5. The Chairman and members of the State Finance Control Board
6. The Speaker, Vice Speaker and the Factional leaders in the MPR and DPR and other members
7. The Attorney General
8. The Central Council of Ulama in Indonesia
9. The Press and other Mass Media
10. Islamic Social Organizations.

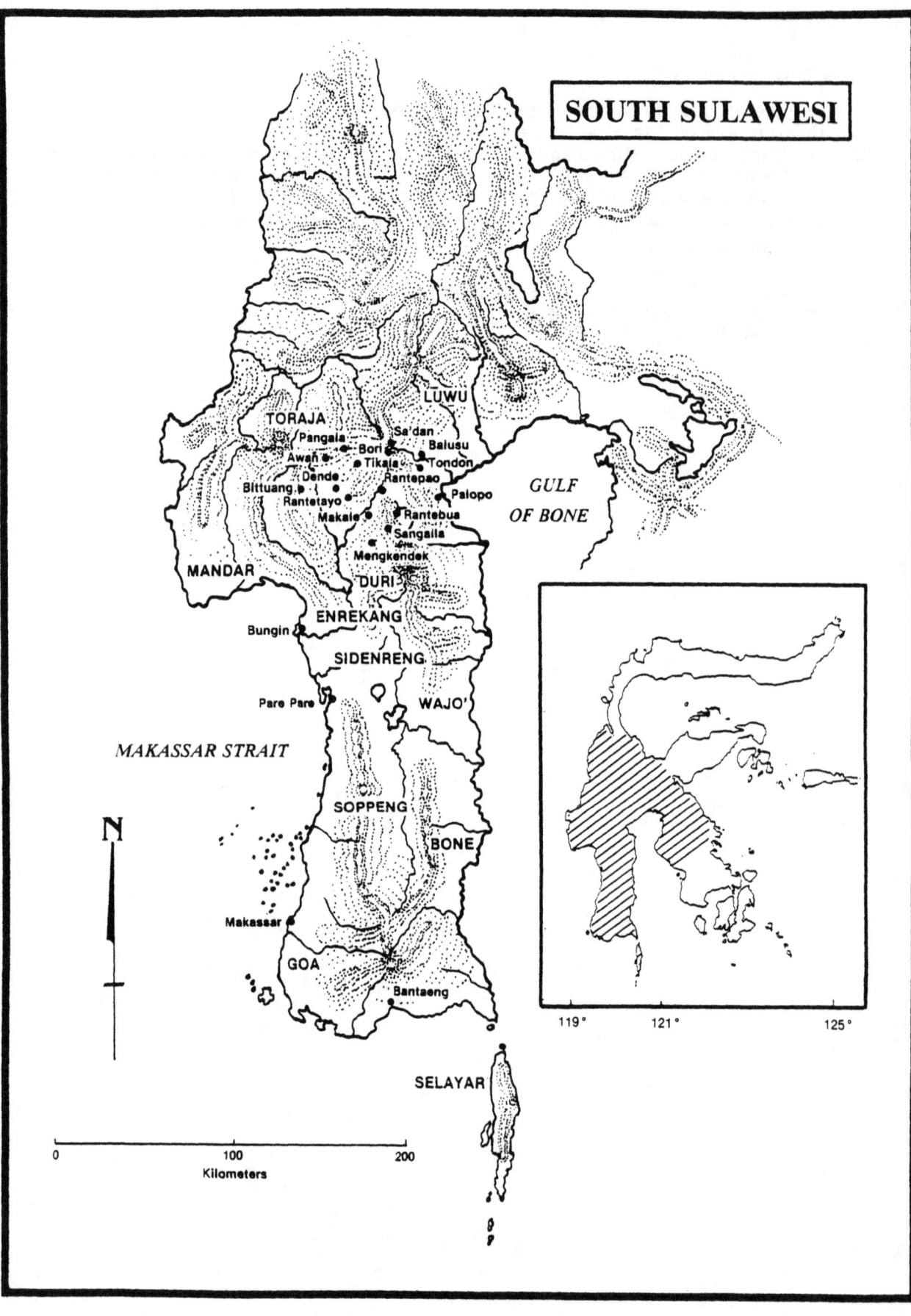

GOVERNMENT AND MISSION IN THE TORAJAN WORLD OF MAKALE-RANTEPAO

Terance Bigalke

Religion, in highland South Sulawesi in the second decade of the twentieth century was not treated with the neutrality claimed by the Dutch for their rule in the Indies. A long and costly war had just been concluded with the Acehnese, and Islamic organizations on Java were showing signs of vitality that troubled the colonial authorities. Dutch officials throughout those islands which had substantial Muslim populations *and* still unconverted groups of highlanders were, then, concerned over the potential of a politically militant Islam. This caused the government to focus more attention on contiguous highland populations in provincial policy planning than their numbers warranted. So it was that the Torajan world was not left to make its slow accommodation with the Islamic lowlands of South Sulawesi.

Dutch officials operated on the assumption that the mere proximity of Bugis Muslims (who had already penetrated and converted inhabitants of the foothills of Enrekang and Duri to the south) would lead to large-scale Torajan conversion to Islam. Islam was perceived as an advancing tide that could only be stopped by building a bulwark in the highlands; isolation was the only way to preserve the heathens from Islamic conversion *and* to save them for later conversion to Christianity. Breedveldt Boer, assistant resident of Luwu, summed up the government position generally put forward in this period:

> Greater security of persons and goods since our arrival [in 1905] had resulted in more contact--chiefly through trade--between coastal peoples and heathen ethnic groups. Thus, a fraternization is underway between the former oppressors and the oppressed, the Muslims and the heathen, a fraternization and mingling which will increase still further as the economic development of the land and people increases. Although there is much to rejoice in about development and it cannot be enough supported by the government, there lies in this fraternization the future evil that the heathen, in the first place in the vicinity of Rantepao and Makale, will more easily than previously be converted to Islam. Torajans who have temporarily moved to Palopo to seek work with traders or Europeans, do not eat pork because they feel self-conscious among Muslims; indeed, the number that undergo circumcision for this reason is also very great.
>
> All this together means, I believe, that it is high time to begin with evangelization, not only in Rantepao and Makale such as the present plans call for, but in the whole heathen region. . . .[1]

---

1. Breedveldt Boer, "Memorie van overgave, van de aftreden Assistent-Resident van Loewoe," pp. 65-66 (Palopo, 1913, in my possession).

Several interesting points emerge from this commentary. One is the way in which the government was so willing to dichotomize the groups involved into "coastal" and "heathen," not ordinarily considered a parallel construction. Coastal, as the Dutch so rightly understood in the Indonesian context, did indeed mean Muslim, and usually this variety of religious outlook was associated with a fairly thorough-going Islam. "Heathen," on the other hand, was correctly used as a synonym for "highlander" at this time, since these were the only pockets of population in the archipelago that remained isolated from at least a nominal conversion to Islam.

Another point is the tendency to perceive the Torajans and Bugis as enemies, as oppressed vs. oppressors. Certainly there was basis for such a generalization, but it missed the essential features of the interaction between leaders of the Torajan and Bugis communities, that in part explained the successful exploitation of Torajans by the Bugis. This undifferentiated view of both the Bugis and Torajan was a convenient one for the Dutch to hold, given their concern over the spread of Islam, and it came to assume a place in the pantheon of unexamined assumptions that dictated Dutch policy. The Bugis were continually portrayed as the strong, the Torajans as the weak. In its stripped-down version presented by a mission spokesman, the argument ran like this:

> The Bugis are a mighty people. One finds among them keen seafarers and their trade activity had already stretched throughout the Indies by the time of the Company.
> As a seafaring folk, they have obtained a certain worldly wisdom. Also by means of their religion they have made contact with Arabic elements, with whom many have gone to live.
> The Bugis are thus more advanced than the Torajans. Where the Bugis appear, they supersede the Torajans. Where they marry Torajans, one finds little of the Toraja-type in their offspring but rather a thoroughly Bugis type.[2]

Extending this reasoning, the same spokesman argued that the Bugis had not wanted to convert Torajans prior to the coming of the Dutch because they were easier to exploit that way. Now however, since the Dutch provided political leadership that prevented these abuses from continuing, the Bugis were out to dominate the Torajans spiritually.

Neither government nor mission representatives gave the Torajans much credit for an autonomous response. Although there had been little actual conversion of Torajans to Islam in the highlands, the Dutch drew examples from those Torajans living in Muslim regions who had appeared willing to acquire some of the outward forms of Islam. We have seen Boer's account of this phenomenon in Palopo. Another major source of examples was the large population of former slaves returning from Bone and Sidenreng who had been released as a result of the conversion of slavery to debt bondage by Governor Kroesen. Of the estimated 12,000 Torajans who had been seized for slavery and transported to the lowlands, about one-third had gone back before the 1911 deadline by which Torajans could legally leave the Bugis lands. Some would not return because they had been well absorbed into lowland life and frequently had converted to Islam.[3] Those converts to Islam who did return to the highlands became

---

2. A. A. van de Loosdrecht, *Alle den Volcke* [hereafter *ADV*], June 1915, p. 40. *Alle den Volcke* was a mission monthly journal appearing in the Netherlands.

3. Boer, "Memorie van overgave," p. 111.

a sudden new focus of concern for the Dutch administration, as shown in this 1910 report:

> [C]onversion (to Islam) is also promoted by the return of many former Torajan slaves, who from much time in slavery in Sidenreng and Bone embraced Islam. The disappearance of [Islamic influence from the highlands] is out of the question, as indicated by a report from the controleur of Mandar that Torajans here and there are beginning to regard pigs as unclean animals.[4]

The author of this report did not carefully distinguish his cases, lumping the returning Torajan slaves together with Torajans in Mandar (the west coast of Central Sulawesi) who were beginning to observe a pork taboo. It would indeed have been fascinating to observe the Torajan slaves as they once again took up residence in the highlands if they were now regarding pigs as unclean. The pressure exerted on them to resume eating pork would have been very heavy, given the ceremonial importance of the meat. Because there is almost no further mention of this phenomenon, however, one is inclined to conclude that the returning slaves did not form a discrete community of Torajan Muslims, though as individuals they may have remained Muslim. But in Mandar Torajans inhabiting the lower hills near the shore had begun to respond to influences from the coast and convert to Islam. Where physical geography did not divide Bugis and Torajans discretely, coastal culture increasingly penetrated the highlands resulting in a religious dichotomization of people locally referred to as "Toraja Salang" (Islamic Torajans) and "Toraja Kapiri" (literally, "Kafir" or "pagan" Torajans, obviously from a Muslim perspective).[5]

The Coming of the Mission

Set against their concern that Islam was penetrating the highlands of South Sulawesi, Netherlands Indies authorities in Makassar sought to encourage mission societies to take an interest in the region. Provincial officials permitted Luwu's assistant resident, Breedveldt Boer, to explore possibilities with mission groups, inviting them to observe the situation in Makale-Rantepao and develop plans for its conversion. Largely for financial reasons the missions proved unable to respond to the government's invitation, though Colonel Covaars of the Salvation Army did visit the highlands in January 1912. Boer was then forced to fall back on engaging an assistant minister from the Protestant Church of the Indies (hereafter "Indies Church") to make a brief visit to Makale-Rantepao in March of that year.

The history of the Indies Church made it a seemingly unlikely candidate for an assignment whereby it would pioneer Christian proselytizing in highland South Sulawesi. An early creation of the VOC, it had maintained its identity as a colonial state church long after the official separation of church and state in the Netherlands. The nineteenth century rise of pietism and religious revivalism that created mission societies in the Netherlands left the Indies Church largely unaffected, though it was put increasingly on the defensive as these societies actively sought permission to open mission fields in the Indies. Almost solely because the state revenues it received enabled it to

---

4. *Adatrechtbundel IX*, Series P, Zuid Celebes, No. 3 (The Hague: Nijhoff, 1914), pp. 239-40.

5. Boer, "Memorie van overgave," pp. 22; 54; 66-67.

hire an evangelist, the Indies Church now found itself expected to advance the faith aggressively into the highland regions of Sulawesi. It found itself in this position because the state perceived its own interests served by the Church's presence there. Thus while the Indies Church changed its mission to meet new circumstances in Holland and the Indies, its historical role as quiet servant of the government's interests remained constant.

Assistant minister Kelling, who made the first visit for the Indies Church to Makale-Rantepao, was subsequently placed in Makale in a position jointly financed by the Church and the Governor General, who intended to subsidize evangelistic work in Central and South Sulawesi until the private missions were financially able to take it over.[6] Not cut from the aristocratic mold of the full-fledged ministers of the Indies Church, assistant minister Kelling was willing to become a circuit-evangelist based for short periods in outlying areas to supervise the building of schools and placing of teachers, all seen as preliminary steps to eventually baptizing the students and (it was hoped) their families. In contrast to the record of most missionaries of the Indies Church, the number of his conversions had been phenomenal in Luwuk (northeastern arm of Sulawesi, not to be confused with Luwu) and in the Binuang district of Mamasa, west of the Sa'dan highlands. In two short visits to the Binuang district he had baptized 5,000 persons.

In Makale-Rantepao, while using less spectacular methods of conversion than elsewhere, Kelling still minimized pre-baptismal instruction before administering the sacrament. He seems to have focused his proselytizing on the sons of chiefs who were attending the government school in Makale, a Second Class Native School popularly called the "landschap" or regional school.[7] A group of twenty students were suddenly baptized without prior permission from their parents or knowledge of the government, touching off a row that left many influential Torajans embittered toward Christianity. The controleur reported that "most of the elders resigned themselves to what had happened but declared firmly that no more of their children would be permitted to convert to Christianity." Significantly in light of later events, the controleur concluded that the incident had stemmed from the failure of coordination between the government and the missionary: "Later more cooperation developed between the government and mission, with the result that in several places private village schools were built."[8]

Many competing interests were brought into sharp relief between 1911 and 1913. Because of its concern that Islam was an advancing tide poised to sweep over the highlands, the provincial government wanted to induce Christian conversion there with all due speed. Meanwhile, despite the activities of assistant minister Kelling, the Indies Church was still largely at odds with the aggressive

---

6. This and the following paragraph are based on van de Loosdrecht, *ADV*, November 1915, pp. 86-87.

7. In principle, each *onderafdeeling* (subdivision) town in South Sulawesi had at least one government primary school. A five year, Malay-medium primary school was opened in both Makale and Rantepao towns in 1909. Dutch authorities sought to restrict attendance to the children of headmen, whose early suspicions of Dutch intentions led some of them secretly to substitute their clients' children.

8. E. A. J. Nobele, "Memorie van overgave betreffende de onderafdeeling Makale," *Tijdschrift voor Indisch Taal-, Land- en Volkenkunde* 66 (1926): 9.

evangelical spirit emanating ever more strongly from mission societies in Holland, and it tried to slow the entry of the private Dutch mission societies into the places where it was beginning to proselytize. The Datu of Luwu, who in the eyes of evangelists and government officials represented militant Islam, was equally opposed to the missions' entry and did his best to see that no funds from the budget of Afdeeling Luwu went to subsidize any Christian proselytizing. Nonetheless, by 1913 both the Indies Church and the Datu had lost out; and it was through a resident missionary sent by the Calvinist Mission Alliance (GZB), subsidized from the Luwu budget, that the government began to lay the foundation for establishing Christianity in the highlands.

The GZB missionary A. A. van de Loosdrecht came to Makale-Rantepao by way of the Mission Institute located near Leiden. Dominated by the methods of the famed pair of Dutch missionaries, N. Adriani and A. C. Kruyt, the Institute's approach combined a wide variety of skills in ethnography, carpentry, medicine, teaching, and, of course, preaching. Teachers at the Institute contended that a good cultural understanding of the people to whom one ministered was necessary before one could hope to manipulate the religious and social system in ways that would lead to Christianization. By finding common elements, pouring new wine into old skins as it were, the religious transformation would come about more profoundly. Tinkering with symbolic systems rather than overhauling them posed less likelihood of provoking an adverse reaction and promised a more genuinely held Christianity.[9]

On his maiden journey inland from Palopo to Rantepao, the GZB missionary, van de Loosdrecht, spent a night at the government rest house midway to his destination. Not speaking much of the Torajan language (Tae') and still rudimentary in his Malay, he attempted to instruct one of the porters carrying his belongings to wake him in the morning by knocking on the resthouse door. The difficulties inherent in transmitting this lesson in alien forms of communication soon became all too apparent when the porter attempted to beat down the door in the manner he believed he was emulating. We are left to assume that the missionary rose on his own the following morning.[10]

After experiencing in miniature, then, some of the difficulties that would confront him in the Sa'dan highlands van de Loosdrecht arrived in Rantepao. Having come to convert its people, he would first have to communicate notions foreign to the Torajan experience. To succeed in his own mission he would have to convince Torajans of the significance of the innovations he offered. And, as with the door, Torajans might receive a message very different from the one he intended to convey.

Before settling in Rantepao, van de Loosdrecht and his wife (who had hitherto remained in the Luwu capital of Palopo) spent three months in Posso with the Dutch missionary Kruyt, observing his twenty-year-old mission.[11] (Though located a considerable distance from Makale-Rantepao in Central Celebes, the Posso highlanders did have cultural traits in common with Sa'dan highlanders.)

---

9. A. M. Brouwer, "The Preparation of Missionaries in Holland," *International Review of Missions* [hereafter *IRM*] 1 (1912): 229-39; and G. A. Gollock, "The Present Outlook of the Preparation of Missionaries," *IRM* 13 (1924): 385.

10. Van de Loosdrecht, *ADV*, February 1914, p. 16.

11. Van de Loosdrecht, *ADV*, May 1914, pp. 37-39.

Four Torajan youths--one a nephew of Pong Maramba,[12] the powerful headman of Rantepao--accompanied the van de Loosdrechts to this foreign highland society as Tae' (Sa'dan Toraja) language tutors to prepare them for their return to Rantepao. During this time the Tae' language appears to have come easily to the determined missionary and his wife, as did impressions about the power a missionary had to transform East Indies societies. Kruyt had in many ways combined the functions of government and mission in the ten years prior to the Dutch expansion of their authority to the region in 1905. With such a foothold, the mission tended to mold the character of the later arriving Dutch administration. Without having to identify with the secular state, Kruyt's mission had received ample cooperation from it. As Ida van de Loosdrecht later wrote to Mrs. Kruyt, "We often say to one another, 'how wonderful for Posso that the mission preceded the Government.'"[13]

Back in Rantepao the ambitious missionary set out to recreate the city on a hill that he had witnessed in Posso under the seasoned master. With a sense of urgency, he visited the major districts of Rantepao, met their headmen, and, in a meeting also attended by the controleur, encouraged them to build schools in their *kampung*.[14] "Of all the means that a mission has at its disposal to gain entry to the people," he wrote soon afterwards, "the school is surely one of the most prominent." And while his approach was aimed at the future adults of the society, he did not concede those already grown up: "The way to the heart of a father and mother in mission work goes through the child. Children attach themselves quickly to their teachers, who have a knack of getting on with them even more than their parents do."[15]

By pushing education, the mission hoped it had found a means by which to enter traditional societies without creating the type of resistance that would be engendered by a direct attack on traditional religious values. The problem remained to convince district headmen and their village clients that they themselves would derive some benefit from the schools. Van de Loosdrecht found the traditional elite initially cautious but generally willing to consider allowing schools to enter their *tondok* (district).[16] In retrospect, it appears that they were probably less enthusiastic than the missionary reported to his home board.[17] The headmen were still in the process of evaluating the behavior of the "Kompania," the name they still applied to the Dutch government over a century after the demise of the Dutch East Indies Company. It appeared to them that the school was one of the forms of tribute demanded by the new patron state. For some years many continued to believe that it was a disguised means of drafting their sons into the colonial army and taking them away from

---

12. Sampe Pandin, interview, January 22, 1978, Ujung Pandang.

13. Letter from Ida van de Loosdrecht to Mevrouw Kruyt, May 25, 1914, Rantepao. (Archive, Hervormde Kerk, Oegstgeest; hereafter AHK.)

14. Van de Loosdrecht, *ADV*, March 1914, p. 23.

15. Van de Loosdrecht, *ADV*, October 1914, pp. 85-86.

16. Van de Loosdrecht, *ADV*, March 1914, p. 23.

17. D. Crommelin, "Rapport over het bezoek aan het zendingsterrein van den Gereformeerden Zendingsbond in Rantepao en Makale, Juni 1918," pp. 2-3 (AHK); E. A. J. Nobele (untitled secret government report on the death of A. A. van de Loosdrecht, by Assistant Resident of Luwu), Palopo, August 20, 1917 (AHK).

the highlands. Thus while on the surface they acquiesced to this peculiar new form of tribute, they also tried to circumvent it in various ways.

Van de Loosdrecht's first year in Rantepao can be seen as a cautious effort to undo what Kelling of the Indies Church had done during his short tenure in the Sa'dan highlands, as well as to counterbalance the "bad examples" set by both the Dutch and Malay-speaking Christians stationed in Makale-Rantepao with the NEI administration.[18] Pragmatically he accepted the hasty baptismal techniques of evangelist Kelling for their value in slowing the advance of Islam, while he maintained that their use had produced a Christianity that was superficial at best. He ridiculed the cautious forays made to the town of Makale by the elitist minister of the Indies Church stationed in Makassar, Kyftenbelt. Kyftenbelt preferred to spend an hour a week with the five Christians in Makale town and the rest of the week recovering, van de Loosdrecht complained; never would he dream of setting foot in the villages. What was worse, Kyftenbelt's wife insisted on parading about under a white umbrella like some royal personage, followed by an entourage of servants bearing her daily necessities.[19]

Van de Loosdrecht himself retained many of the stereotypes of "the native" common to the Dutch colonials of his time and tended to patronize Torajans as children who needed tutoring. Yet he understood the inherent limitations of the elitism of Kyftenbelt and others like him in the Netherlands Indies Church who were content to wait for potential converts--shorn of their traditional explanatory systems through education, employment, or migration--to surface in urban centers. By contrast, the strategy of the hill country evangelist of the twentieth century was to bring about that transformation in place.

Convinced of the importance of the elite to any successful mission venture in Makale-Rantepao, van de Loosdrecht sought to develop personal relationships with key district and village headmen. Within a short time he identified Pong Maramba of Rantepao, Ne' Mattandung of Balusu, and Tandibua of Pangala as central figures among the *onderafdeeling* (subdivision) Rantepao elite. Frequently he visited their kampung, especially those of Maramba and Mattandung whose houses were not far away from his own. Maramba did not go out of his way to reciprocate the missionary's interest in him, but, after a few fruitless attempts, van de Loosdrecht finally managed to find the headman at home, having just returned from a death feast. Their exchange that evening was, by the missionary's account, a warm one in which he avoided outright proselytizing. The women in Pong Maramba's household paid a return visit to Mrs. van de Loosdrecht some days later, displaying great curiosity over the bed, sewing machine, and church organ as they led the somewhat astonished woman about her own house.[20] An amiable enough relationship had begun to develop, it would seem.

With Ne' Mattandung of Balusu, relations were similarly cordial at first. Van de Loosdrecht was sensitive to the fact that Balusu district was located on the western border of Luwu and he was alert to possible signs of Islamization

---

18. "Yes, the Christians here in general provide a poor example. They look upon the Torajans as lowly but not too low to enter into the most intimate of relationships with them." Van de Loosdrecht's letter to Kruyt, December 30, 1914, Rantepao (AHK).

19. Ibid.

20. Ida van de Loosdrecht, *ADV*, November 1914, pp. 95-96. "If Pong Maramba were to become Christian, the strength of heathendom would be forever broken," wrote the missionary's wife.

emanating from this old Islamic kingdom.[21] Historically the Balusu "Puang"[22] had married into the Luwu court families, quite like their Islamicized neighbors in the adjacent Luwu Highlands; Ne' Mattandung's daughter herself was married to a close relative of the Datu. Perhaps attuned to the missionary's fear that this pattern of intermarriage signalled the beginning of the Islamization of Balusu, Ne' Mattandung apparently assured him that, despite the birth of a child, the father's two-year absence meant that the marriage was as good as dissolved. The missionary counted on Mattandung to provide a prime point of contact with Torajan society, just as invading Dutch troops had relied on him eight years before, when they extended their administrative control into the highlands. Nonetheless van de Loosdrecht harbored the suspicion that Mattandung retained an "inclination toward Islam."[23]

While attempting to build cultural bridges directly to the headmen, the van de Loosdrechts sought allies in their children as well.[24] They invited several youths from influential families to board with them, providing Biblical instruction and a Dutch Calvinist moral framework. Van de Loosdrecht depended on his boys to teach him the language and, more importantly, to form the core of the first indigenous group of *guru* (teachers), and *guru injil* (evangelists). Their high social status insured that these pioneer figures would draw attention.

Girls were trained as prospective wives for the Malay-speaking and Torajan *guru*.[25] Ida van de Loosdrecht taught them a Victorian morality quite alien to Torajan custom, schooled them in the basics of nutrition, hygiene, and housekeeping, and instructed them on how to use the sewing machine. These women would provide the moral and spiritual fiber for the children at home that would set the Christian household apart from the heathen. Without a pool of suitable marriage partners from which to draw, the teachers would be more likely to become embroiled in scandal with village women, and decrease the effectiveness of their religious message in a society where "[t]he children understand the whole village chronicle, know who has a quarrel with whom, who speaks scandalously of others and who has deceived another, who is esteemed and who is disdained."[26]

Initially the missionary adopted a conciliatory approach toward the indigenous religion and ritual that underpinned the elite with whom he was so concerned. He took the high road of emphasizing schooling while avoiding talk about religion in his initial meetings with people. "As soon as they hear that the morals and customs of their ancestors must be changed, their favorable disposition immediately disappears and they refuse to do anything," he wrote.[27] If he took the back door and stimulated widespread acceptance of schools, religious

---

21. Van de Loosdrecht, *ADV*, October 1914, pp. 88-89.

22. "Puang" was the highest term of nobility in the southern portion of the Sa'dan highlands (Makale, Mengkendek, Sangalla) as well as the eastern *tondok* of Sa'dan and Balusu.

23. Van de Loosdrecht, *ADV*, July 1915, p. 44.

24. Van de Loosdrecht, *ADV*, March 1914, pp. 23-24; van de Loosdrecht, letter to Kruyt, February 22, 1916, Rantepao (AHK).

25. Van de Loosdrecht, *ADV*, May 1916, p. 40.

26. J. Belksma, *ADV*, June 1918, p. 42.

27. Van de Loosdrecht, *ADV*, September 1914, p. 84.

education would naturally follow. This, he assured any skeptics in the home church in Holland, was because the heathen mind did not easily distinguish between the sacred and the profane; in due course it would seem natural that religion was being taught in school.[28] Surprisingly, he did not anticipate that Torajan opposition to the schools might arise out of that same unitary world view.

Van de Loosdrecht's directness and the nagging image he retained of the flourishing mission in Posso prevented him from circumventing religious issues for long, though he initially chose his themes with discretion. He told the creation story frequently and selected Abraham, Noah, and other Old Testament patriarchs to appeal to the Torajan ancestral reverence.[29] The Biblical myth of the flood, which he found to be very popular, strongly resembled a Torajan myth. His use of the Prodigal Son parable further exemplified his early efforts at finding commonalities between Torajan religion and Christianity.[30] Van de Loosdrecht held a view of primitive religions having declined from an earlier purity to a corrupted state. This view implied that Torajans had originally believed in the same high god as the God of the Christians, but that through the centuries the belief had become corrupted by spirit worship. Therefore Torajans need only strip away these corruptions to reveal the high god; they need only return to belief in "*Puang Matoa*." The use of the indigenous name of a prominent Torajan deity for the Christian "God" as much as the missionary's emphasis on a "return"--i.e., the Prodigal Son--set a context for religious discussion that accepted much that was authentically Torajan. This fitted nicely with a strategy of conversion focused on attracting the elite.

If working through the traditional elite composed one leg of the initial mission strategy, cooperation with the Dutch administration constituted the other. Van de Loosdrecht was an acutely political man, who knew the meaning of lobbying for his causes and appeared able to locate the points in the various tiers of the East Indies administrative hierarchy where he could exert pressure. His interest in gaining active support from the government stemmed from the view he took of religious, or more broadly, cultural change: that the efforts by the mission to loosen Torajans from their cultural moorings had scant impact compared to changes induced by the East Indies administration.[31] The outlawing of headhunting and trial by ordeal, abolition of the slave trade, and forced resettlement ("kampung-forming"), to take several examples, had given the traditional order a shock from which it would never recover. In providing a buffer between Torajans and their "former oppressors" the Bugis, the Dutch administration had given the formation of Torajan ethnic consciousness a "great shove."[32] But through its various modifications of tradition (in the name of preserving tradition), the government had succeeded in loosening people from their animism while providing them nothing directly to replace it. In this anomic state, "[the Torajan] himself waits for something to replace" his earlier beliefs, the missionary anticipated.[33] The mission would provide that something in the wake of government-induced social change.

---

28. Ibid., p. 86.
29. Van de Loosdrecht, *ADV*, April 1915, p. 21.
30. Letter from van de Loosdrecht, February 22, 1916, Rantepao (AHK).
31. Van de Loosdrecht, *ADV*, August 1915, p. 60.
32. Van de Loosdrecht, *ADV*, October 1914, p. 86.
33. Van de Loosdrecht, *ADV*, June 1915, p. 41.

During the first year of GZB activity in Makale-Rantepao, relations with the East Indies government officials were not notably cordial. The government's deep anxiety that Islamic adherents would penetrate the highlands and convert the hill peoples was counterbalanced for a time by their misgivings about the blunders committed by the overly eager evangelist Kelling. His mass baptism of school-aged children without regard to the wishes of their parents raised concerns that perhaps one potential threat to "peace and security" would be replaced by another. The quality of the teaching personnel loosed upon the highlands was brought into question by the dismissal of a teacher for his swindling activities in the Makale village to which he had been assigned. Though the Indies Church mission was soon displaced from Makale-Rantepao by the arrival of van de Loosdrecht in 1913, a cloud of zealotry still hung over the highlands.

It is most ironic that zealotry should ever have been associated with the Indies Church, given its tepid record of proselytizing in other parts of the Netherlands East Indies. It was a zeal, in the Sa'dan highlands, born of the hasty efforts of the provincial government to use whatever Protestant vehicle was at hand to begin erecting a Christian buffer in South Sulawesi.

During the six years following the introduction of government schools in 1908, the authorities had regularly resorted to using troops to round up truant children of the elite and bring them to school in the towns. Van de Loosdrecht believed that such an approach could be an effective lever to help him build attendance at his village schools. He pressed for permission for elite children attending the government school to be given the option of attending the mission village schools. The controleur of Rantepao finally conceded this point, and, with that, van de Loosdrecht was able to employ the implied force of military truant officers to the mission's advantage. He reported absentees to the controleur, who had the parents of truant children arrested in their villages and taken to the Rantepao jail.[34] With such heavy-handed practices, an absentee rate of 5 to 10 percent was considered high.

While attempting to maximize both direct and indirect benefits of government policy in Rantepao and Makale, the missionary and his supporters sought to have officers more sympathetic to the mission installed in the highlands. Lobbying the bureaucracy appears to have paid off by the end of 1915, just over a year after the missionary had arrived. The newly appointed controleur of Rantepao, M. R. Brouwer, was a man who shared the religious outlook of the GZB mission and who, van de Loosdrecht predicted, "will not withhold his unqualified support from us."[35] At about the same time, Breedveldt Boer was replaced as assistant resident of Luwu by E. A. J. Nobele, whose sympathy for the mission and concern for *rust en orde* had grown with the incidence in uprisings that had begun to characterize South Sulawesi after 1914, some of them inspired by Islamic religious leadership. The assistant resident began to push for the GZB to extend its mission activities into the highlands of the onderafdeeling of Palopo which was the Islamic stronghold in Luwu. By late 1915 any reluctance within the Dutch administration to cooperate with the mission in afdeeling Luwu had been removed: "it is wonderful that Assistant

---

34. Letter from A. A. van de Loosdrecht to A. C. Kruyt, June 8, 1914, Rantepao (AHK).

35. Letter from A. A. van de Loosdrecht to A. C. Kruyt, December 30, 1914, Rantepao (AHK).

Resident Nobele so strongly cooperates," wrote Kruyt in reply to a letter from van de Loosdrecht.[36]

Torajan headmen had gone through nearly a decade of readjustment since the coming of the Dutch administration. New rules of competition had been thrust upon them, with the Pax Neerlandica imposed upon highlands that had seen so much fighting during the Bugis struggle from 1870 to 1905, in shifting alliances with Torajan headmen, to control the coffee and slave trade from the highlands.[37] Firearms, once so prevalent in the hands of the powerful chiefs, had been turned in to the Dutch or lay rusting in the limestone caves that concealed them. The traditional system of *Ra'*, the ultimate determination of an argument by ritualized battle, had been replaced by a government court to handle those quarrels that could not be peacefully resolved by village or district heads. Duplicating the feats of great headmen such as Pong Tiku, Pong Maramba, or Andi Lolo, who forcefully expanded their land holdings just prior to the Dutch arrival, was out of the question with the regularized order that the Dutch had imposed on the Sa'dan highlands. Control of retainers had passed from such leaders' hands, except for the days of service specifically granted them as compensation for their chiefly duties, and whatever extra-legal claims they could get away with. The benefits of the coffee trade had become somewhat questionable now that the controleur of Makale-Rantepao prevented Bugis trading agents from bargaining directly with the chiefs for access to their coffee; once coffee collection was organized for government taxation in Makale and Rantepao towns after 1910, a sizeable source of chiefly wealth and power slipped from the hands of the headmen.

Although many of the traditional forms of competition for power had been diverted into more routinized channels, the elite still did retain perhaps the primary means of attracting clients, the distribution of meat. Through the ceremonial system, the patron-client relationship that for much of the year might be difficult to distinguish came clearly into view. Patrons at the death feast, for example, distributed portions of meat that "repaid" the labor clients had provided during the year. Now, without the overtly coercive mechanisms that had been available before the Dutch administration (the most direct being outright attack and seizure of individuals or an entire kampung for slavery), the sacrificial system assumed even greater importance as a vehicle of cementing patron-client relationships.

The new administration and the coming of the mission brought about opportunities as well as challenges. New symbols of power were introduced: the Dutch awarded medals of service to chiefs who had helped to put down Torajan resistance; officers' dress jackets replaced the chief's traditional clothing; and the office of *pangarak* (caller) was created to place some distance between the chief and those he might wish to summon.[38] Through the missionary came another

---

36. Letter from A. C. Kruyt to A. A. van de Loosdrecht, April 4, 1916, Pendolo (AHK).

37. For details on the slave trade, see Terance Bigalke, "Dynamics of the Torajan Slave Trade in South Sulawesi," in *Slavery, Bondage and Dependency in Southeast Asia*, ed. Anthony Reid (New York: St. Martins Press, 1983), pp. 341-63.

38. L. Weber, *Verbaal* 12-8-1914-76, *mailrapport* 1817/13 (Colonial Archive, The Hague), pp. 75-76. Laso' Sombolinggi, interview, March 2, 1978, Rantepao. G. R. Seinstra mentions *pangarak* along with *patikin* ("sword bearers," a kind of village police) and *mandoro kampung* (assistant village head) as officials

potential symbol of influence, the village school. While the chiefs did not clearly understand the reason for building schools and harbored some suspicion of them, it was widely known that the government supported their construction. By building a school a chief looking for increased influence put himself closer to the light of government patronage.

Most Torajans who knew van de Loosdrecht seem to have viewed him as an extension of the Dutch administration.[39] The short period during which he avoided attacking Torajan religious beliefs was generally cordial, however. Chiefs enjoyed receiving a visitor, exchanging stories with him, inquiring about his tondok, and making observations about the unusual aspects of *To Belanda* that they had observed. One remarked that Dutch mothers must be lax in teaching their children language, since the Dutch always went around asking Torajans what the words were for various things they saw. Another noted that he had never seen a mug like the one the missionary's wife had used to serve him coffee, and according to custom asked to take it home with him.

As Torajan chiefs began to hear messages that contradicted their system of beliefs, they responded variously. Some, such as Tandiseru, a kampung head from Tikala, announced that he would "rather be exiled than believe in Christianity"; another felt it was "preferable to die than to leave the religion of the forefathers."[40] Others sought comments on the missionary's stories from Islamic teachers they knew in the towns of Makale or Rantepao or in Luwu. They were, like Ne' Mattandung of Balusu, seriously considering conversion to Islam after years of contact with Islamic elites; or they were, like Pong Maramba, continually seeking alliances that would provide the most room for maneuver: Christian when Islam pressed, Muslim when Christianity threatened. There were chiefs who saw an unabashed syncretism as the way to deal with the god of the Kompania, finding "a place for Pong Isa" (Jesus) among the *deata*, the host of spirits complementing Torajan deities.[41] During the missionary's first year this suggestion to incorporate a new element into their beliefs was the warmest response that he received.

Much in the early teachings of the missionary sounded quite funny to Torajans but some of the stories contained similarities with those they had heard from their Muslim neighbors. The story of the crucifixion was not impressive, given their belief in the efficacy of trial by ordeal. In their view, if this god was powerful he would never have died that way.[42] Even more difficult to accept was the belief that each man was a sinner. The Torajan view of religious responsibility corresponded more to a system of rituals and duties that were carried out at the proper time and for the proper persons or deities. Thus a typical Torajan response to hearing that he was a sinner was that his heart was good; how could he be a sinner? The full flavor of this attitude was carried in a quotation that comes a year later than the period under review but aptly emphasizes the point: "Oh Tuan, my heart is right; I am a friend

---

assisting the kampung headman. All were initiated under the Dutch administration. G. R. Seinstra, "Memorie van overgave, betreffende de onderafdeelingen Makale en Rantepao" (Rantepao, 1940, in my possession), pp. 133-34.

39. Van de Loosdrecht, *ADV*, August 1917, p. 69.

40. Van de Loosdrecht, *ADV*, October 1916, p. 97; August 1915, p. 60.

41. Van de Loosdrecht, *ADV*, May 1915, p. 31; July 1915, p. 44.

42. Van de Loosdrecht, *ADV*, April 1915, p. 21.

of the Kompania ... and my heart is right toward you, as well as toward Puang Tarongkon [the Puang of Makale] and is right toward the deatas to whom I never forget to provide offerings."[43]

The Torajan fascination with death and the afterlife did, however, provide some common ground for discussion. Their most appreciative responses to the missionary came when he described the Christian vision of the hereafter. Pong Maramba, at a time when he was encouraging visits from both Islamic teachers and the missionary, once told the latter that it was as if his stories made the heavens open up for him, Maramba, to catch a glimpse.[44] This sort of reinforcement naturally skewed the content of early Christian proselytizing among the Torajans, at least insofar as the missionary could still see some promise in the elite. But there were seeds of conflict in an approach that down-played the message of love and the sacrificial lamb while emphasizing the afterlife. Taking that as a point of departure, it was hard to avoid a basic commentary on Torajan funeral practice and conceptions of the hereafter. This opened the way to fundamental differences between the Christian conception of heaven and the Torajan conception of *Puya*, where the social hierarchy was believed to continue much as it had on earth. Once the more egalitarian aspect of Christianity was exposed, the fascination with "making the heavens open up" was replaced by a concern that the existing social order not be turned upside down.

While proselytizing did not force an immediate response from the headmen because there was little danger of anyone converting, the building of schools did. Generally schools received an ambivalent response from the powerful chiefs, with somewhat more enthusiasm coming from the less powerful in small districts. The school could be interpreted as another symbol of the chief's power, located as it was near his house in most villages that had a school. It could also be seen as a threat to his control of the village, since it introduced through the guru, usually a non-Torajan, a foreign element beholden to the missionary.

In principle, most of the major tondok that were pressed to build schools acquiesced, with their chiefs providing manpower and access to the materials needed for construction. Since the chiefs' retainers were doing the building, it was customary for them to be provided with meals in return for their labor. Only in Tondon did the headman refuse outright to allow a school to be built. This refusal stemmed from a dispute between the guru in the Rantepao government school and the ruling headman of Tondon over the treatment of the latter's child. After the guru was relieved of his position the resistance declined, and a new school was built in Tondon in 1916.[45]

The posture of the chiefs was critical in the initial years of a school's existence. Children needed a great deal of coaxing to go to school; indeed, the first few times they saw the missionary approaching for school inspection they ran from sight, crying out the characteristic whoop formerly associated with warfare.[46] The sight of a "belanda" was still rare enough to inspire tremendous apprehension; eventually van de Loosdrecht sent his teachers out

---

43. D. C. Prins, *ADV*, April 1918, p. 27.
44. Van de Loosdrecht, *ADV*, December 1914, p. 102.
45. Van de Loosdrecht, *ADV*, August 1917, p. 70.
46. Van de Loosdrecht, *ADV*, October 1914, p. 87.

alone to get the schools functioning and came himself only for their official dedication.

Once the children had been initiated into the school system, other problems arose to cause the chiefs concern. The guru regularly administered corporal punishment, disturbing not only the victims of the poundings but their parents as well.[47] This was not merely a dispute over the proper locus of corporal discipline, the home or school. Rather, it cut deeply against the Torajan ethic of how children should be raised. They believed that, if a young child were hit, his spirit could desert him, and the child would become seriously ill. Toby Volkman reports that only after a child has suffered from smallpox, the most feared disease, is it considered proper to administer a physical blow.[48]

Another cause for concern stemmed from the students' reactions to life in the village once they had attended school in the town. Some refused to return home to live an agricultural life, or to engage in manual labor of any sort. In Buntao, children refused to work in the fields after schooling, leading van de Loosdrecht to note with some alarm that an "educated proletariat" was in the making. While this may have been the result of life in the town as much as of the education received there, the chiefs associated the tears in the social fabric of the village with their children's going away to school. The missionary's reassurances that this was not the intended response from the children and his encouragement of education in the villages quieted some but not all their fears.[49]

A good indication of the depth of the mistrust among the elite was the nearly universal practice of substituting their retainers' children for their own in the schools. This, naturally, made the children's resistance to manual labor all the more chilling, for it promised an unmanageable clientele in the future. The elite was afraid from the outset that the government's motive in recruiting their children was to send them to the military and take them away from the highlands.[50]

Another measure of mistrust was the small number of girls sent to the schools despite constant reminders from the authorities that schools were intended for both sexes. This restraint was most notable in the large, powerful tondok, such as Rantepao, Pangala, and Makale.

We can summarize the initial period of interaction between the missionary and the elite as one of caution on both sides. The missionary exercised restraint in his choice of religious themes, his pressing for schools, and his response to the ritual systems of the Torajan. The elites listened with curiosity and a tolerance based on their awareness that local Dutch authority solidly supported the mission.

Resolution: The Dutch

When van de Loosdrecht first arrived in Rantepao he had the keen eye of a traveler who has not yet become numbed to the new things he sees around

---

47. Van de Loosdrecht, *ADV*, August 1917, pp. 69-70; April 1918, p. 27.
48. Toby Volkman, personal communication.
49. Van de Loosdrecht, *ADV*, August 1915, p. 60.
50. J. Belksma, *ADV*, June 1918, p. 43.

him. He was immediately drawn to observing the social hierarchy around him, and apparently felt it necessary to justify the existence of the large number of "slaves" (*kaunan*) in the Torajan social structure. It was somewhat difficult for him to do so because of the narrow ascriptive way he defined the kaunan as "slaves," or "former slaves" rather than seeing them functionally as clients.[51] Even so he found it possible to rationalize their condition in Biblical terms, resorting to the Pauline exhortation that masters and slaves must each know their own roles.[52] Indeed, his motivation was not unlike Paul's, in that van de Loosdrecht had gone to Rantepao with the desire to appeal to the elite with his religious message, not to turn the society upside down.

In comparison with his later position, his early observations appear remarkably dispassionate and tolerant of indigenous social behaviors and structures. He attempted to sketch the social "status groups" (*standen*) in terms of the rulers and the ruled (the former being the puang and *tomakaka* classes, the latter being the "slaves" [kaunan] and debt slaves [*to sandang*]), limiting his remarks merely to the contention that most to sandang fell into servitude through gambling, which continued clandestinely despite strong government prohibitions.[53] With regard to the position of women, he simply noted that they appeared to be socially more equal to men in the Rongkong hill country (northern Luwu) than they did among the Sa'dan highlanders of Rantepao.[54]

Within a few months, however, after the missionary had begun to encounter some resistance from the elite whose position he had initially sought to rationalize, he took a much more critical view. He began sending home to mission headquarters unflattering information on the Torajans, information he had undoubtedly noted previously: "human heads adorn the facades of houses in Bori" and the inhabitants there used to practice cannibalism, according to an old Tominaa.[55] In July 1915 having come up square against the powerful headman of Rantepao he pessimistically assessed the chances of conversion: "Pong Maramba is not for it, though the missionary is on a good footing with him. Brother van de Loosdrecht expects a violent struggle in Rantepao."[56] Indicating that he had moved on from his view of the Torajan as "child-like" in many ways, he now concluded that "(t)he worldly wisdom is much greater than one thinks and the sins are more awesome." As van de Loosdrecht came to view the elite less as naive wards than as shrewd adversaries, his approach to evangelizing became more bold. It was as though he had decided to reject the recalcitrant old notables and to begin making an appeal to the lower orders of Torajan society.

Our first clear indication of this comes in the western tondok of Rano. It was from this outlying district and from Simbuang further west that the missionary had received his first rural expressions of interest in conversion, which prompted him to declare that "the signs are such that Makale may be

---

51. For a discussion of this terminology, see Bigalke, "Dynamics of the Torajan Slave Trade," pp. 357-60.

52. Van de Loosdrecht, *ADV*, December 1914, p. 102.

53. Van de Loosdrecht, *ADV*, March 1915, p. 11.

54. Van de Loosdrecht, *ADV*, April 1915, p. 21.

55. Van de Loosdrecht, *ADV*, August 1915, pp. 62-63.

56. Summarized from letter written July 22, 1915, reported in *ADV*, May 1916, p. 40.

won over to Christianity before Rantepao."[57] It is unclear just why he should have chosen to open his offensive against the elite in a place where the elite itself was most interested in converting; it may have been a strategic blunder. But open it he did, with a Torajan-tailored version of the "rich fool" parable, told in terms of rice barns, water buffalo, and fat pigs owned in profusion by a rich man named Pare La'bi ("Excessive Rice"). The crowd that gathered to hear this parable expressed great sympathy and affection for the wealthy Pare La'bi whom van de Loosdrecht painted as a gross materialist. He labeled this rich man a fool because his wealth had prevented him from attending to what really mattered, the spiritual dimension of his life. Van de Loosdrecht records that the inhabitants of Rano responded with shock to the contention that Pare La'bi could be out of favor with *any* deity, given the man's great wealth: "My application fell like a thunderbolt on the many gathered. Such a message was wholly new to them: a 'rich' man called a 'fool' by God. People sat dismayed; with open mouths they listened further to my explanation and the reasons that it was foolishness in God's eye. That God loves the poor as well as the rich was not something that came to the Torajan mind."[58] More significant than the message that a rich man could be a spiritual fool was the correlation that the missionary began to draw between the wealth of some and the oppression of others: "A rich man is held in a kind of holy fear by the Torajan. People put him on a pedestal. Let him extort villagers, swindle, in a word be heartless, but he remains in their eyes great and men call him 'good' because the blessing of the gods is upon him." Over the next eighteen months his class critique sharpened. He began openly to censure the basic inequalities in Torajan socioeconomic relationships, portraying them as having been exacerbated by the complicity between the Bugis and Torajan elites during the days of the slave trade. "The rich are loveless and hard toward the poor," he lamented. "Adat and people's rights have suffered a great deal . . . under this unchaining of passions. Some families have especially known how to profit from this situation and how to gain access to excessively large landholdings.[59] The result of this greed for rice land, he said, had been to reduce most Torajans to tenants or laborers without control of even a small piece of wet-rice field. "For the greatest part of the year they possess no rice and feed themselves on greens that their wives collect in rice fields."

The plight of those labeled "the dispossessed" became his major focus, replacing his initial focus on the old guard, whom he now defined as oppressors. And he broadened the application of "the dispossessed" to include the impoverished tomakaka as well as kaunan, attributing the plight of the former not to land seizures but to the Torajan death cult. He correctly assessed that a landholder would, under economic duress, pawn his rice fields to get buffalo to meet his sacrificial obligations at a death feast. Often, this land would pass permanently from its owner's control to that of the pawnholder, who gained ultimate right of disposal. He argued that to halt the trend toward landlessness, the extent of sacrificial cutting had to be restricted: "So long as the death feasts are not limited, this process will continue and the gap between deep poverty and great riches will assume still graver forms."[60]

---

57. Ibid., p. 40.

58. Van de Loosdrecht, *ADV*, February 1916, p. 15.

59. Van de Loosdrecht, *ADV*, January 1918, p. 6.

60. Van de Loosdrecht, *ADV*, February 1918, p. 9.

While one might applaud the social conscience that stirred the missionary's soul, and acknowledge the genuine sense of revelation that came through his inquiries into Torajan history and social structure, one must remain aware that the motivations driving his inquiry did not exclude self-interest. Behind his revelation lay the gradually awakening realization that the ritual order and the socioeconomic order upheld one another: "No wonder most chiefs are against Christianity," he mused, stripped of his own naivete.[61] During the time he had conceived of his task as converting the whole of Torajan society through converting the elite, he had taken a Pauline view of the relationship of ruler to ruled, each with his duty to obey. Once he saw the inefficacy of this strategy for purposes of conversion, he allowed himself to entertain the possibility of social engineering--for which he so admired the power of the government--as a substitute.

Radical as was his attack on the death feast, it assumed even greater gravity as it came in the wake of a determined attack on gambling and cockfighting. Little had been done effectively to prohibit gambling in its various Torajan forms (including some imported by the Bugis) until the mission arrived in Makale-Rantepao. The government had gradually reduced the number of days permitted for cockfighting, which took place in the period between the death feast and burial, and was associated with religious conceptions of conveying the *sumanga* (life-force) of the deceased to the afterlife. Van de Loosdrecht sought further to reduce the number of days permitted, and restrict the practice solely to the elite.[62] His active opposition to cockfighting became so well known that headmen often teased him about it. One man assured the missionary with a straight face that he would happily turn Christian if the government would first permit him one uninterrupted year of cockfighting; on another occasion, when the missionary approached him at a village gathering on Sunday, the headman prodded: "Why not allow us to fight cock at this service?"[63] The humor, however, barely concealed the growing tension between van de Loosdrecht and the elite, who feared a total ban on the sporting ritual.

The GZB mission became politically very secure after the appointment of Brouwer as Rantepao controleur and the promotion of Controleur Nobele from Makale to the assistant resident position in Palopo. The new Makale controleur was less openly sympathetic to the GZB and to Prins, its neophyte missionary in Makale, but he did not pose an obstacle to the spirit of mission-government cooperation that had emerged with the blessing of the new assistant resident. Both Brouwer and Nobele were sensitive to the deterioration over the course of 1915 of what van de Loosdrecht had termed "the more gratifying spirit that had prevailed in Toraja initially...."[64] They saw this more surly spirit as a spillover from the series of local rebellions that had broken out in Luwu that year, and resolved to use a show of force to prevent any further spread of dissension to Makale-Rantepao. Thus when van de Loosdrecht's probings into village life brought to light some of the unsavory but conventional activities of headmen in preserving or expanding their wealth and influence, the Rantepao controleur, backed by the assistant resident, elected to open official investigations.

---

61. Ibid.

62. E. A. J. Nobele, untitled secret report over the death of A. A. van de Loosdrecht (AHK).

63. Van de Loosdrecht, *ADV*, January 1918, p. 4.

64. Van de Loosdrecht, *ADV*, August 1917, pp. 68-69.

This was a reversal of the government's earlier decision, arrived at after some initial hesitation, that the activities of the elite prior to Dutch arrival were not subject to official prosecution; the ongoing implication for the elite had been that, within certain limits, things would go on as usual at the village level. By December 1915 the government was beginning to show its new policy in dealing with headmen's affairs.

In light of the official support van de Loosdrecht had begun to receive, he planned a show of strength by holding a Christmas feast in Rantepao which he hoped would be attended by the influential headmen of the district. The feast would blend the Torajan custom of slaughtering and feasting upon large numbers of livestock with the singing of school children and a Christian religious service. He received absolutely no response from the headmen until after Controleur Brouwer intervened by bringing pressure to bear on the key figure in the defiance, Pong Maramba. Maramba was persuaded to contribute a pig to the festivities, which brought a counteroffer from his major rival, Ne' Mattandung of Balusu, to contribute a buffalo. After other chiefs followed suit the success of the festival was assured, with some twenty-four pigs and a buffalo offered for slaughter and the promise that all the headmen would attend as well. The government's timely intervention on behalf of the missionary signalled a new cooperation between government and mission in an effort to break what they jointly perceived as stubborn resistance from the powerful old headmen.[65]

The full extent of their cooperation became clearer in the following two months. Pong Maramba spent several short periods in the Rantepao jail on various charges before he was finally hauled off to Palopo to stand trial for extortion.[66] While the headman of the most populous district in Rantepao awaited trial, van de Loosdrecht spelled out the motivation behind the charges in a letter to his mentor, Kruyt. He felt depressed about the response in Rantepao to his evangelizing, which was proving less favorable than that from Makale where much less effort had been expended. While local knowledge of Christianity had increased in Rantepao, the political situation had deteriorated:

> ... the political situation is still wretched, which all the old chiefs have a hand in; the worst enemy is Pong Maramba. Mr. Brouwer [the controleur] is beginning to clean up the situation, supported by the new Assistant Resident Nobele.
> I think that Pong Maramba, who already sits in Palopo, will be the first to go; Brouwer is presently investigating his vile case. This fellow has stolen almost all the sawahs he has. People assess his worth at a tidy million. He does nothing of benefit with all his wealth, merely extorting from the people. It is too bad that this man is so impervious to the truth. He is our greatest adversary and maintains everyone here against us. But we will go steadily forward and in God's time the harvest will come here as it has in Posso.[67]

---

65. Van de Loosdrecht, *ADV*, October 1916, pp. 96-97.

66. S. Pandin, interview, August 15, 1978, Ujung Pandang; F. K. Sarangallo, interview, February 1, 1978, Ke'te (Toraja); *ADV*, November 1916, p. 104.

67. Letter from A. A. van de Loosdrecht to A. C. Kruyt, February 22, 1916, Rantepao (AHK).

Maramba's reluctance to convert to Christianity was a great disappointment to van de Loosdrecht, one that he took personally. It was all the more galling since he was aware that Maramba himself had originally requested that missionaries come to Rantepao.[68] He sensed that the powerful headman was now going out of his way to show more interest in Islam than in Christianity while van de Loosdrecht was seeking to convert him. Maramba's presence loomed over the missionary almost wherever he went in the onderafdeeling. Earlier in 1915 van de Loosdrecht had confronted his own powerlessness in the face of a dysentery epidemic in Bori. His previous admonitions not to provide sacrifices to the deata to ward off disease went unheeded when Maramba, on advice from Islamic teachers, instructed the headman there that each affected household should throw an egg and a needle into the river. On another occasion, when van de Loosdrecht made an unannounced visit to Maramba's house, he walked in on an Islamic teacher talking with the headman.[69] In subsequent conversations with the missionary, Maramba displayed the kind of knowledge of Christianity (apparently gained through his discussions with Muslims) that thoroughly dismayed van de Loosdrecht. Fluent in Bugis, befriended by Islamic teachers, having built a burial structure for his mother topped by the unmistakable dome of Islamic architecture, Maramba was showing ominous signs of not only rejecting Christianity but also possibly embracing Islam. If the great headman of Rantepao converted to Islam, his immeasurable influence threatened to sweep his thousands of clients with him.

The government's criminal court in Palopo found Pong Maramba guilty on twenty-four counts of extortion, and sentenced him to fifteen years in exile. Until the ship came to take Maramba to Java, van de Loosdrecht sought to convert him in his prison cell. The headman's refusal did not have the drama or the finality of the oaths taken against Christianity by some of his fellow headmen; he simply maintained, the mission journal records, that he was still unable to convert.[70]

Maramba's exile was merely the opening scene in a coordinated effort to undo the old guard. Similar criminal charges followed against Ne' Kulu and Danduru of Buntao, and Ne' Mattandung of Balusu was rumored to be next, because of accusations from van de Loosdrecht. The missionary also leveled charges of both incest and extortion against the Nanggala Parenge, while complaints filed by the missionary led to headmen in Sa'dan and Bori being punished for neglect of duty.[71] Van de Loosdrecht insisted he would pursue this offensive, "so long as extortion is not totally rooted out, so long as the belief is not abandoned that our Government will leave Toraja before long, so long as the hope is not given up that the old conditions of plunder and thievery shall once again return, so long ... so long, in sum, until the Lord with his Holy Spirit comes to breathe (life) into these spiritually dead and God's wonder is seen. ..."[72]

Van de Loosdrecht's invective brought together the strands of his somewhat muddled conception of what was "wrong" with Torajan society. It was less

---

68. Letter from A. C. Kruyt to A. A. van de Loosdrecht, April 4, 1916, Pendolo; *ADV*, November 1916, p. 104.

69. Van de Loosdrecht, *ADV*, August 1915, p. 63; December 1914, p. 101.

70. *ADV*, November 1916, p. 104.

71. Van de Loosdrecht, *ADV*, January 1918, p. 4; August 1917, p. 68.

72. Van de Loosdrecht, *ADV*, February 1918, pp. 9-10.

an attack on wrongdoing as such than on what was holding back conversion. There can be little doubt that from the standpoint of a Western-legal view of justice, the charges leveled at selected members of the old guard were justified; the point is, however, that nearly any of their contemporaries could also have been convicted by the same criteria. By driving a wedge between those with the determination and power to resist the changes being introduced and those persons sympathetic to a new order, the missionary hoped to create a "movement" toward Christianity. If the government's presence were to become fixed as a given in the people's minds rather than another in a series of passing waves of influence to be ridden out, influential persons would be tempted to accommodate it. In this process, if social conditions were to stabilize to the point that the lower classes did not remain so dependent on the powerful to protect them from starvation and raids (or the current variant), they might be drawn to a religion offering them a new status.

Resolution: Torajan

By 1917 a complex mosaic of grievances toward mission and government existed in the Sa'dan highlands. If the government was seen as the agent for making decisions that affected people's lives in the tondok, the mission was viewed as the intelligence-gathering apparatus funneling reports from teachers, students, and the missionaries themselves to the controleur. While gathering damaging information through his active participation in village affairs, the missionary dispensed unsettling pronouncements on Torajan custom and the god of the Kompania, confirming with words what his actions had already told them: "the Kompania wills that you become Christian." The controleur, by sending troops and armed police to haul off to the Rantepao jail the parents of truant students, put steel into the missionary's request for manpower and materials to build the schools, and enforced his passion against gambling and cockfighting. While van de Loosdrecht might say "that the mission asks and urges but the government orders and punishes," the Torajan was more likely to conclude that "the mission asks and urges, *then* the government orders and punishes."[73] The distinction was indeed too fine to have meaning in the Torajan context of 1917.

The combined weight of mission and government cooperation put a new strain on the indigenous religion. The missionaries told villagers to test the falsehood of the *pemali* (taboo) against such things as eating rice during the time between a family member's death and burial, and asserted that the souls of sacrificed animals did not go with the deceased to the afterworld--a belief that underpinned so much of Torajan religion and social behavior. The fears that the Dutch were out to obliterate the indigenous religion reached their height when the governor journeyed to Rantepao on March 2, 1917 to meet with the missionaries in what Torajans widely held to be a plot to convert all Torajans to Christianity.[74]

---

73. Van de Loosdrecht, *ADV*, August 1917, p. 69.

74. Unless otherwise noted, the discussion of the governor's visit is based on the reports of two government investigations: W. Fryling, confidential report from the investigation into the death of A. A. van de Loosdrecht, *Verbaal* 27-5- 1918-97, *mailrapport* 1836/17 (Colonial Archive, The Hague), E. A. J. Nobele, secret government report over the death of A. A. van de Loosdrecht), Palopo, August 20, 1917 (AHK).

The rumor had some basis in truth. Indeed, the governor was meeting with the controleurs from Makale and Rantepao and the mission personnel (including Prins and van de Loosdrecht) to discuss van de Loosdrecht's proposal to abolish not only cockfighting but the death feast itself and ban markets on Sundays, essentially transforming the market system from a six-day cycle to a seven-day cycle, with the Sabbath off. The meeting ended with the governor supporting a reduction in the number of days allowed for cockfighting during a funeral ceremony and vigorous enforcement of the prohibition against gambling, which had been regularly ignored by headmen. He apparently rejected the idea of banning the Sunday market, but conceded that no corvée be performed by Christians on Sunday. His position on the death feast is not mentioned, but we may assume that he probably agreed with van der Veen that abolition would be premature, though heavy cutting at death feasts should be discouraged.

The incomplete information leaking from this meeting made a profound impression on Torajan headmen. Many of them met at the Rantepao headmen's hall and made strong statements of protest against the anticipated forced Christianization. The rumor soon spread that the death feast, cockfighting, and the Sunday market would all be abolished. Indeed, the signs had been around them for some time. It had become so difficult to gain a permit for cockfighting at a funeral ceremony that only one in ten applications was favorably received. If the controleur thought that a cockfight had been held too recently, he would deny permission even to the most prominent of applicants, on the grounds that otherwise people would make the rounds from cockfight to cockfight, squandering their money.

The immediate fears stimulated by the governor's presence in Rantepao exacerbated long-standing animosities generated by the village schools. These schools, in the minds of most villagers, were a kind of corvée. New construction required too much hauling of wood from distant sources, especially in the heavily populated Sa'dan heartland, and too often the wood gathered was rejected as unsuitable; this angered both the laborers, who had hauled it, and the headmen, who were punished for not having seen to it that the work was properly completed. People in two districts felt badly aggrieved because they had had to supply deliveries of wood for a total of three schools, four houses for teachers and missionaries, as well as numerous stalls for two new markets. This was in addition to the regular corvée labor they had to provide on local roads and the main road to Palopo. Having little sense of the school's utility to the village, people focused on their own losses, in terms of children's labor in the fields or at home, and the cost of clothing them for school. They resented being jailed or fined when their children were absent from school, and many objected to the taxing of death feasts to support the school through the "fonds sekolah," even though this supposedly voluntary contribution of 10 percent had actually been proposed by Pong Mangassa of Tondon. In sum, while most headmen and their people may not initially have objected to the idea of having a school in their village, once it was built they found it objectionable and gave it little support.

In the final analysis, the perceived attack on indigenous religion and custom, combined with the villagers' objections to the schools, might not have produced the eventual violent reaction they did had not the mission and government made such a determined effort to undercut some of the stalwarts of the old elite. By selectively removing and sending into exile the linchpins of the elite, the Dutch may have failed to recognize the general sense of alarm this caused among the headmen. If it could happen to Pong Maramba, Ne' Lapu, and Danduru, why not to Ne' Mattandung or anyone viewed as opposing the mission? As Kruyt concluded, "... it never would have come to a death if something else had not been added, namely van de Loosdrecht's cooperation to bring to light the crooked ways of the chiefs."[75] Combined with his airing of such matters as land seizures and elite participation in slave trading, and his shift in sympathy toward the "dispossessed," the missionary's thrust against the stalwarts raised their fears to the breaking point.

Opposition began to mount against the increased interference of mission and government in village affairs. In keeping with the still fissiparous nature of Torajan political organization, the response was largely spontaneous, and it cannot be said to have characterized the highlands as a whole. To the extent that there was a perceivable pattern, the opposition came mainly from the more populous, politically influential tondok of the Sa'dan valley in onderafdeeling Rantepao. In contrast, far greater tolerance, to some extent even support, for the mission's penetration came from the peripheral tondok that had been forced to accommodate to their more powerful neighbors prior to 1905, and which continued to play a subordinate role in the onderafdeeling administration constructed by the new overlords. The picture in onderafdeeling Makale shows similarities to that of Rantepao, particularly in the rapport that had begun to develop between the mission and the tondok peripheral to the Tallu Lembangna (the three populous tondok Makale, Sangalla, and Mengkendek). Perhaps because the mission did not become very active in Makale until 1916, opposition did not grow as fast as in Rantepao; it appears to have peaked there about three years later, with the mysterious burning of missionary Prins' house.[76]

A few specific instances drawn from 1916 and 1917 serve to illustrate the rising resistance in Rantepao. Van de Loosdrecht had long identified Pangala and Balusu as key districts in which to gain support. His initial optimism there totally faded as Tandibua and Ne' Mattandung gave no backing to the schools in their districts. Pangala, it seemed to him, was *the* bastion of heathenism, meaning that adherence to the indigenous religion had remained firm there, with little evidence of movement among the elite toward either Islam or Christianity.[77] The animosities generated on both sides began to take on personal overtones as these two district heads confronted the missionary. Tandibua was suddenly relieved of his position as district head on the usual extortion charges, which doomed the Pangala school as long as he resided in the district. Surreptitiously the sacked headman began to assemble supporters and arms in an old fort west of Pangala. Mattandung, pressed by rumors that he would be arrested, also began to rally his supporters, while the missionary dredged up unsavory charges based on the headman's allegedly bloodthirsty past as a warrior. Mattandung adopted a young tomakaka in the traditional "anak angkat" manner, a practice particularly prevalent in periods of unrest. His adopted son, Pong Massangka of Pangli, was widely known as a daring youth, skilled in cockfighting, who swore he would sooner fight the Kompania than go to jail for gambling.[78]

---

75. Letter from A. C. Kruyt to D. Crommelin, September 1918, Pendolo (AHK).

76. J. Belksma, *ADV*, April 1921, pp. 26-27.

77. Van de Loosdrecht, *ADV*, January 1918, p. 3.

78. W. Fryling, "Korte verslag over de maand, Juli 1917," *Verbaal* 8-4-1918-7, *mailrapport* 2135/17 (Colonial Archive, The Hague).

In Sa'dan, opposition centered on the missionary's instructions that a better house had to be built for the guru. The present accommodations were wretched from the mission's point of view, but the unpopularity of the guru and general dislike of the school caused the villagers to refuse to supply labor or materials for anything better. Even when several headmen were prosecuted for "neglect of duty" their resistance did not weaken, which was particularly notable since the Sa'dan district head was not known for his ability or influence.[79]

In Nanggala the headmen directed a barrage of accusations against the guru, and student attendance at the school slowed to a trickle. Because of their determination, the headmen finally forced the guru out of the village and the school closed down.[80] In tondok Bori (Tikala district) the opposition took a different course, and was directed at halting construction of the school and the guru's house before either could be completed. Initially the elite engineered a slowdown, which brought angry complaints from the mission. Ultimately their resistance took a more determined form, when the headmen denied food to any of their retainers who worked on the buildings. Starving out the kaunan in this manner brought construction to a standstill, until the controleur sent armed police into Bori to put down what he chose to interpret as a breach of the corvée obligation there.[81] To break the boycott the government appointed a member of the elite to supervise each day of construction activity, making him responsible for seeing that the kaunan were properly fed. There is no indication whether or not the controleur's threat to jail any headman continuing to resist was tested.[82]

Tondon, the first district to deny labor and materials for use in school construction, remained a source of bitter complaints, ostensibly over a misunderstanding between the chief and a guru from the government school in Rantepao. It later became apparent that the conflict ran deeper and van de Loosdrecht, encountering continued subdued hostility among the elite there, remarked that "a spirit of quiet rebellion rules in Tondon."[83]

Behind the scenes of isolated resistance, the headmen had begun to take positions that envisioned the expulsion of the Dutch. From the beginning, some of them had seen the Dutch as passing overlords destined not to control the highlands for long. As early as 1909, some of the headmen hatched a plot first to attack the Dutch in Makale and Rantepao, then to move on to conquer Palopo and Makassar.[84] Now in 1917 a variety of plots and subplots swept through the more rebellious tondok while in most other, less volatile, villages, the headmen usually chose to keep silent about them. A Tikala village headman did report one arms cache in March 1916, shortly after the exiling of Pong

---

79. Van de Loosdrecht, *ADV*, January 1918, p. 4.

80. Van de Loosdrecht, *ADV*, August 1917, p. 68.

81. At the time of this incident, and for several years afterwards, there was still no firm decision from the residential authorities as to whether or not school construction could be considered an obligatory duty. Van de Loosdrecht sought a policy statement from the governor in support of such a position, but appears not to have succeeded. Disappointed, he concluded that school construction was dependent on the good will of the local official.

82. J. Belksma, *ADV*, June 1918, pp. 42-43.

83. Van de Loosdrecht, *ADV*, January 1918, p. 4.

84. W. Fryling, confidential report, p. 16.

Maramba; it amounted to three Beaumont rifles, nearly a dozen barrels and bolt assemblies, and a ten-kilo keg of powder.[85] On July 21, 1917 the Tikala district head, Arung Langi, and the Bori headman, Pong Arung, reported to the Rantepao prosecutor that Ne' Mattandung's adopted son had organized a gambling party in his kampung; they broadly hinted that "the named persons harbored plans to revolt."[86] There was no love lost between these two informers and Ne' Mattandung, their animosity originating in the days of Tikala raids into Balusu for slaves and ransom. However, Dutch authorities proved unable to find Mattandung's adopted son.

Vague plans for rebellion had been in the wind since 1916, but they assumed a sense of urgency only after the incendiary rumors emanating from the governor's visit to Rantepao swept through the onderafdeeling. Accounts of who was involved vary, but by one Torajan version the conspirators included Tandibua of Pangala, Ne' Mattandung of Balusu, and Mattandung's adopted son Pong Massangka.[87] The official Dutch investigation also implicated Pong Arung of Bori, who had tried to play both sides. The rebels planned simultaneous attacks on all Dutch compounds in Makale and Rantepao towns, and on the houses of the four missionaries, to drive all the Dutch from the highlands. Arms were collected and stored in preparation for the rebellion, though they apparently consisted mainly of traditional spears and long knives. Given the lack of political unity at the time, the plan, and the preparations for implementing it, seem quite impressive. Before the principal plan had a chance to develop fully, however, the subplot initiated by Ne' Mattandung and his followers prematurely came to a climax.

About July 15, 1917 Pong Massangka led a dozen followers into Rantepao on market day to wait in ambush for Controleur Brouwer, who typically took a walk around the market each day in the late afternoon. Hiding knives in their *sarung*, the band watched the controleur, with his wife and young son, approach to within two hundred meters (by Brouwer's later reckoning) of where they were hiding behind some trees. Suddenly the child stumbled and fell, beginning to wail. Rather than take the protesting child through the crowded market, Brouwer and his wife decided to return home at once, thwarting the plot of the would-be assassins.[88]

When Massangka and his supporters returned to Pangli, Ne' Mattandung held a gambling party for them. They then made a second plan for an assassination, this time of van de Loosdrecht at his house in Barana, just north of Rantepao. On

---

85. W. Fryling, "Kort verslag over de maand Maart 1916," *mailrapport* 1301/16 (Indonesian National Archive, Bogor Repository).

86. W. Fryling, confidential report, pp. 5-6.

87. S. J. Sarungu, "Sejarah Peperangan Pong Tiku dengan Belanda tahun 1906-1907" (Rantepao, 1971), pp. 48-49.

88. M. R. Brouwer, Letter to A. C. Kruyt, February 18, 1918, Rantepao (AHK). Torajan accounts of this story coincide with the account Brouwer gained from interrogating Pong Massangka about the incident; in current Torajan accounts, such as Tandilintin's popularized history, the young boy's wailing is given as the reason the controleur returned home, while the fact that his wife was pregnant is given as the reason the Torajan plotters did not then fall upon them (it is taboo). I initially suspected the veracity of this account, but Brouwer's letter confirms that his wife was then in about her fifth or sixth month of pregnancy.

the evening of the 26th the group, joined by others who had not participated in the earlier attempt, slaughtered a pig and prepared rice for a ceremonial meal before starting off for the missionary's house. A courier had just returned with word from Ne' Mattandung that he agreed with their plan to attack the missionary. According to one account, lances were stuck into the ground as the conspirators swore an oath of war. Suddenly someone appeared with the news that van de Loosdrecht had been seen at a guru's house in Bori, some twenty minutes away. Under cover of darkness, thirteen of the celebrants then hurried off to carry out their plan.

After the band reached the Bori bridge, the designated assassin left them and approached the porch where the missionary was reading to the guru. Leaping onto the porch, the young warrior plunged his lance through van de Loosdrecht's lower chest; as he slumped to the floor, the dying missionary knocked over the lamp, and flames engulfed the porch as the band slipped away.

Passions pent up over the period of several rice harvests poured out that night and the next. With the active or passive support of many villagers Pong Massangka and his followers swept through Tokarau market an hour away, burning the newly constructed market stalls. They then returned to Pangli where they burned three bridges linking the village with the road to Rantepao--a road resented by Massangka because, without consulting him, the government had confiscated a portion of his rice fields for a right-of-way.[89] The inhabitants of Pangli were whipped into an anti-Dutch frenzy, and they built barricades around village entrances, preparing to fight the Dutch troops that they knew would soon arrive. Reports to the assistant resident indicate that the Dutch expected a fierce battle in Pangli.

Controleur Brouwer, with his half-brigade of armed police, proceeded from Bori to Balusu, bypassing the stronghold at Pangli. Two brigades of infantry from Palopo and two from Enrekang were already on their way to deal with any heavy resistance. Brouwer went to Balusu, because he suspected that Ne' Mattandung was somehow involved in the murder of the missionary, a suspicion that was confirmed when the old headman not only refused to meet him but also sent "a ridiculous, skinny pig and a pair of old sick chickens" as full measure of his esteem for the ranking Dutch official in Rantapao.[90] At dusk all the surrounding kampung lit fires in support of Mattandung's truculence, and by the next morning five hundred armed supporters hovered in the hills surrounding the unwelcome authorities. Half a day of cat and mouse left one Torajan dead, shot as he advanced on the messenger bearing a summons to Ne' Mattandung. The stalemate ended with the arrival of the assistant resident with his troops from Palopo and another half-brigade of police from Makale. In the face of this triangular advance, Mattandung's warriors dispersed throughout the hilly terrain, fighting ineffectually with lances and long knives against the Dutch firearms. Several more Torajans were killed and captured and the resistance crumbled. The round-up of rebels and active sympathizers continued for two weeks, with hundreds being detained.

Mattandung's capture and the surrender of Pangli without a fight exposed the weakness of the leadership behind the plots to kill Brouwer and van de Loosdrecht. The more comprehensive plans for rebellion, however, were implicating Tandibua of Pangala, Pong Arung of Bori, and numerous other headmen. By mid-

---

89. Ne' Banding, interview, March 11, 1978, Bori (Toraja).

90. J. Belksma, *ADV*, December 1917, p. 103.

August, interrogations had produced arrests of the conspirators involved in the more ambitious plot, and ultimately Pong Massangka surrendered, together with his co-conspirators in the missionary's killing. The various plots to expel the Dutch from the highlands had misfired, and fifty-six persons from onderafdeeling Rantepao were exiled. With the departure of Tandibua and his lieutenants, Ne' Mattandung and his, Pong Massangka and the tragic Pong Arung (who committed suicide in jail), the steel went out of the Torajan resistance to change--particularly the change dictated by the mission and a sympathetic government. Pong Maramba and Danduru had preceded them, Tangki Langi', an influential headman in Pangala convicted in a sawah dispute, followed. The missionary who succeeded van de Loosdrecht recorded the whispers passing through Bori, the tondok which lost the most prominent tomakaka, as news of their deaths in exile trickled into Rantepao: "the Dutch are killing all our great men."[91]

Conclusion

Why this outbreak of rebellion in July 1917? It arose after several years of grievances that grew out of a tightening of colonial administration throughout South Sulawesi. Reports of refusals to pay taxes and evasion of corvée labor assignments had been increasing since about 1915, around the time when the Dutch administrative machinery was coming to be set firmly in place.[92] The demands for construction of new roads, school and administrative buildings, and assessment of the head tax were by then becoming unavoidable, as they were enforced by local armed police reinforced, if necessary, from the afdeeling capital. Headmen were no longer the masters of their own realms; many of the decisions they were compelled to support emanated from the onderafdeeling capital and beyond. What at first may have seemed little more onerous than the exaggerated tributary claims of Luwu looked very different to the headmen as their own powers came to be circumscribed by a new and more penetrating form of external political control.[93]

In Makale-Rantepao, the coming of the mission amplified the effects of this penetration. In addition to the taxes and corvée labor with which people throughout South Sulawesi had to contend there was now the difficult-to-ignore presence of village schools. Villagers often resented providing labor and materials for purposes that they barely understood; while officially the headman had to give his consent before school construction could begin, this condition was easily overlooked. Even more important, it was by no means certain that the consent of the "village" head, a creation of the Dutch administration, reflected the feelings of those heading indigenous formal or informal power structures. Most headmen who broke with the administration in 1917 had previously singled out some aspect of the school for criticism.

---

91. J. Belksma, *ADV*, February 1921, p. 11.

92. Van de Loosdrecht, *ADV*, May 1916, p. 40.

93. Sampebua makes this point about Pong Massangka and other politically ambitious men like him: "They had their path to influence and riches impeded by the Dutch and the application of a different legal standard. Plunder had been an important part of his income, and this was much more difficult to carry out under Dutch law." Interview, March 11, 1978, Bori (Toraja).

The school was simply the most visible target for protest. It reminded sensitive headmen of the broader encroachments on their lives that had occurred over the decade of Dutch control. Had these feelings been handled with more sensitivity, more guarantees that their world would not be turned upside down, the rebellion in 1917 probably would not have occurred. Instead, the period 1913-1917 was one of increasingly close cooperation between government and mission to bring about fundamental change in the highlands, with less public assurance that tradition (adat) would be protected here than was generally the case in areas of Dutch rule. Van de Loosdrecht found an ally in the controleur of Rantepao, who was one of a small minority of Netherlands East Indies civil servants who shared the missionary's Gereformeerde (Calvinist) Christianity rather than the more relaxed, liberal Reformed Christianity against which the Dutch Calvinists had rebelled in the late nineteenth century.[94] This alliance moved the controleur much further along toward providing official support to the GZB than would otherwise have been possible, contributing to the strong impression that the government and mission were working together to convert Torajans to Christianity. They were, in fact, doing so, with support from the highest levels in the Netherlands Indies administration, but the process was to be a much more subtle and long-range project than the rebelling Torajan headmen could have realized. What probably precipitated the rebellion in mid-1917 was the governor's visit to Rantepao, which touched off rumors, not totally unfounded, that the Dutch meant to abolish the death feast and gambling, and Christianize all Torajans. A growing sense that few options but open resistance remained was undoubtedly strengthened by Pong Maramba's exile and the investigations being conducted against other headmen who had openly opposed van de Loosdrecht.

Indeed, it is striking that the most dramatic resistance to Dutch rule since Pong Tiku's lengthy resistance to the occupation in 1906[95] should have been so devoid of ideological content. One could try to attribute this to the nature of the Dutch inquiry into the rebellion, inclined as most such investigations were to classify peasant rebellions into a few easily dismissable categories, such as "Ratu Adil" (millenarian) in Java and "religious fanaticism" in such strongly Islamic areas as lowland South Sulawesi. Yet even indigenous oral sources bear out the Dutch conclusions. It may be that colonial penetration was not sufficiently advanced to have given rise to religious revivalism. Those resisting the advance still stood firmly enough on an indigenous religious foundation that was almost unconsciously a part of their lives. The entire episode rather seems to have been initiated by an elite that felt it was losing control and was being goaded by a missionary attempting to bypass the elite in order to convert the masses, and thereby attacking the very basis of the social hierarchy.

The number involved in the 1917 rebellion was not large, but its leadership was prominent. This promised possible further disruptions unless the tensions that had precipitated the outburst could be reduced. The government was aware of the fragility of a bureaucracy staffed and supported by so few Dutchmen; "peace and security" depended on the support of the traditional elite. Thus the Torajan rebellion could not be lightly dismissed.

---

94. Van de Loosdrecht, *ADV*, February 1914, p. 14.

95. On this resistance, see Terance W. Bigalke, "A Social History of 'Tana Toraja' 1870-1965" (PhD dissertation, University of Wisconsin, 1981), pp. 98-116.

The controleur, with full compliance from the mission, issued orders that Torajans could no longer be summoned from their field labor for impromptu meetings with missionaries nor could they be coerced to attend mission functions. Any request for a village school must come directly from the kampung head, supported by a majority of his villagers, and only voluntary labor could be used to construct future schools and teachers' houses, except when there were extreme shortages of manpower.[96] Soldiers and armed police, who were stationed in the towns, could no longer be dispatched to round up truant village children and drag their parents off to jail, nor could the latter be fined for their children's truancy.[97] All these restrictions probably helped to relieve some of the major irritants to high status persons, from whose ranks the mission recruited most of its students at this time, and to reduce the disruptive effects of the school on village society.

These changes in government policy clarified the hierarchy of Dutch authority in Makale-Rantepao, differentiating the compulsory power of the administration from the (in theory) merely persuasive authority of the mission. For the village elite, this meant more freedom to reject out-of-hand the advances of the missionaries and teachers. Yet the changes still left the rivals to the ruling elite with an alternative path to power through the mission, and middle and lower status villagers were not foreclosed from rejecting the prevailing social hierarchy and finding a new source of patronage. This had important consequences for subsequent Torajan history.

---

96. J. Belksma, *ADV*, July 1919, pp. 51-52.

97. D. J. van Dijk, "Enkele grepen uit den 25-jarigen Zendingsarbeid te Rantepao," in *Om te Gedenken* (Delft: van Barneveld, 1938), p. 158. This missionary mentions that after 1917 children could be heard to say, "Tae' namadin diparuku" ("he can't force us"), indicating that they realized coercion could no longer be used to make them attend school.

THE LOGIC OF *RASA* IN JAVA

Paul Stange

Intuitive Consciousness and Charisma

We may have the adage that "knowledge is power," but beneath it lies an epistemology implying that "knowledge" is primarily a matter of intellect, of qualities of thought and quantities of information. Closely linked to this is a sense of "person," profoundly conditioned by Enlightenment notions of equality, which results in sharp resistance to suggestion that there may be qualitatively different orders of consciousness. Yet as Louis Dumont points out, ". . . it is only in our egalitarian ideology that reality appears on a single plane and as composed of equivalent atoms."[1] Through work such as his, which explores the pervasive implications of hierarchy and inequality in the Indian context, we become fully conscious of the degree to which our thought is shaped by a one-dimensional ontology. If we are aiming to understand the logic which underlies the nexus of mystical consciousness and social power, as those are conceived and expressed within cultures which attend to it, then we need to consider the implications of differing epistemologies.

Insofar as the social sciences are disciplines of intellect, it is natural that the dimensions of life and forms of logic most accessible to the intellect are the ones most easily subjected to analysis. So, in attempting to unveil the logic of social and cultural systems, we may also be seduced by the tendency to treat symbolism as an autonomous realm, then attempting to discern the pattern of relationships between symbols in cerebral terms. But Malinowski's injunctions, which underlie much contemporary ethnography, include emphasis on the fact that:

> . . . the foundations of magical belief and practice are not taken from the air, but are due to a number of experiences actually lived through, in which man receives the revelation of his power to attain the desired end.[2]

This statement points us toward the new emphasis, I am inclined to say "revival," of concern with "praxis" in contemporary social theory.[3] In any event, an

---

1. *Homo Hierarchicus* (Chicago and London: University of Chicago Press, 1979), p. xxx.

2. Bronislaw Malinowski, *Magic, Science and Religion* (New York: Doubleday, 1954), p. 82.

3. For a discussion of the new "practice" orientation within anthropology, see Sherry Ortner, "Theory in Anthropology since the Sixties," *Comparative Studies in Society and History* 26, 1 (January 1984): 144-57. The sense of "praxis" which underlies my approach here is at a tangent from those discussed

emphasis on contextualizing beliefs not only in their social but also in their personal and experiential contexts is especially pertinent if we are attempting to interpret the logic of the relationship between consciousness and power.

In the Javanese traditional context, and among those now still experiencing a continuity with it, "knowledge" in its significant form is "ngelmu." Though in Indonesia "ilmu" now closely approximates Western senses of "knowledge," the Javanese term clearly refers to gnosis, to a mystical or spiritual form of knowledge which is not just intellectual but also intuitive. Another way of clarifying what is meant by "ngelmu" is that, in the end, it is the whole body, and all organs within it, rather than just the mind that "knows." This sense of knowledge underlies Javanese mystical theory not only of consciousness, but also of its relationship, which is essentially reflexive, to social and political power. "*Rasa*," my focus in this paper, is among other things the cognitive faculty which, as Javanese mystics understand it, we use to "know" the intuitive aspects of reality. It is, in Javanese terms, through intuitive experience and knowledge that people may sense the "*wahyu*," the charistmatic glow, of a person of power.

The Javanese mystical idea of power may be unique in some of its particulars, but it is clearly also part of a wider pattern of belief. Wolters has recently suggested that one of the underlying patterns within Southeast Asian cultures may be the notion of "men of prowess," of the existence of "unequal souls" in Kirsch's terms.[4] Errington's essay on "Embodied *Sumange'* in Luwu" shows that in the Malay world the central concept of "semangat" is linked to mystical senses of power.[5] There is clearly a resonance between these ideas of "power" and the concept of "*mana*," which entered the vocabulary of English after Codrington identified it in the Melanesian context. Anderson's treatment of "The Idea of Power in Javanese Culture" is the definitive exposition of the theory, both explicitly and implicitly, which in Javanese terms links political expressions of power to magical and mystical cosmology.[6] But by stressing "beliefs," and the way they contribute to conditioning of social actions, it remains possible for Javanese notions to be considered as simply another ideological formulation, different from ours but another gloss of the same "reality."

Anderson's essay builds on Weber's work in that he has clarified both the systematic coherence of the political theory implicit within Javanese tradition and the substantive differences between the underlying conceptions of power in traditional Java and the contemporary West. Weber himself had

---

by Ortner, but remains related: in both contexts emphasis is shifted to what people "do."

4. O. W. Wolters, *History, Culture, and Region in Southeast Asian Perspectives* (Singapore: Institute of Southeast Asian Studies, 1982), pp. 6-7.

5. Shelly Errington, "Embodied *Sumange'* in Luwu," *Journal of Asian Studies* 42, 3 (May 1983): 545-70; on the centrality of the notion of "semangat" within Malay thought see Kirk Endicott, *An Analysis of Malay Magic* (London: Oxford University Press, 1970). Also closely aligned to this "school" of thought is Michelle Rosaldo, *Knowledge and Passion* (Cambridge: Cambridge University Press, 1980). In her discussion of Ilongot society Rosaldo speaks of the sense her informants had that "*liget*," energy experienced in the heart, fluctuates through experience and constitutes a major focus of attention within the culture.

6. In Claire Holt et al., eds., *Culture and Politics in Indonesia* (Ithaca: Cornell University Press, 1972).

already highlighted the essential logic of charismatic modes of authority:

> The holder of charisma seizes the task that is adequate for him and demands obedience and a following by virtue of his mission. His success determines whether he finds them. His charismatic claim breaks down if his mission is not recognized by those to whom he feels he has been sent. If they recognize him, he is their master--so long as he knows how to maintain recognition through "proving" himself.[7]

Weber's formulation, based in part on Chinese theories of the "mandate of heaven," draws attention not only to the circularity of logic underlying this sense of "supernaturally" bestowed power, but also to the fact that it reflects a linkage between leader and following which, in the ideal, is "felt" on both sides. The term "charisma" has since entered popular vocabulary, and Weber's explanation has been used as a way of outlining, in phenomenological terms, the manifestations of charisma. His concept has been criticized, in some quarters discounted, for lacking an explanation of the mechanism which links leader to follower within a charismatic system.

In this essay I am suggesting that within the terms of *kejawen*, of traditional Javanist culture, the logic which underpins ideas of power is that of rasa. In Javanist terms "rasa" is not only a term applied to sensory experiences, implying a particular aesthetic, but also a cognitive organ, used actively within mystical practices. From the perspective of practicing mystics within the culture, the "ideas" of power within it are secondary reflections or statements which are logical and sensible in that they are reports of what may be experienced when rasa is activated as a tool within ngelmu *kabatosan*, the "science of the spirit." As mysticism underlies much of Javanese cultural theory, the perspective of those expert in it does offer grounds for uncovering the "logic" which may elude us at the ideological level. Though I am arguing that the "logic of rasa" underlies central patterns of ideology and experience, this is not to say that rasa explains the whole orientation of the culture. Important as it may be within the complex of the culture, it remains only an element.

Given the resonance of the word "intuition" with popular cliches of a "spiritual East," with romanticism about the qualities of traditional cultures, a number of caveats are essential. In the first place, my argument does not require a particular ontological position. It is simply an attempt to explicate the significance of rasa in Javanese terms, as can be observed in social practice and through Javanese statements about it. Second, it is crucial to distinguish between discussion of orientation and emphasis and conclusions about everyday realities. In arguing that Javanese culture encourages cultivation of intuition I am simply pointing to an orientation, not making conclusions about the degree to which intuitive sensitivity may be present in social practice. Finally, though I am dealing with the role of intuition in Java that is not meant to imply that the Javanese are either unique or typical.

I will build out of description of the way intuition is perceived, understood, and placed within one Javanese mystical movement. Through the Sumarah case my aim is to draw attention to the "rules of rasa" or "logic of intuition" as they apply within meditation practice and group interaction. Then I will turn to suggesting some of the ways in which those same rules can be seen

---

7. In Hans Gerth and C. W. Mills, *From Max Weber* (New York: Oxford University Press, 1946), p. 246.

to underlie, and hence elucidate the logic of, general patterns of Javanese belief and action. The link between the case and its context does not rest on assumption that Sumarah is a perfect microcosm of the whole, nor even on suggestion that the sense of rasa within it is perfectly representative. It rests rather on the degree to which the logic and rules which we can observe within the case can be used as a key to unlocking the underlying logic of general patterns.

Rasa in Sumarah Practice

Within Indonesia there are literally hundreds of movements, ranging from informal local groups to formally organized national associations, which see themselves primarily as extensions of an indigenous tradition of spiritual wisdom, rather than as derivative of imported religious models. These mystical movements, generically termed "*kepercayaan*" or "*kebatinan*," are to varying degrees national in orientation, but most are primarily Javanese in both origin and composition. Sumarah is among the more prominent national organizations, one of the dozen or so most active at the national level. The Javanese word "*sumarah*" simply means "the state of total surrender," and it is a name not only for the organization, but also for the practice which provides its focus.[8]

Sumarah was founded in the mid 1930s in the court city of Yogyakarta by Sukinohartono. Together with his friends Suhardo and Sutadi, he attracted a following of about 500 by the end of the Japanese occupation. In the midst of the revolutionary fighting of the late 1940s the membership expanded to several thousand; at the end of that period it became formally organized under the leadership of Dr. Surono, with its center still in Yogya. Under his leadership, until 1966, it grew to include roughly 6,000 members throughout Java, with regional organizations existing in all the major towns of the island. Since 1966 the organization has had its center in Jakarta under the leadership of Drs. Arymurthy, and it currently has a membership of perhaps 10,000.

The practice of *sujud* sumarah, as the meditation is called, is carried out both individually and in group meetings by a guide, or *pamong*. Individually, members spend periods of time in "special meditation" (sujud *khusus*) but they are also supposed to be integrating meditative awareness into their everyday lives. Members are "socially invisible," as is the case with most Javanese movements, in the sense that they lead ordinary social lives, have no distinctive dress, and use no special symbols. Individual members are not bound by any outward rules, and their participation is conditioned only by the degree to

---

8. The following treatment of the Sumarah case is based on my fieldwork, over the period from early 1971 to early 1974 and during four brief visits since. Very little has been published, providing insight into practices within Javanese mysticism. General introductions to "*kebatinan*" can be found in Clifford Geertz, *The Religion of Java* (Chicago: University of Chicago Press, 1976); in Niels Mulder, *Mysticism and Everyday Life in Contemporary Java* (Singapore: Singapore University Press, 1978); and to teachings in Harun Hadiwijono, *Man in the Present Javanese Mysticism* (Baarn: Bosch and Keuning, 1967). Full treatment of Sumarah history is in my thesis, "The Sumarah Movement in Javanese Mysticism" (PhD dissertation, University of Wisconsin, 1980); Sumarah practice has also formed the focus for a separate thesis--see David Howe, "Sumarah: A Study of the Art of Living" (PhD dissertation, University of North Carolina, 1980).

which they internalize, within their consciousness, the commitment to total surrender which, in principle at least, brings them together in the group.

Group meetings are held regularly, usually in the homes of people who act as guides or in those of organizational leaders. There are no special places associated with the practice, no particular buildings are especially appropriate for it, nor is there concern with sacred sites. The atmosphere of meetings is relaxed and informal, including extended discussion of practice mixed with periods of collective meditation led by the guide, or pamong. The guides have differing styles and approaches, but despite considerable variation the principles of Sumarah guidance are consistent. Although the individuals who serve as guides are called pamong, in principle guidance does not come from them, but through them, and only when the true function of guidance is activated by the right spiritual circumstance.

There is consistent emphasis within Sumarah on the fact that "pamong" are not "*guru*" (teachers). The "teaching" is a function only activated when the circumstances are right and not one that can be attached to the personality of the guide. As Arymurthy has said:

> ... Duty as a guide, as a *pamong*, only happens in the instant that the task is given by *Hak* [truth]. A person is a *pamong* only in that instant of duty, otherwise we only call him a *pamong* for administrative convenience. Whether he then actually performs as one or not depends on the functions that arise within him. Outside of that he had no special rights or authority over others.[9]

Even if the Sumarah system of guidance has been expressed differently over time and from guide to guide, and can also vary in accordance with regional styles, in all cases a mechanism of "contacting" or "attunement" forms part of the interaction.

In Sumarah it is axiomatic that the inner life flowers through introspection (*mawas diri*) and self correction, that no "faith" in the authority of an external teaching or teacher is necessary, and that the only significant verification of an external statement is the individual's direct recognition of its truth within his or her own conscious awareness. To quote Arymurthy again:

> Within Sumarah a *pamong* does not announce himself as such. He becomes *pamong* through signs from the guide in which the reality of it is simultaneously obvious. A person could say a thousand times that he is a *pamong* and yet not be one. It cannot be faked. In spiritual things this is evident even if the person says nothing. ...[10]

Nevertheless, the understanding within the practice is that the guides, whether in leading group meditation or in responding to individual questions, are

---

9. This statement of Arymurthy's was made in the context of a formal meeting in September 1973 in Surakarta. In Arymurthy's terms this statement, and the others by him which follow, came through reception of *Hakiki*, that is, it has authority beyond that of personal knowledge. At the time of the meeting, with Western followers of the practice in Solo, I was interpreting. Subsequently I was asked to provide an English translation based on the tape recording of the session. My translation is reproduced in my *Selected Sumarah Teachings* (Perth: Department of Asian Studies, W.A.I.T., 1977). This quote is from p. 22.

10. Ibid., p. 21.

"tuned" to the inner psychic condition of those they are leading. This is directly related to the notion that there are distinct levels of consciousness, that not all individuals are equally aware, and that some may be aware of the inner state of another person. The transmission of "sumarah" is based on this sense of experiential contact rather than on a specific technique or ritual practice. The guides are emphatic in reminding people to take nothing on faith, but rather to "test" within themselves whether a statement or suggestion is appropriate.

This mechanism was implicit within the very first exchange which led to the movement. After Sukino's individual experience, the "revelation of Sumarah" (wahyu Sumarah) in 1935, he explored it with his longtime friend, Suhardo. In Suhardo's subsequent description of the encounter, he related that he had first spoken with Sukino, then experimented on his own. During his own meditation he felt the validity of Sukino's experience and so went back to him to check. According to the official Sumarah history, based on Suhardo's own recollection, their conversation went as follows:

> Suhardo: Is this the correct way to surrender to God?
> (And then Suhardo practiced meditation.)
> Sukino: Aha, you really can meditate correctly. Who taught you how?
> Suhardo: I heard a voice from within saying,
> "Sukino's way of worshipping God is correct. If you want to do the same then calm your senses and desires, center your mind and feeling in the heart, and repeat the name of God." I did follow the advice from within and it genuinely did lead to calm and peaceful feelings.[11]

Suhardo's narration clearly implied, though it drew no special attention to, the understanding that a spiritually advanced person may have the capacity to "know" the inner state of another.

The general pattern of guidance within the first phase of Sumarah, up to 1949, followed the same pattern. Everyone who received instruction in the practice had explicit one-to-one corrective guidance, called *nyemak*, from a pamong. Practice has changed, and nowadays guides make their comments more often in general terms, leaving it to the individuals present to assess whether a statement is specifically relevant to them or not. Within some groups the practice of one-to-one correction is still common, in others it is implicit, and in most of the branches of the organization at times it is explicit. From the Sumarah perspective, it is important to emphasize that the capacity for contacting is something anyone can develop; it is not seen as the preserve of unique, special, or gifted people. Instead, it is understood as an extension or normal byproduct of the meditation all members practice.

The fact that contacting is related to normal practice is linked to one feature of Sumarah meditation that does distinguish it from many other practices:

---

11. The Indonesian version of Suhardo's explanation is: "Saya mendengar suara batinku demikian: 'Sukino berbakti kepada Tuhan memakai cara (laku) yang benar. Kalau kau mau, tenangkanlah pancaindra dan nafasmu, kumpulkan cipta (angen-angen) dan rasamu, dudukkan di indraloka dengan dikir Nama (Asma) Tuhan.' Anjuran dari suara batinku itu saya jalankan dan ternyata membuat hatiku benar-benar menjadi tenang dan tenteram." The above is recorded in *Sejarah Paguyuban Sumarah 1935-1970* (Jakarta: Direktorat Pembinaan Penghayat Kepercayaan, Departemen Pendidikan Dan Kebudayaan, 1980), pp. 59-60.

it emphasizes openness to, and reception of, awareness of the environment, even in the initial stages of practice, rather than withdrawal from or exclusion of stimuli from "outside" the individual. Although some members feel that the Sumarah use of contacting is unique, most see it as simply a systematic cultivation of a facility which is present within many traditions of spiritual practice.

Rasa is at once the key to individual entry into Sumarah meditation and the initial agent for the contacting through which guides lead people into meditation. In Indonesian the word "rasa" means "feeling," both in the physical and emotional sense; in the more spiritually resonant Javanese it also means "intuitive feeling." Rasa is at once the substance, vibration, or quality of what is apprehended and the tool or organ which apprehends it. I will return later on to the spectrum of meanings associated with this Sanskrit term in Java, but for the moment will concentrate on the specific sense of it most relevant to Sumarah practice.

In this context the sense of "rasa" I am concerned with is that of the "organ" or "agent" of perception, or, if you like, the "function," of "intuition." Within Sumarah "rasa" is considered an organ or constituent of our psychology in precisely the same sense as "thought" is. In fact it is commonly said that "mind" is the tool through which we register and process information received through the five senses from the outer world, *alam lahiriyah*, while "rasa" is the tool through which we apprehend inner realities, that is alam *batiniyah*.

Sumarah practice begins with relaxation of the physical body and with the stilling of the senses and thoughts. In itself the shifting of attention from outer events and thoughts to releasing the tensions within the physical body implies a shift from thought to feeling. Stillness of the senses and thoughts means, in Sumarah terms, not "turning off," "freezing," or "repression" but rather an open and receptive state within which attention is not focused on sensory perceptions or thoughts. Instead "attention," the point at which we are aware, is supposed to enter into rasa so that there is not simply increasing awareness *of* feeling but rather awareness *through* feeling. "Feeling" in its turn may in the first instance mean awareness of physical sensation within the body, but that gross-level rasa becomes progressively more subtle—it shades through inner physical sensation into awareness of the emotions and ultimately into rasa *sejati*, the absolute or true feeling which is itself mystical awareness of the fundamental vibration or energy within all life.[12]

The necessity of making the transition from "thought centered" to "feeling centered" awareness is repeatedly emphasized during meditation sessions. Sudarno Ong, one of the most active Sumarah pamong in Surakarta during the 1970s, stressed that:

> As we speak of all these things we need to be aware that none of them can be grasped concretely with the mind or senses. The closest

---

12. More extended treatment of the concept is provided later in this paper. Howe ("Sumarah," pp. 71-72) also emphasizes the significance of *rasa* within Sumarah. He says: "The fundamental element in Javanese psychology is *rasa*, and it is probably the most difficult concept in the Javanese language . . . (and) . . . Rasa is the experiential context of human life . . . (and) . . . *Rasa Murni* is the feeling of feeling and as such does not constitute any particular affective response."

> we can get to picking up on them is with our intuitive feeling. As we are asking questions there is no use doing so simply to satisfy some mental curiosity. Our question should be based on whatever concrete experience we are having in our meditation. Then as we ask it we need to be genuinely grappling with it inside ourself. In receiving answers we have to be following with our feeling so that we can experience rather than simply understand what is meant. Not only do we need to be understanding and experiencing, but we also need to be aware what we are experiencing so that it does not just pass right through us. The most important thing is to learn directly in our own consciousness so that we are not just noting down theoretical points but actually making the realization ourselves.[13]

In somewhat different terms Arymurthy, then the national leader of the movement, explained:

> Frequently we become tools of our own tools. Take the mind for example. We might have hopes which are useless so that then the whole self becomes oppressed by the mind. It is not enough just to know the mind, but we need to know how it functions within the whole. If you want to learn Sumarah then you have to do it with the whole self, to receive the impact of experience on the total framework of being. Unless you do that then the human being is becoming a tool of his own tool.... Within the *sanubari* we have been referring to there is opportunity to calmly and clearly know your own identity. The point is that then aspects which are not good can be purified. We cannot cleanse ourself, but we can become purified through the guidance of *Hak*. This develops through the natural course of events. Purification only becomes possible as an experience when we are located in the *sanubari*.
> ... You have probably frequently heard *pamongs* speak of the '*sanubari*'. It is just a term but there is no way to relate to where it really is unless we begin with entering the realm of meditation ... here we use the work "*dirasakan*" meaning to feel the state rather than to understand it. To begin with the meditation has to be felt in much the same sense that we feel when we are physically enjoying something, listening with pleasure or eating tasty food.[14]

The "sanubari" is also related to the chest area, within which the function of rasa is located. Within that lies the *kalbu*, the inner or esoteric heart which is the center of yet more highly refined spiritual awareness.

Though rasa is the tool or vehicle through which individuals enter into awareness beyond the mind and senses, it is in the end seen only as a pathway toward a final awareness in which no distinctions exist between inner and outer or between one tool and another. It is a pathway through the fact that individuals direct their attention into rasa, becoming aware then of the blockages and resistance within their own make-up so that these barriers can be removed. According to Sumarah theory, as blockages are released there is increasing

---

13. This conversation with Sudarno, in the context of a meditation session, took place in Surakarta on December 11, 1973. This is a reconstruction recorded in my field journal on the following day.

14. Stange, *Selected Sumarah Teachings*, pp. 18-19.

surrender or openness to the Absolute which is at once everything and nothing that can be "known" in the ordinary sense. Most people within Sumarah use the term "God," some avoid terms and speak only of union and oneness. In any event, and this is all that matters here, rasa is not the endpoint or object, even though it is fundamental as a step on the Sumarah path.

The "processing" of individual awareness through Sumarah practice leads toward the condition in which it is possible to function as guide. The general understanding is that normal consciousness is dominated by an attention which is focused in thoughts, filled with attachment to the data received through the senses, and directed, for the most part subconsciously, by desires and emotions. With increasing stillness and receptivity of the thoughts and senses, through surrender, attention becomes more and more firmly rooted in rasa. If the practice reflects commitment, then this will mean not only a change within "special meditations," but also an increasing awareness of rasa, and an increasing openness within everyday life. Beyond the senses and thoughts there lies a cleaning of internalized subconscious blockages, so that gradually perception is less filtered through subjective structures. As a person becomes open, as even inner blocks are released, he or she becomes increasingly conscious of precisely what information enters the sphere of awareness--it becomes possible to distinguish "inner noise" from messages received. A pamong, or guide, is a person who is, at least when the "function" of guidance is activated, fully aware within rasa and clear enough in consciousness of what happens within his or her individual meditation to relate it to others. This is not an adequate definition of pamong, nor does it clarify the range of qualities of guidance, but it is sufficient in this context.

There are a number of analogies used within Sumarah to suggest how progress in individual meditative consciousness relates to the practice of guidance. Arymurthy has used the imagery of "mirroring." He suggested that it is as though in our normal awareness, our "internal mirror" is clouded. As a result, we benefit when facing a clear mirror because we can see ourselves better, hence realizing our inner limits so that we can release them. In explaining the process of guidance to Western followers of Sumarah in Solo Arymurthy clarified that:

> Once this has happened, once you are relatively blank, you become like a mirror. You can see your own identity more clearly: that you are grey, or very black, or red, or that you are becoming rose. You can see it all yourself. When I say that you become like a mirror I mean that then you become aware of your total identity. This means that functioning as a *pamong* is also directed within the self, that a *pamong* is headed in healthy directions internally. A mirror takes shape within which we can see our own reflection. . . . What we can do is to give witness. Once the mirror within us had begun to clear enough so that we can see ourself, then when it is turned toward others they can see themselves reflected to whatever extent their own mirror has not cleared. If we do not have the use of our own mirror then it is as thought we can borrow that of another. At the same time that other mirror does nothing except reflect. A *pamong* is only truly one when we see ourselves more clearly in his purity of consciousness. Ultimately those who make use of a *pamong*'s guidance can cleanse themselves to the point that they can see with their own mirror. But while our own mirror remains scratched we can benefit from willingness to temporarily borrow the mirror of another.

In any case it is the spirit rather than body of the *pamong* which provides the mirror.[15]

Sudarno has suggested an analogy with the gamelan orchestra. He points out that, if two identical gamelan are side by side and only one is played, precisely the same notes will resonate on the other gamelan. The guide, in these terms, is the silent gamelan, ordinary awareness a state of "being played," which eliminates awareness of resonance. In the same vein, Joyosampoerno compares guides to finely tuned radio receivers. The radio waves are there to be received by anyone, but most tuners are either turned off (e.g., people unaware of rasa) or confused by static (e.g., too much inward noise or not enough sensitivity).

The analogies draw attention to several characteristics of rasa and guidance as they are understood within Sumarah. The mirroring image highlights the fact that, even when experiencing guidance, it is what the meditator sees for and of himself that increases awareness. The gamelan image clarifies the guide's characteristics. The radio analogy emphasizes that the information is available to anyone and that the differences between people are simply questions of reception. In all three images it is clear that rasa is conceived as an organ present within all people, even if only consciously developed in some. While the process of "reading" another person's inner state in Sumarah guidance is at first glance a leap into the paranormal, the emphasis in these images, and indeed in Sumarah understanding generally, is on the fact that it simply involves refinement, through conscious discipline, of an intuitive facility possessed by everyone.

Attunement and Authority in Sumarah

So far I have been focusing on individual awareness of rasa and the way that relates to meditation guidance. If we turn now to the principles which are related to the role of leadership and process of collective decision making, we see the same logic applied to a larger stage. On the surface, the Sumarah organization has been structured in the same way as most modern organizations. Ever since it was formally organized in 1950 it has had a constitution, clearly defined leadership and branch structures, conferences and congresses, minutes, membership lists, and most of the other trappings of "formal" associations. At the same time, leaders are supposed to function for the collective in very much the same way that guides function for the groups they lead in meditation. Collective decision making is based, insofar as practice approximates the ideal, on consensus achieved through group meditation--that is on what is confirmed through rasa, though once again this does not mean that "rasa" is the "source" of the decision.

From the inception of the organization it has been emphasized that the basis for all important decisions must lie in *Hakiki*, that is, in Truth. The Javanese word "hakiki" derives from the Arabic "*khak*," meaning "right" in the sense of privilege, and "*haqiqa*," which in Islamic terms refers to basic or absolute Truth, to what is incontrovertibly correct. Suhardo, the second of Sumarah's founders, confirmed that the Sumarah sense of Hakiki is identical to the "guru sejati," the true teacher, and to the figure Dewaruci in Javanese mythology.[16] It refers, in other words, to direct inner reception

---

15. Ibid., pp. 21-22.

16. Interview with Suhardo in Yogya, during July 1972.

of the highest order of Truth. Constitutionally, the highest authority in Sumarah lies in congress decisions based on Hakiki.

Naturally there are in practice difficulties in recognizing Hakiki. On the one hand everyone in the movement accepts that individuals are of varying degrees of consciousness and by implication that some are more capable of receiving and recognizing Truth than others. Conversely it is understood that Hakiki is only confirmed when it "meshes" with collective experience during the attunement achieved through group meditation. The distinction between these two principles helps explain some of the problems and tensions which have surfaced in organizational history. In any case, the confirmation that "Hakiki" exists is meant to work in the same way as a pamong's guidance of meditation does. During discussions of the group decision-making process at the initial congress of Sumarah in 1950, Dr. Surono, who became the first leader of the reformed movement, explained:

> Even if it is *Hakiki* it also has to be proven. It is up to us to experience the Truth in all these matters, not just to adopt suggestions on faith. We differ from religions, within which people accept God on faith and without knowledge. Even Sukino asks us for our agreement.[17]

Thus, though individuals, usually those of high spiritual standing, may be the receptors of Hakiki, only the collective could certify it as such.

Hakiki does not, in Sumarah terms, come from rasa, nor is rasa finally even the tool of awareness through which it is apprehended. Nevertheless, the recognition of a fully harmonized feeling within rasa is one of the key indicators that a consensus based on Hakiki has been achieved. As a consequence it is understood that the organization's correct functioning depends on a meditative atmosphere achieved both through group guided meditation and continuous awareness of rasa on the part of all present. This explains why the frame for group meetings, including business sessions, is collective guided meditation. At points of doubt, deliberation, crisis, or division, the group returns to deep meditation, and, in addition, everyone aims to remain centered in rasa and thereby "tuned" to the collective "sphere."

Underlying this meditative approach is the conviction that the "correct" decision, insofar as there is one, is implicit in the situation. If the context is one of division, then that is thought to reflect attachment to surface forces rather than surrender to divine will--which is itself of course understood to be unitary rather than divided. Ultimately there is conviction that God's will is actually being expressed through natural law within all events--men need only open themselves to align their awareness and actions fully with it. These convictions frame and in one sense explain Sumarah actions. But focus here lies on practices rather than on the beliefs to which they may be related. The point is that exercising awareness of, and receptivity within, rasa is not only a key to Sumarah meditation but also a basis for organizational processes and finally an approach to everyday life.

So while the format of Sumarah meetings is defined on the surface by standard modern patterns of representation, regulation, and leadership, the process of decision making is meant to follow a logic which is only perceptible through rasa: the focus of attention is not exclusively intellectual. This does not

---

17. In Ismoe Soebagyo, *Rentjana Tjatatan Konggres Paguyuban Sumarah* (np/nd [Yogya, 1951?]), p. 38.

mean that mental and critical facilities play no part in the proceedings. On the contrary, they are meant to "speak for themselves," and this is implicit in the Sumarah understanding of consensus. Statements which offend reason are seen as automatically leading to division in "feeling" as well. It is understood that people react spontaneously if they are being open. This, however, is to speak of principles, while in practice there is a tendency to repress criticism due to "belief" in the need for unanimity. But leaving aside deviations from principle, achieving consensus, a verification of Hakiki, is seen as occurring when a statement or directive emerges from group meditation and leaves the collective "feeling" right.

It may be impossible to explain fully the dynamics of attunement within Sumarah, but it is possible to suggest the "direction of attention" involved. What Sumarah people "do" when "centering in rasa" is aptly suggested by thinking in terms of everyday experiences to which we can relate. Perhaps, while attentive to a tearful friend, we have noticed empathetic tears, stemming from sympathy rather than from any grief of our own. We may notice the difference between the atmosphere of an argumentative committee session and a spring celebration in a sun-flooded park. Surface events do not always correlate to inward qualities of feeling, and we can recall times when we have been aware of registering feelings originating beyond ourselves. For the most part we notice them only in an extreme situation, where they seem to "intrude" into our awareness rather than constitute a focus for it. Albeit imperfectly, we can grasp something of what it means to approach life through rasa if we imagine continuous awareness of this inner feeling and of the changes within it in response to the fields of our interaction. Sumarah practice implies, as one step on the spiritual path, exercising continuity of awareness within, and refinement of sensitivity to, this sphere of rasa.

If by this point the role of rasa within Sumarah meditation is clear, and also how it extends from individual practice into social situations, then we already have the basic point on which I wish to build. Before shifting to discussion of the ways in which this intuitive approach relates to general Javanese practices and ideas, several additional points need to be drawn from Sumarah experience. These points are particularly useful in making the transition to the general level, because, within Sumarah, practice of surrender which begins through rasa is explicit. As a result, it also relates more explicitly within the group than in other contexts to social patterns and historical evolution. From the micro level of individual practice, then, we can extend first to the functioning of leadership within the movement, and from there to the relationship between the movement and its context--only then considering rasa in the general context of Javanese culture.

Organizational leadership within Sumarah is not directly correlated to degrees of spiritual awareness. Nevertheless, there is a close correspondence between a pamong's relationship to those he is guiding in meditation and that of a leader, at any level, to those to whom he is responsible. The function of pamong is only genuinely activated when, among other things, there is a "sphere" indicating contact in rasa. Once that precondition is met, it may be possible for the guide to speak on the basis of a direct link to the actual inner condition of others present. If that happens, then it will be as though the guide is a receptor, highlighting forces which had been only subconscious in others. At the same time, confirmation that the "contact" is genuine depends on the practical relevance of what is said to those receiving guidance.

Similarly, the appropriateness of a leader can be, and within Sumarah is, tested by the degree to which he is tuned both to the inner condition of the collective and to the outer circumstances to which it relates. When leaders are appropriate then they will be doing and articulating what feels right to the group. It was a confirmation of Arymurthy's leadership, for instance, when his guidance of the opening meditation at the 1973 conference touched on and clarified all of the major issues which had been preoccupying the branches.[18] On the other hand, when leaders have been increasingly preoccupied with matters which do not concern, or are in conflict with, the corporate experience, such a situation has led to rejection. In the years preceding Dr. Surono's replacement in 1966, the break between leadership and collective was clearly reflected in Surono's unwillingness even to hold the meetings which would have "tested" the Hakiki he claimed. To function properly, a Sumarah leader needs to be tuned to and speaking for the collective.[19] While in one sense this could be said of any theory of representative leadership, the implications here are different. In Sumarah the underpinning is conviction in an immediacy of contact and directness of intuitive awareness that is not normally entertained.

Insofar as leaders have articulated what may have been latent within the collective, then the source of action, leaving aside teleological questions, lies in the clarification of what "already is"—not in innovation or expediency, though each of those also has a place in Sumarah interpretation. Leaders are not so much pioneers, pointing the way to new ground, as "focalizers."[20] As such they are meant merely to crystallize, and thereby raise consciousness of, developments which have already been taking place.

This stance is especially evident in the way Sumarah leaders have spoken of the emergence of new phases in spiritual practice. So far there have been six distinct phases, and in announcing them the leadership has generally aimed to draw attention to changes which have been related at once to the Javanese context and to the maturation of individual practice. The movement from one phase to another is presented as a sequence of evolutionary stages rather than as a shift in direction.

Two points about the changes, especially the depth of change within Sumarah, are relevant here: the first concerns the Sumarah interpretation of the changes, and the second the general relationship between changes within Sumarah and changes in its context.[21] After Sumarah came into existence in 1935, significant

---

18. This point is based on my own participation in the 1973 Sumarah annual conference held in Surakarta. At that point I had been involved with the organization intensively for two years. Immediately prior to the conference I had completed a circuit of visits to all the major regional centers, spending several weeks in each. During the course of the visits I became aware of the issues which preoccupied regional groups--issues differed from place to place, although, of course, some concerns were common. I was therefore especially struck, during this opening meditation, both by the degree to which and the way in which Arymurthy touched on all of these issues.

19. Further details of the problems which surfaced in the mid-1960s can be found in my thesis, or in my "Javanese Mysticism in the Revolutionary Period," *Journal of Studies in Mysticism* 1, 2 (1978).

20. My use of this term is drawn from the way it is used within the Findhorn community in Scotland, where precisely analogous principles are used. See David Spangler, *Revelation: The Birth of a New Age* (Middletown, Wisc.: Lorian Press, 1977), pp. 173-77.

21. For the nature of these changes, which constitute the major focus of

changes in its organizational structure occurred in 1950 and 1966; distinct phases of spiritual practice are associated with the years 1935, 1949, 1956, 1974, and (less clearly to me) the late 1970s. It is not surprising that major organizational changes coincide with the attainment of national independence, the transition to Sukarno's Guided Democracy, and the coup which introduced Suharto's New Order. What is striking, however, is how thoroughly changes have ramified through the organization, with the movement paralleling national changes profoundly rather than just at its surface levels.

Within Sumarah the interpretation of this parallelism is that the movement stands in precisely the same relationship to the nation as leaders within it do to the collective, or as pamong to those they guide: as a focalizer or receptor of unusual clarity throwing into relief the murky or hidden realities around. Here we are simply moving up the scale from the microcosm of the individual, through the group as a collective, to the nation. Within the group it is thought that the degree to which, at any of these levels, a structure reflects its environment can be related in practical terms to how "open" it is to "whatever is."[22] Since Sumarah defines itself by commitment to increasing openness, its sense of union involves not only a remote and abstract absolute, but also a dissolution of the boundaries between people, and thereby an increasing interpenetration between individual, collective, and society.

For my purposes, that is in using the Sumarah case to make suggestions about Javanese culture, we can leave aside discussion of whether Sumarah in fact "mirrors" national events, or whether it does so more or less than other movements. We can ignore the question of whether leaders in Sumarah are actually attuned to the collective; nor is there any reason to be concerned with whether a pamong is actually able to "know" the inner state of another. All we need to note is that there is a consistent structure within those three relationships, and that the interpretation within Sumarah links them all through a *systematic* understanding of the way consciousness relates to social interaction. The key to that structure lies in an approach to meditation through rasa, or intuitive feeling, thus emphasizing a different psychological facility in approaching both cognition in general and social life in particular. Sumarah people are not just interpreting reality through a different theory; they are cultivating rasa within their meditation and approaching interactions through it. While we might devote energy to fine analytical distinctions; they are refining and sharpening awareness of intuitive feeling.

Rasa in Javanist Theory

Sumarah is profoundly rather than incidentally Javanese. It is unique only in the sense that individuals are unique, or in the way that particular villages might present variations in the general pattern of rural life. While

---

my thesis, see Stange, "Sumarah Movement in Javanese Mysticism."

22. "Mysticism" and "religion" interpenetrate, but in this we may have a way of identifying different characteristic emphases. Within mystical styles of spirituality there is usually emphasis on the fact that all forms, including those of the movement or practice itself, are simply vehicles for, or pathways of, the ultimate; within the religious approach there is a tendency to identify the ultimate with its manifestation through specific forms—whether doctrinal, personal, ritual, or corporate. While the latter may lead to resistance to change, the former (insofar as practice reflects ideals) may be more open to it.

this means we cannot assume that Sumarah is a perfect microcosm of the society, it also implies that we need not. The usefulness of the case lies in the explicit and elaborate understanding of rasa existing within Sumarah. Through that we can draw out patterns which remain implicit within general thought and practice. In making this transition, I will begin by considering the meanings attached to the term "rasa" both within other mystical movements and within the culture as a whole. Then I want to show how rasa is interlocked with other key ideas within Javanese culture. Finally, I suggest how the logic underlying Sumarah practice corresponds to traditional patterns of social relationship and political power.

The special potency of the concept of rasa stems in part from the spectrum of meanings attached to it. Because rasa links the physical sense of taste and touch to emotions, the refined feeling of the heart, and the deepest mystical apprehension of the ultimate, it provides a continuum which links surface meanings to which anyone can relate to inner levels of experience which normally, at least within our context, appear discontinuous. At the same time it is central not only to Sumarah "spiritual psychology," but also to Javanese mystical theory in general, and through that it is related to Javanese perceptions of society and politics.

Gonda comments that the Javanese have combined the original Sanskrit meanings associated with "rasa" ("taste, flavor, essence, enjoyment, sentiment, disposition, meaning, etc.") and *rahasya* ("secret, mystery") within their use of the term "rasa." Javanese interpretation certainly does involve an emphasis different from that within Sanskrit, where "rasa" is primarily aesthetic rather than psychological. Nevertheless, there has been a remarkable continuity of interpretation, extending from Sanskrit through Kawi and into contemporary Javanese usage. This continuity combines with the resonance of "rasa" in Javanese language and thought to provide one measure of the degree to which the Javanese have interiorized Indian patterns of thought. In commenting on the use of the term within old Javanese texts, Gonda clarifies both the varieties of usage and depth of meanings associated with it:

> ... it is not easy exactly to say what connotations were meant by these mystics when resorting to the favourite term *rasa*. It often served to translate the Arabic *sirr* "secret, mystery," which refers to the most subtle and most hidden and latent elements in the human heart in which God is said to reside, the "spot" where God and the soul are in contact. ... In Javanese mystic texts this divine principle is also called *rasa*, "but not the ordinary *rasa*," "it is not the *rasa* ('feeling') which we feel in our bodies, but the *rasa* which is felt in the heart." The clear and pure heart receives the supreme *rasa*, which is pure and without any defect ... [and] ... On one hand *suksma* and *rasa* are regarded as related, but not identical principles ... on the other hand they may be interchanged or *suksma* is called the true *rasa*, the *rasa* of the body.[23]

In the same context, Gonda goes on to point out that in Javanese mysticism there has been a special emphasis on the heart, which is associated with rasa (from Sanskrit) but also with Sufi stress on the *qalb*, which in Javanese is "kalbu."

---

23. J. Gonda, *Sanskrit in Indonesia*, 2nd ed. (New Delhi: International Academy of Indian Culture, 1973), p. 256.

If we trace back through the esoteric lore of Java, we can relate emphasis on the heart, and with it rasa, to the importance of Vishnu, as represented by the inclination of rulers such as Airlangga to be associated with him. This is not to suggest that "paths of the heart," either in the form of Vishnu cults or Sufism, have been developed to the exclusion of others in Java, for there have, of course, been many different forms of mystical practice in Java. Although each cult or spiritual practice tends to emphasize a particular occult center of perception (referring here to such centers as they are understood within either Tantrism or Sufism, both of which apply in Java), each also carries awareness that the center it may emphasize is but part of a complex system. While it is possible to identify a variety, even the full range, of potential "emphases" among Javanese spiritual paths, it can be argued that both historically (as reflected in texts such as the *Dharmasunya*) and in contemporary spiritual practice, emphasis on the heart (whether as the esoteric locus of Vishnu, as kalbu, or as the locus of true rasa) is a characteristic of Javanese spirituality.[24]

This emphasis, and its association with those senses of rasa I have been detailing above, is represented clearly in the teachings and practices of contemporary Javanese mystics, as scholars of the subject have noted. One of the larger Javanese sects is called "Rasa Sejati," or "the absolute, pure, inner feeling." Hardjanta, a leader of a Hindu sect in Surakarta, has confirmed that emphasis on the heart is a characteristic approach in Java.[25] In the teachings of Sapta Darma "the radiance of God in man is called *rasa* or spirit" and its understanding of the network of inner psychic centers is called "*tali rasa*," literally the "rope of inner feeling."[26] In Bratakesawa's teachings the "*rasa djati*" is the organ unique to man through which he can contact his essence.[27] Within Pangestu, as Hadiwijono puts it:

> *Rahsa Djati* is not something organical, it is a definite sphere in the psychological life. It is also indicated as the essence of the emotional life. It is the entrance or the threshold to the immaterial possibility of being. . . .[28]

In his report, based on the understandings of his informant Pak Dwidjo, Weiss says the "feeling of the heart" is called "rasa *khodim*," and he places it

---

24. On the *Dharmasunya* I am drawing from G. Forrester, "The Dharmasunya: The Philosophy of the Void" (Honors subthesis, The Australian National University, 1968). This is a basis on which we could construct a useful comparative mysticism. While in Sufism there is an emphasis on the heart; within Zen or Taoism the stress falls on the navel. Different centers within the body are given different emphasis by variant practices.

25. Based on discussions with Hardjanta in Surakarta. He is the leader of a Javanese-based association called "Sadhar Mapan," and was previously a regional leader within the national structure of Hinduism. Details of his career are treated in Julia Howell, "Vehicles for the Kalki Avatar" (PhD dissertation, Stanford University, 1977).

26. The quote is from Hadiwijono (*Man in the Present*, p. 165), but for the rest I am relying on instructions about the practice from Ibu Sri Pawenang in Yogyakarta during 1972 and 1973.

27. Hadiwijono, *Man in the Present*, p. 194.

28. Ibid., p. 213.

on the gradient of rasa leading to "rasa sejati." Pak Dwidjo immediately linked "rasa" to "elmu rasa," that is "the science of intuition," and for him this was coterminus with kebatinan, or Javanese mysticism as a whole. At the same time, he presented his theory that many psychic powers are extensions of rasa sejati and that, if rasa is developed, then there is no need to rely on tools of divination, such as the *primbon*.[29] Leaving aside questions of relative emphasis, it is clear that Sumarah is not alone among Javanese mystical groups in attributing great significant to rasa.

In their general interpretations of the Javanese world view, Clifford Geertz and Niels Mulder point to rasa's significance within it. As Mulder puts it:

> The Javanese high road to insight in reality is the trained and sensitive *rasa* (intuitive inner feeling). In mysticism, the essence of reality is grasped by the *rasa* and revealed in the quiet *batin*. ... It is only by training the *rasa* that man can bridge the distance to "God." ...[30]

Mulder goes on to relate the Javanese emphasis on rasa to the principles of harmony, oneness, and even coincidence, which are expressed in Javanese social life.

In a similar vein, Geertz gives us an extremely useful outline of some of the many uses and permutations of rasa. He stresses the dual meanings of "feeling" and "meaning," and also points to its association with the heart. Although he provides an excellent statement, the emphasis on "meaning" within it is at the expense of the more appropriate "essence," and the term "intuition" is unfortunately absent from his vocabulary. His greatest contribution on this point was to clarify:

> The three major foci of *prijaji* "religious" life are etiquette, art, and mystical practice ... these factors are so fused as to make their separate consideration nearly meaningless. ... The connecting link between all three, the common element in them all which ties them together and makes them but different modes of the same reality, is what the Javanese ... call *rasa*. ... By taking *rasa* to mean both "feeling" and "meaning," the *prijaji* has been able to develop a phenomenological analysis of subjective experience to which everything else can be tied. ...[31]

He goes on to point out that the concept is used to link subjective experience and objective religious truth and to explain that, through the emphasis on "feeling," there is implied a direct link between rasa, ultimate spiritual knowledge (in Javanese terms), and the quality of *"halus"* or extremely refined feelings cultivated through Javanese etiquette. While Geertz accurately, in my opinion, pinpoints the centrality of rasa within Javanese cosmology, while he shows great sensitivity to its permutations in mystical theory and the social etiquette to which it is bound, the logic evident within Sumarah practice provides a basis for extension from his point.

---

29. Jerome Weiss, "Folk Psychology of the Javanese of Ponorogo" (PhD dissertation, Yale University, 1977), pp. 278 and 285-89.

30. Mulder, *Mysticism and Everyday Life*, pp. 15 and 30.

31. Geertz, *Religion of Java*, pp. 238-39.

Rasa and Social Relations

The logic of rasa is the mechanism underlying the interpenetration of "etiquette, art, and mystical practice"; it is the mechanism underlying the complex of Javanese ideas relating to the nature, manifestations, and ideals of power (*kasekten*) in the political realm. Rasa occupies a fundamental place within the Javanese map of spiritual consciousness, and that in turn is fundamentally related to notions of power and authority. In this context there is neither the possibility nor the need to catalog complexes of Javanese thought and action which relate to rasa. Instead, my aim is to concentrate on just a few examples to identify the "logic of rasa" as a substructure underlying Javanese cosmology and actions. If the "logic" becomes apparent, then it will be possible to conclude that the "fundamental" rules we are dealing with are not simply those of a "thought system," but rather extensions of perception resulting from practical cultivation of sensitivity to rasa, as is suggested in the Sumarah example.

Within Javanese village society there is a consistent emphasis on harmony, peace, balance, and consensus. This is, of course, characteristic of peasant cultures in general, it is not unique to the Javanese case.[32] Justus van der Kroef speaks of it in terms of a "stasis-seeking mechanism," virtually an obsession with balance, one that has its natural counter in the prevalence of millenarian movements.[33] Geertz identifies the *selametan*, or communal feast, along with its associated offerings to the spirits, as the basic ritual of rural society.[34] The word "*selamet*" means "peace" or sometimes "safety," and is closely paired with "*rukun*" or "harmonious," as an ideal of village life. These concepts are related to an emphasis on "smoothness" in social relations, on the importance of cooperation (*gotong-royong*) within village enterprise, and on the ideal of consensus (*mufakat*) as a model for decision making. Individual behavior is guided in theory by the imperative to harmonize, and collective decisions are meant to reflect achievement of a "corporate" union of wills which is supposed to be simply articulated, or brought to the surface, by the village head. Despite the degree to which these may be merely ideals, often in stark contrast with behavior, there can be no doubt that they are widely held and invoked as ideals, even by ordinary villagers.

At the national level, the same ideas entered most forcefully into synthesis with other ideologies through Sukarno's political philosophy, especially during the period of Guided Democracy. Sukarno's thought is simply the most powerful and accessible example--there are many others with a similar bent, and those who follow him in "spirit" remain numerous up to the present. Sukarno referred actively to village values and sought to construct a national ideology which had an indigenous, for him mainly Javanese, basis. As this feature of his

---

32. For instance see Eric Wolf, *Peasants* (Englewood Cliffs, N.J.: Prentice-Hall, 1965) or Robert Redfield, *Peasant Society and Culture* (Chicago: University of Chicago Press, 1956).

33. "Javanese Messianic Expectations," *Comparative Studies in Society and History* 5, 1 (1958-59).

34. On the *abangan* see: Geertz, *Religion of Java* (Part One: The "Abangan" Variant); and on forms of village cooperation see Koentjaraningrat, *Some Social-Anthropological Observations on Gotong-Rojong Practices in Two Villages of Central Java* (Ithaca: Cornell Modern Indonesia Project, 1961).

enterprise has been repeatedly outlined, even filtering into press coverage of Indonesia, only brief suggestions bear repeating here.[35]

Consensus through deliberation (*musyawarah*-mufakat) was taken as an ideal to replace the notion of representative democracy through elections. Sukarno presented himself as the "mouthpiece of the people" (*penyambung lidah rakyat*), implying that through his attunement to popular consciousness he spoke for the whole. The national motto of "unity in diversity" (*bhinneka tunggal ika*), is in this context explicitly linked by many to the mystical sense that "union" lies in the realm beyond forms, just as is the parallel pronouncement that "all religions lead to the same goal." Whether in the statements of Sukarno and Suharto or in critiques of them, it is suggested that the fundamental basis of power lies in the wahyu, the cosmic sanction which bestows both legitimacy and a spiritually charged authority.[36]

The classical notion of the ruler held that the king's heart (sanubari) needed to be "oceanic," embracing the realm so that his consciousness became a pure embodiment or reflection of the collective. Conversely, criticism becomes justified when it begins to seem that *pamrih*, selfish motive or self-interest, rather than collective interest, guides government. These notions are still current, even contributing to the framing of dissent within Suharto's New Order.[37] The leader is supposed to have, and this is a closely related conception, "keenly attuned inner feelings"--implying capacity to "receive" and register the qualities of sentiment moving through the public, so that direct consciousness rather than simply an intelligence system contributes to awareness of the kingdom.[38] Finally, explicit traditional ideology of kingship attributes higher qualities of spiritual awareness, in the end merging into ideas of

---

35. Clifford Geertz, *Islam Observed* (Chicago: University of Chicago Press, 1971), ch. 3; Anderson, "Idea of Power"; Bernhard Dahm, *Sukarno and the Struggle for Indonesian Independence*, trans. Mary F. Somers Heidhues (Ithaca: Cornell University Press, 1969); and many others.

36. Anderson, "Idea of Power"; and Soemarsaid Moertono, *State and Statecraft in Old Java* (Ithaca: Cornell Modern Indonesia Project, 1968).

37. Criticisms of the Suharto regime are concentrated on its moral qualities. Incidents such as the Sawito affair of 1976 underline the significance the regime itself attaches to these forms of criticism. On the Sawito affair, see David Bourchier, *Dynamics of Dissent in Indonesia: Sawito and the Phantom Coup* (Ithaca: Cornell Modern Indonesia Project, 1984). Bouchier's analysis suggests that the "mystical" aspects of the affair were magnified by the government to discredit the challenge implied by it (pp. 7-8 and 94). I do not see an opposition but rather a convergence between the framing of dissent in cosmological and moral terms and the "reality" or "substance" of the political challenge--which is what his analysis implies. In terms of the point I am making in this article, it is in any event incidental whether the challenge was in substance "moral" or "political." In either event the framing of the challenge and the government's response confirm the existence of an idea of power which relates it to the presence or the absence of a cosmological mandate.

38. The quote, "to be a leader you must have keenly attuned inner feelings: ("*dadi pemimpin mono kudu duwe rasa rumangsa kang landep*"), is from Elinor Horne, *Javanese-English Dictionary* (New Haven and London: Yale University Press, 1974), p. 495. It is not incidental that this appears as her final illustration in defining "rasa."

incarnated deity to the ruler. The highest ideal of traditional kingship called for a consciousness through which rulers could demonstrate attunement both to the natural world, through the mediation of the ancestral spirit realm, and to the social world of the realm.[39]

This emphasis on the *spiritual* consciousness of the ruler is directly related to the sociopolitical sensitivity of mystical men and movements. The structure of that relationship is clear in Anderson's discussion. He points out, following Schrieke, that the prevalence of politicized mysticism has been viewed in Javanese society as a "barometer," increasing incidence indicating growing imbalance and ill-health in the state. Conversely, if those who are thought to have spiritual awareness of a high order, and, by direct correlation, a high degree of actual attunement to the social realities of the time, are aligned with the ruler, then this is interpreted as an important confirmation that the wayhu indeed rests with those in power.[40]

Insofar as the logic which is evident in Sumarah does underlie general Javanese beliefs, either in the case of the village ethos or in terms of ideologies of power, the implications are obvious. Mystical practice is precisely concerned with dissolution of ego and, in the Javanese case at least, with an increasing sensitivity of intuition which makes people directly aware of currents of energy, sentiment, or vibration beyond the ego. Whether as leaders, advisors, neutral people, or critics, mystics are thought to have direct access to and awareness of the *actual* conditions of individuals, the collective, and the natural world. Their power, because that is implicit in this quality of consciousness, is presented as a consequence of attunement to objective realities, an openness and clarity which hence "allows in" and registers events which remain confused or unclear to most. One paradox in this lies in the fact that it is precisely through transcendence of ego, self, and the concern for material gain that access to influence increases—this explains the Javanese preoccupation with pamrih in those exercising influence over others.

Finally, just as a village head or national leader is analogous, in the terms outlined above, to a Sumarah pamong (a term which, not incidentally, is of course also used for the bureaucracy), the significance of individual mystics or their movements as "barometers" is explained by the fact that they are believed to have not just an unusual consciousness of the ineffable, but also a particular clarity, as receptors, about the environment. Javanese kings were supposed to be "warana," "screens" registering neutrally; Sumarah leaders, such as Sukino and Arymurthy, apply the same concept to themselves.[41] As receptors they do not simply register, but also internalize and embody the forces around. So the pamong is meant to experience consciously what

---

39. The classical, though now also dated, discussion of kingship in Southeast Asia is Robert Heine-Geldern, *Conceptions of State and Kingship in Southeast Asia* (Ithaca: Cornell University Southeast Asia Program, 1956).

40. See Anderson, "Idea of Power"; and B. J. O. Schrieke, *Indonesian Sociological Studies*, vol. 2 (The Hague: van Hoeve, 1966), pp. 76-95. In general Schrieke emphasizes succession as a basis of legitimacy, as opposed to the cosmological mandate; however in this section he deals with the ideal theory of royal power and the way that relates to protests which have been directed against rulers. He also points to the particular emphasis on Vishnu in Javanese ideals of royalty.

41. See Moertono, *State and Statecraft*, p. 35 on "warana" and kingship.

his follower does; the leader to feel precisely what is implicit in the collective; the collective to mirror the currents within society. "Mystical union" is once again conceived here as having a practical implication—and it is this that underlies Javanese thought.

The Javanese conviction that there is a parallelism, even an identity, extending from microcosm (*jagad cilik*) through to macrocosm (jagad *gede*) becomes in this context a secondary reflection of practices of union cultivated through rasa; it does not remain simply a philosophical belief inherited from India and carried by tradition.[42] The mirroring suggested between pamong and student, leader and group, or Sumarah and nation is of course identical to that of ruler and realm. Each is explicitly linked, through the mediation of rasa, to meditative consciousness. The ideal ruler is then one who *practices* awareness attuned to the collective he rules—and, as we would expect, there are a variety of ways in which rulers are said to have, or according to traditions supposed to have, actively exercised meditation.[43] Insofar as the ideals are embodied, then the understanding is that leaders have actually *been* aware of their environment, directly experiencing currents of feeling from the collective of those ruled.

Conviction concerning the fundamentally unitary nature of reality and, from the perspective of "realized" mystics, the actual experience of it is then *reflected into* the dimension of cosmologies and beliefs in the form of the idea that microcosm and macrocosm correspond. The underlying logic within Javanese cosmology is an expression of its experiential basis. But if we merely suggest that Javanese have been shaped in their actions by their beliefs and leave it at that, our image is incomplete—the dialectic of belief and experience proceeds both ways. At a simpler level, we can observe in this logic a more practical bent than is normally associated with the Javanese world view. Within Sumarah the validity of a pamong's guidance or a leader's Hakiki is tested by whether it strikes home in the group. By implication the measure of a ruler's wahyu lies not simply in debates about hypothetical imponderables, but quite practically at the level of whether the leader does in fact act on the basis of a recognized consensus, one that is spontaneous and rooted in well-being.

The practical implications of this suggestion are not confined to the dimensions of formal authority and power, but also extend to everyday social relations. While my focus here has been on the special sense of rasa which applies within Sumarah practice and mystical perceptions of power, I have also been suggesting that Javanese culture is generally characterized by an emphasis on intuitive modes of knowing and relating. The Javanese language is in itself an indication that this may be so, as fine distinctions in the realm of emotions and feeling contribute so much to its vocabulary, and the word "rasa" itself has so many permutations. If we are concerned with interpreting the nature of everyday social transactions in Java, awareness of the significance of rasa within them provides a new angle for insight. Without an understanding

---

42. On the centrality of the notion of correspondence between microcosm and macrocosm see Heine-Geldern, *Conceptions of State and Kingship*, p. 3. As an element within the structure of Javanist ideology, this notion deserves more emphasis than it has generally been given.

43. For example see Prof. Zoetmulder's discussion of Kertanagara's spiritual practices in "The Significance of the Study of Culture and Religion for Indonesian Historiography," in *An Introduction to Indonesian Historiography*, ed. Soedjatmoko et al. (Ithaca: Cornell University Press, 1965).

of its significance, we might conclude that endless repetition of formulae within ordinary social discourse is a way of avoiding "meaning"; once we are aware of rasa, we can see that the transaction finds its substance not in words, but in the establishment of a harmonious "feeling contact" between the parties. Instead of concluding that discourse draws consciousness to the "surface," as though devoid of content, we will see the locus of substance in communicative exchange, in intuitive feeling.

To conclude suggestively, and at the most general level, one of the implications extending from this argument is that we need to pay more attention to the cognitive and psychological differences of emphasis between cultures.[44] If we "read" cultural systems as primarily consisting of different ideological glosses on the same "reality" then we have only noted part of the matter. Cultures clearly do involve different ideological formations which then condition or shape perception and behavior. At the same time, however, these cultures may also direct "attention" and awareness to different cognitive functions, to different aspects or dimensions of the exchanges involved in social discourse.

---

44. Here I am thinking of suggestions such as that of Robert Ornstein, in *The Psychology of Consciousness* (London: Cape, 1975), that traditional Asian cultures give more emphasis to the intuitive mode of awareness--a suggestion clearly convergent with mine here.

TALES FROM THE ISLAND OF ROTI*

Compiled by D. Manafe

Translated by Thomas John Hudak

Providing moralistic training as well as entertainment, folk tales represent an important part of oral and written culture in Indonesia. As a multilingual and multicultural society, Indonesia has a wealth of such tales. Over the years, concerted efforts have been made to collect and preserve as many of them as possible. The Balai Pustaka, for example, has issued five volumes of folk tales collected from nearly all the islands in the archipelago. In another effort to preserve the varied cultural heritages of Indonesia, the Indonesian Department of Higher Education, in 1977, instituted a research project to describe and record the major dialects throughout the country. A secondary goal of the project was to collect folk tales and other folk literature in the original dialects. While the tales gathered for this project have not been published, other collections from single language and dialect groups have appeared in Indonesian. Among such collections are the following tales from the eastern island of Roti.

1. How Two Children Turned into Pigeons

Once upon a time the sky and earth were so near to each other that people from the earth could climb up to the sky and people from the sky could go down to earth. By means of a wooden ladder, crowds of people went up and down, each going about his own business. In the sky, not very far from the ladder, lived a grandmother with her two grandchildren. One day the old woman sent the two grandchildren down to earth to get some fire.

When the children reached the earth, they walked here and there, wondering which place or house might have some fire. Finally, after a long time, the two of them reached a hut with some fire. Then the older said, "Ah, are we lucky! We've found some fire. Let's take it back to grandmother. She'll really be glad to get it."

"Right, but how are we going to carry it?" asked the younger.

"Easy," answered her brother picking up the still burning coal. "Watch out!" he cried, flinging the hot coal away. "This fire has teeth. It almost bit my hand in two!"

"Teeth?" asked the youngest. "I'll get some string to tie it up and then we can drag it behind us." When she found the string, she tied the coal up and

---

* These stories first appeared as *Dongeng-Dongeng Dari Pulau Roti*, compiled by D. Manafe (Jakarta: Balai Pustaka, 1969), and were reprinted in 1974 and 1975.

called to her brother, "Let's go! Now we can pull the fire behind us." But even before she finished speaking, she saw that the fire had burned the string in two.

"Wow! The fire's teeth have already cut the string in two," continued the younger sister. "Now what are we going to do?"

"Easy," answered her older brother. "Let's grab the coal again and put it into my pocket." The two of them then grabbed the coal and put it into the elder brother's pocket, but in a second the coal burned through and fell out. The children became increasingly desperate as they discovered that a fire, even as small as that one, could not only hurt their hands but also burn a string in two and make holes in pockets.

"Just where are the fire's teeth?" asked the youngest.

"I don't know," asnwered her brother, "but if I did, I'd knock them out."

Both of them turned the coal over and over to see whether it had any teeth. When they could not find any, they sat down in desperation. Suddenly the older child cried out, "I have an idea. Let's grab the fire and put it into my blanket. I'll wrap it up so tightly that it can't bite." Then he took the coal again, wrapped it up with his blanket, and said to his sister, "Let's go home. This fire can't do anything more now."

The flames got bigger

Carrying the coal wrapped up in the blanket, brother and sister walked toward the ladder. What they did not know, however, was that the coal was already burning through the blanket. When he felt the heat, the older child cried out, "Hey, let's run, little sister; the fire's beginning to bite again!" Both of them then ran toward the ladder, but before they reached it, the coal burned through the blanket and burned the older child. Throwing the burning coal down, the children let it burn all the grass and dried leaves piled up near the ladder. The flames kept getting bigger and bigger, and soon even the ladder burned up. Then the people from the sky could no longer go down to the earth, and the people on the earth could no longer go up into the sky. When the children saw the ladder burn up, they became frightened and ran away to hide in the forest.

As soon as the old woman heard the news about the ladder, she knew that it was her two grandchildren's fault. In a fury she went to the burned ladder and shouted to them, but no one answered. As her anger increased, the grandmother cursed her two grandchildren. After she cursed them, the sky raised up higher and higher. Changed into pigeons, the cursed grandchildren flew toward the sky. Unfortunately, before they could get there, the sky was out of reach. So, returning to earth, the two grandchildren lived as a pair of pigeons and gave birth to the thousands and thousands of pigeons that we see today.

2. How Seven Boys Turned into Stars

Once there were seven boys who came from the sea searching for work on the land. Walking about, they went from village to village asking if anyone needed help. Several of them were lucky and found work searching for firewood while others found work herding ducks. Those who succeeded in finding work stayed on the land while those who did not returned to the sea.

Among those who stayed on the land was one who lived in the king's palace and worked as a cow herder. He was said to be a clever and obedient child, and because of that, he was much loved by the king. Early in the morning he would herd together the king's cattle and take them out to pasture, and then in the afternoon he would lead them back into the corral.

At that time the people from the sea and the people from the land were enemies; thus, when the land people learned that the king's clever herder came from the sea, they captured and killed him. Afterwards, they threw his corpse into the forest. No one from the palace knew where the herder had disappeared to, although there were some who guessed that perhaps he had died from some disease.

The king ordered his people to search for his beloved herder, but all their searching was in vain, for the cow herder's body had already been eaten by the wild beasts of the forest and only his bones remained scattered about. When the other six boys heard the sorrowful news about their friend's disappearance, they came to search for his body.

Never knowing exhaustion, the boys searched for their friend, going in and out of the forest and crossing rivers and wide fields. Several days later, when they were near desperation, they found the bones scattered in the forest. Sadly, the six friends gathered the bones together and put them under a banyan tree. Then the oldest said, "Go to the sea and bring some water here." Obeying, the five other friends went to the sea and in a short time returned carrying the sea water. They poured the water on top of the pile of bones and instantly the bones were changed back into the cow herder, but he was weak and unable to walk. When the six boys saw the cow herder alive again, their hearts were filled with joy. Each taking turns, the six boys supported the weak cow herder and walked towards the sea, fearing that the land people would discover them.

But just before they entered the sea, the sea people came out and chased them away crying, "We don't know you! You went to the land looking for work and left the sea for a long time. Because of that, you're now counted as land people."

With troubled hearts, the seven children returned to the land, but even there they were chased and people tried to kill them. Finally, the oldest said, "Because we cannot return to the sea and because on land we are always pursued, it's better that we should go to the sky." The six other boys agreed and so they went up into the sky where they were changed into seven stars that remained side by side forever, a cluster of stars that joined together to send rays to the earth. The rays from one of the seven stars, however, were pale and dim, for they came from the star that had been the cow herder who was still weak and weary when changed into a star.

3. The Monkey and the Turtle

(1)

One day a monkey met a turtle on the beach and said, "What are you doing here, my friend?"

"Oh, I'm taking a rest because I've been swimming all day and now I'm very tired."

"Do you want to be friends with me?" continued the monkey.

"Certainly," replied the turtle.

"If that's so, then it'd be wonderful if we could prove our friendship to each other."

"And how are we going to do that?" asked the turtle.

"Well, for example, we could look for fleas on each other."

"That's fine, but it's obvious that there aren't any fleas on my head because I don't have any hair," replied the turtle scratching his head.

"Even though you don't have hair, that doesn't mean that you don't have fleas. I can see a lot of fleas hiding underneath the skin of your head right now. If those fleas aren't killed, I'm sure they'll eat up the skin on your head. And after they've done that to your head, they'll get into your skull and, I'm afraid, maybe eat up your brain."

When he heard what the monkey had said, the turtle uncovered his head and let the monkey search for fleas. Several times the monkey bit the skin and caused the turtle to moan, "Why are you biting my head?"

Convulsed with laughter, the monkey replied, "I'm not trying to hurt you, my friend; you're feeling pain because the fleas have already penetrated a long way into the skin on your head. If you want to save your head, this skin has to be taken off!"

"Don't, don't," cried the turtle pulling his head away. "If you do that, later my brains will dry out and be baked solid by the sun."

"OK," said the monkey brushing off his friend's head. "If that's what you want, I won't skin you anymore, but I'll do my best to kill all of those damned fleas." Then the monkey bit the turtle's head several more times. The turtle complained, but the monkey said, "Don't cry, my friend; a little pain doesn't matter as long as you're freed from these fleas." The monkey then bit the turtle's head again and again until it was bleeding. When the turtle cried, the monkey cheered him up saying, "Patience, my friend. You've got to have pain before you can get rid of those fleas. Later on it'll be better."

The turtle brushed away his tears, and his friend continued scraping until several sections of the skin were loosened. As soon as the brains were visible, the monkey began eating and continued until he had finished them off.

When he was full, the monkey jumped on top of a rock and said, "Good-bye, my friend. Before this I was hungry, but now I'm full and can be on my way again." The turtle scratched his head and discovered to his horror that the monkey had eaten all his brains. With that, the turtle began to plot his revenge.

4. The Monkey and the Turtle

(2)

When the water had ebbed, the monkey went out into the sea to catch some fish. Turning several stones over and over and deep in thought, the monkey suddenly heard a voice behind him, "Good afternoon, my friend. How are you?" When he turned around, he saw a turtle with his head bound with a red cloth sunning himself on top of a rock.

"Good afternoon," replied the monkey.

"What are you doing here?" asked the turtle as he approached the monkey.

"I'm looking for fish brains."

When he heard the monkey's answer, the turtle grew very angry. He felt ridiculed and insulted, for he remembered that it was this very monkey which had eaten all his brains. With great effort, the turtle subdued his anger and said patiently, "Oh, I know where all the brains of the fish are hidden. Only recently have the fish realized that there are a lot of enemies trying to steal their brains, so they've gathered all their brains together and hidden them not far from here."

"Is that true?" asked the monkey licking his lips.

"Up until now, I've never lied to anyone, not even to one of my enemies. I don't want to hurt anyone even though they've hurt me."

Laughing, the monkey asked, "Just where is this place you're talking about, my friend?"

"Over here," answered the turtle, taking his friend's hand and leading him to an oyster. The oyster shell was open and the white meat sparkled as the sun's rays struck it. When the monkey saw the meat, his mouth watered.

"Since when have the fish hidden their brains here?" asked the monkey.

"Since we turtles lost ours," answered the turtle.

"And who showed them such a safe place?" laughed the monkey.

"Me," replied the turtle, adjusting the bandage on his head, "so don't take any fish brains while I'm still here. Later I'll be accused of telling the secret. Be patient until I leave and then you can eat to your heart's content." With that, the turtle left the monkey watching over the oyster.

Seeing the turtle disappear behind a rock, the monkey could wait no longer and stuck both hands into the oyster shell. He tore at the meat, but it was in vain because in a second the shell closed tightly and caught both of his hands. The monkey almost cried out, but fortunately, he did not lose his senses. Instead, he said, "I'm really luckier than all the other animals because I've found this good place for my urinal." When the oyster shell heard the monkey, it quickly opened its shell up and the monkey jumped away saying, "Good-bye, my friend. Give my regards to the kind-hearted turtle. Tell him that I want to borrow his *destar*."[1]

---

1. *Destar*—Javanese head covering. The monkey mockingly refers to the turtle's bandage as the head covering worn by Javanese men.

5. The Monkey and the Turtle
(3)

After the monkey had freed himself from the grip of the oyster, he began to plan his revenge. Every day he went to the beach and spied on the turtle. Nearly every morning he saw the turtle sunning himself on top of an *upih pinang*.[2] When the sun got higher and the weather hotter, the turtle would then go back into the sea.

One afternoon, after the turtle had returned to the sea, the monkey got a rope, tied it to the upih pinang, and hid one of its ends in some bushes. Early the next morning the monkey returned and hid in the same bushes. Not long after that, the turtle came and climbed on top of the upih pinang and at the same time stretched his body several times.

A cool sea wind blew and the sky grew cloudy causing the weather to cool down. As a result, the turtle fell asleep on top of the upih pinang. Seeing his opportunity, the monkey crept out of the bushes and carefully pulled the upih pinang into the forest. With the upih pinang rocking gently like a cradle, the turtle only slept more soundly.

Not long after that, the turtle was awakened by pains in his body as he was pulled over rocky and bumpy ground. When he saw himself in such a dangerous situation, he was desperate and almost cried out for help. But seeing how far away he was from the sea, he remained silent and looked for a way to escape.

Every time the monkey turned around, the turtle pretended to be sleeping. Frequently the monkey would check to see if the turtle was still living. He would put his ear to the turtle's nose or carefully touch his stomach. When he was sure the turtle was still alive, the monkey would start pulling again very carefully.

Not long afterwards, several other monkeys came up and asked, "What are you pulling?"

"I'm taking this sleeping turtle to my place and tonight my family and I are going to have a feast."

"That's fine, but how are you going to carry that turtle over the small bridge near your place?" asked a young monkey. "Isn't it impossible to pull him over that bridge? It would be good if we helped you and carried him on our shoulders--as long as you don't forget about us."

"Good," replied the monkey, and he began asking his friends to help pull.

When they reached the small bridge, one of the monkeys said, "Let's put the upih pinang on our shoulders. But be careful! Lift it slowly so the turtle doesn't wake up. If he moves even a little bit, we'll fall into the river for sure."

The turtle laughed silently to himself when he heard what the monkeys said. As soon as he saw the monkeys getting ready to put him on their shoulders, he shut his eyes and pretended to be sleeping soundly.

---

2. *Upih pinang*--a large piece of bark from the areca palm.

Carefully, the monkeys began to carry the turtle over the bridge. When he knew they were moving with great difficulty over the bridge, the turtle began to struggle and move about, causing several of the monkeys to fall into the river, together with him and the upih pinang. In the water, the turtle turned to his "friend" trying to swim and said, "Good afternoon, my friend. How are you today?" The monkey did not say a word and continued to swim towards the bank. When he received no answer, the turtle said, "Have a good swim, my friend. I thank you with all my heart because you so willingly brought me on this excursion. Now it's time for me to go back. Until we meet again." And with that, the turtle swam towards the sea.

They fell into the river

6. How a Boy Turned into a Monkey

Once upon a time a grandmother lived on the edge of a forest with her grandchild. The old woman was a weaver, and every day she went to someone's field and helped to pick cotton. In the afternoon she went home with the cotton the owner of the field had given her for her work. At night she ginned the cotton, spun it, and then wove it into cloth which she sold to buy food for her grandchild and herself.

One afternoon when the old lady was deep in thought spinning thread, her grandchild came up whining and begging for something to eat. Quickly the old woman got up and went to the kitchen. Not long afterwards she came back carrying some rice in a coconut shell. She gave the rice to her grandchild, but he flung it to the floor furiously. Patiently, the grandmother picked the coconut shell up and went back to the kitchen to get some sugar. But even the sugar did not satisfy the child, and he threw it too onto the floor. As his crying got louder and louder, he grumbled and rolled around on the floor.

"What do you want?" asked the old woman.

"I want some fried corn."

"The corn is all gone," said the woman, continuing her work. But this did not stop the child; and his cries kept up and became even harder to stop.

When she no longer had any patience left to listen to the unending crying, the grandmother took the spinning wheel into the kitchen and spun her thread there. When he saw what the old woman had done, the grandchild got more and more angry and finally went into the kitchen where he whined and rolled on the floor.

Losing her patience again, the woman reached for a ladle and struck her grandchild on the head. Instantly, the child turned into a monkey and jumped on the roof of the hut calling out, "I don't like sugar and corn anymore. Now I only want fruit from the forest and water from the rock pools."

The old woman regretted what she had done and she tried to call her grandchild back with words of flattery, "Come here, my beloved grandchild. Here's some corn and sugar. Eat to your heart's content."

But the monkey quickly leaped into the forest and disappeared. And it is because of this story that the old people of Roti are forbidden to hit their children on the head with a ladle.

He jumped on the roof

7. How Boys Turned into Mice

Once upon a time there was an old woman who lived with her two grandchildren on the outskirts of a village. The woman was a weaver and she exchanged her woven goods for rice or corn to use as food. One day the old woman said to her two grandchildren, "I'm going to the sea to catch some fish today. You must stay at home and fix our meal. Take one grain of rice and boil it in one coconut shell of water." After telling her grandchildren what to do, the old woman left.

The two children began to light the fire to boil the rice, and while washing the cooking pot, the older brother said, "Grandma told us to boil one grain of rice to fill one cooking pot full of rice. That seems to me impossible to do with only a single grain of rice."

"Take as much as will fill up this coconut shell," replied his brother. "The cooking pot will be filled for sure and then we'll have a lot to eat."

"That's true," continued the older brother. "Maybe Grandma will catch a big fish today, so we'd better boil as much rice as possible."

The two of them took a coconut shell of rice and began to boil it. The longer it cooked, the more rice overflowed out of the cooking pot. Finally, it flowed through a ditch beside the hut into the river. Then the rice flowed into the sea, and in the wink of an eye one part of the sea was filled with piles of rice. When the old woman saw all of that rice, she knew what had happened at home. Immediately, she left; and when she got home, the old woman whipped the two grandchildren. Then she asked the eldest, "How many grains of rice did you boil?"

"A lot, Grandma, a coconut shell full."

"Didn't I tell you to boil only one grain?"

"He told me to boil a coconut shell full," replied the older brother accusing his younger brother.

"No, Grandma. It wasn't me who told him to do that. He just took it!" contradicted the younger brother.

The old woman got madder and madder listening to the brothers accuse each other. Finally, she took a spindle and struck them on the head; and in an instant they turned into mice.

When the two grandchildren saw what had happened, they ran off and hid in a hole. The old woman cried and begged the two of them to come out of the hole; but the two children replied, "It's impossible. We're mice and we can't live with you anymore. Go home! Don't be sorry, but remember this: if your children and grandchildren make a mistake, don't hit them on the head with a spindle."

The two turned into mice

8. How the Cow Got Skin That Sags

The day was very hot and all the trees standing in the middle of the field were withered from the drought. Several cows and water buffaloes which had been contentedly eating grass ran into the shade at the edge of the forest, leaving only two or three horses still eating greedily.

"Wow, it's really hot today!" said a thin cow to an old water buffalo that was chewing its cud at the edge of the forest.

"You said it," replied the water buffalo. "This heat really tires me out, and what's more, my skin really gets scorched if I stand in the field too long."

"Let's take a bath so we don't get scorched," continued the cow starting to walk away.

"Taking a bath is really a lot of fun, but it's hard to find a good spot."

"I know a good place," replied the cow. "There's a river with fresh water over there behind the forest. I usually take a bath there after I've plowed the fields with my master."

"I'd rather go to a buffalo's watering hole," said the water buffalo. "The water's colder there because there's a lot of mud."

"I know you feel that way," replied the cow, "but since there isn't a watering hole near here, it's better if we go to the river. We can drink as much water as we want to."

"OK," answered the water buffalo lazily.

When they reached the river, the two of them took off their skins and jumped into the water. The water was cool, and the weather was no longer quite as hot because the sky had begun to cloud up. The two of them relaxed and played in the water, chewing their cud and talking without stopping. Then the clouds upstream turned black. Suddenly, while the two were deep in conversation, the river rose up and they had to scramble for their skins. In their haste the water buffalo accidentally took the cow's skin and the cow the water buffalo's. Looking for a safe place, the two friends got separated so that the cow no longer knew where his friend was.

Around the neck it felt very loose

When he reached a safe place, the cow realized that he had taken his friend's skin by mistake. The skin was so large that when it hung on his thin body it looked as though it were empty. Around the neck it felt very loose. Feeling his neck, the cow knew there was extra skin hanging because the skin from around the neck of his friend was too big for him.

It was the same for the water buffalo. When he reached a safe place, he felt how tight his skin was; and then he, too, realized that he had taken his friend's skin.

And it is because of this mistake that we see cows' skin sag.

9. Why Crows Have Black Feathers

Once upon a time before crows had become fugitives, their feathers were as white as snow. Unfortunately, of all the birds it was the crow that was regarded as the most harmful. It was almost always the sparrows and the magpies that cried because their children had been kidnapped by the crows. And children of pigeons and thrushes were as often eaten by the crows. Even though the mother birds tried to fight them off, the crows still weren't discouraged from kidnapping the newly hatched baby birds.

Fighting well with their large strong beaks, the crows easily defeated their enemies. Many mother pigeons sacrificed themselves, many were seriously wounded, and the others could only surrender. So the crows remained the rulers of the wilderness.

One day in a discussion, the pigeons, the thrushes, the magpies, and the sparrows all agreed that this matter had to be brought before the king of the birds. An old eagle, acting as king at that time, ordered several other eagles to catch all crows big and small. All the captured crows were then killed, so that soon almost all of the crows in the land were destroyed.

Only a single pair of young crows remained, and with heavy hearts they took shelter in a hole in a banyan tree. With fear and loneliness, the two of them discussed ways to save themselves from the dreadful eagles. One night the male said, "Next to a village not far from here, I saw a man boiling some indigo in two cooking pots. Don't you think it would be a good idea if we went over there and made our feathers black?"

"Yes! Is it really possible for us to disguise ourselves?" replied the female.

"Of course it is, and I intend to do just that. If we're disguised, it won't be easy to recognize us."

"Good, good," cried the female. "Tomorrow we'll go."

The next morning the two crows went to where the man was making indigo. They jumped into the pot and dyed their feathers. When their feathers had turned black, the two of them got out and dried themselves off on a turi tree. Several eagles passed the tree, but not one of them knew that the black birds perched on the branch were the fugitive crows. Smiling, the female said, "Your idea was really good!"

The male flapped his wings arrogantly and said, "Without ideas, you'll become the enemy's corpse for sure."

"Yes, that's true, but I'm sorry that my white feathers have turned black," replied the female.

"Never mind the black color as long as you're safe," returned the male.

And from that time until now, the crow and its grandchildren have had black feathers.

10. The Magic Fishhook

Once there was a fisherman who went to the point of a cape every day; but from morning until afternoon not even one fish nibbled at his hook. Exhausted, he got up lazily and grumbled, "Unlucky hook, you're only suitable for firewood. I sweat all day, but I can't catch even one fish!"

"Oh, my master," cried the fishhook. "Don't be so quick to blame me. Examine yourself, lest you have any shortcomings."

"You dare to accuse me, fishhook? I don't have any shortcomings. I'm perfect. It's only you --- you're too lazy to catch any fish for me. You wait; I'll put you into my stove."

"Forgive me, my master. I've already asked lots of fish to stop for a second, but they always refuse."

"Why do they refuse?" asked the fisherman in a rage.

"They say that the bait you use doesn't give them any pleasure."

"What'll make them happy?"

"Baby wasps, my master."

"If that's so, I'll go look for some for them later."

"Forgive me, my master, but don't tire yourself looking for the wasps because as soon as I mentioned them, the fish swam away; and I don't know where they went."

"If that's the case, then it's certain you've lied to me. I'm going to burn you up."

Then the fishhook cried out, "Forgive me! Don't burn me! Take me home, and every day I'll give you as many fish as you need."

"Good," replied the fisherman. I'll make you keep your promise all the time. And in case you don't, I'll use you as firewood." Then he went home happily and put the hook by his bed.

In the morning the fisherman took a basket, went to the hook and said, "Let's go, fishhook. Give me enough fish to fill up this basket."

"First, my master, try to answer this question. Who on earth is able to command and then get everything he has asked for? No one except God can do that. Everyone has to sweat in order to get a mouthful of rice; and for that reason, it's impossible for me to give you a basketful of fish this morning."

When the fisherman heard the answer, he became furious. Taking the fishhook into the kitchen, he said, "You liar! Today you're finished. This is the second time you've lied to me. Now you're going to get your punishment. I'm going to burn you in my stove until you're nothing but ashes!"

"Don't tire yourself, my master. Don't you know that it's impossible for me to be harmed by the flames? Don't you know that I'm a magic fishhook?"

"Then I'll cut you to pieces with my adz."

"It'll be in vain, my master. I'm invulnerable."

"Then I'll shoot you!"

"Don't you realize what I've told you? I'm magic! Bullets can't hurt me."

"I'll take you to the river and drown you!"

Hearing those words, the fishhook cried out, "Please don't do that, my master. I'll die if you throw me into the water."

"No, there's no more time for you. Soon you'll be washed away in the river." Then the fisherman took the hook and threw it into the river.

Laughing, the fishhook called out, "Oh, stupid man! Why have you thrown me away? I could give you as much as you wanted if you'd only work without grumbling and complaining. Today I tested you by not giving you any fish, but all you could do was grumble and threaten to destroy me. If you had worked patiently and trusted in God, then I would have given you as many fish as you needed every day." With those words the fishhook disappeared at the bottom of the river and the fisherman went home empty-handed.

SECOND THOUGHTS ABOUT A HISTORY OF BATAVIA

Tony Day

In a beautiful "*catatan pinggir*" (marginal jotting), which is printed around the edges of a nineteenth-century Batavian residential scene, Goenawan Mohamad thinks about what it means to be an "orang Jakarta."[1] One night, he writes, he meets a friend outside a Jakarta restaurant. "You know, we're foreigners here," the friend says. "Visitors. We peddle everything in this town: things, bodies, integrity as well. Afterwards we feel like going home." Left alone, Goenawan thinks about going "home," to where he lives in the city, to his birthplace in the countryside for Lebaran. The nagging question is: why come back? Jakarta asks neither affection nor commitment. Those who work in the city day after day for their mouthful of rice return to their homes exhausted but unassimilated. Jakartans are people "who suffer from the nausea of a traveler who hasn't cast anchor: someone who has turned his back on his origins yet fails to form an attachment to a new home." As he tries to characterize his city, Goenawan feels caught in a rip tide, pulled in one direction by urbanization only to be swept away in another by "ruralisasi," as a flood of rural migrants pour into the city with their babies, corpses, superstitions, their lack of freedom, so that the city is carried back out into the *udik*, the backcountry. What power does Jakarta have to resist such retrogression? "The wall which Jan Pieterzoon Coen built in the style of Amsterdam has fallen. But it wasn't destroyed by an assault from Mataram. It was destroyed by something else even more powerful: the overwhelming reality of the fact that a city in Indonesia cannot stand on its own. It was encircled and finally mastered by economic and political forces all around it." This sensation of being at the mercy of impersonal, world-historical forces leads to a recognition of the difference between Jakarta and the cities of Europe, those "sources of freedom and modernity" which turned fleeing, half-enslaved peasants into free citizens and protected them against the incursions of the udik, where the feudal castles of the territorial state lay. Batavia's Castle has fallen, but where are the city's protective walls, where are its citizens? "'Cities, like dreams,'" Goenawan concludes, quoting from Italo Calvino's *Invisible Cities*, "'are made of desires and fears.' . . . Then I remembered my friend: his are perhaps other desires, other fears, which will keep him from wanting to help make Jakarta a reality."

The reality of Jakarta's desires and fears, of a city "the thread of whose discourse is secret, its rules absurd, its perspectives deceitful," where

---

1. Goenawan Mohamad, "Kota" [City], *Tempo*, June 23, 1984, p. 23. A collection of these popular weekly essays, written by Goenawan for *Tempo* between 1976 and 1981, can be found in Goenawan Mohamad, *Catatan Pinggir* (Jakarta: Grafiti Pers, 1982).

"everything conceals something else,"[2] is what matters to Goenawan Mohamad and his friend. They are part of the urban "plural society," held together in language by the inclusive Indonesian pronoun "*kita*," to which the essay is addressed.[3] We (*kami*) non-Indonesian historians of Indonesia are rather like Calvino's Kublai Khan, who has never seen the invisible cities of his Asian empire but only knows about them through the tales of the traveler Marco Polo, who confesses that he is really only ever describing one city, Venice. If we pretend to make Goenawan Mohamad our Marco Polo his Jakarta will only become doubly invisible. The city which he describes is one which we cannot ever see or dream about, from within as he does. And we are only pretending to listen to his tale. Our Jakarta is like the reproduction of van de Velde's 1840s lithograph in Goenawan's essay,[4] his a marginal jotting around its edges.

Even if an encounter with the exclusiveness of Goenawan's language, his "kita," makes us feel superfluous, even if we are troubled by the enormity of the challenge his essay presents, to write a history of *his* Jakarta, we are still likely to take heart from the dictum enunciated more than twenty years ago by John Smail: "There is no philosophically absolute barrier to prevent a Western historian (or a modern Asian historian) from achieving a valid Asia-centric perspective."[5] This belief is an article of faith with most of us. It is one which has inspired Jean Taylor in her recent book, *The Social World of Batavia*,[6] and has put her as much at ease with her subject as the top-hatted Dutchman appears to be with his as he converses in front of his colonial *dalem* with a pigtailed Chinaman, in van de Velde's lithograph.

Without that confident faith in the possibility of "a valid Asia-centric perspective" we would not have Taylor's study, the first book-length social history of an Indonesian city to be published in English, one of a handful in any language which deals in an accomplished manner with the urban or social history of Southeast Asia in any respect. But to dwell on Taylor's scholarship, clarity, and wit would be to participate in, rather than critically examine, the Western historical discourse about Indonesia which her book reproduces. Imagine for a moment that Taylor's history is to be substituted for van de Velde's lithograph, inset within and juxtaposed to Goenawan's Indonesian text. Among other things such a juxtaposition of discourses and "perspectives" would raise the question: What is the nature of the historical language and form which Taylor has inherited, via Smail, from the Dutch economic historian J. C. van

---

2. Italo Calvino, *Invisible Cities* (London: Picador, 1979), p. 36.

3. Goenawan's essay recalls the following passage from J. S. Furnivall, *Colonial Policy and Practice* (New York: New York University Press, 1956), p. 304: "In Burma, as in Java, probably the first thing that strikes the visitor is the medley of peoples--European, Chinese, Indian and native. It is in the strictest sense a medley, for they mix but they do not combine. . . . As individuals they meet, but only in the market-place, in buying and selling."

4. A larger copy of the same print is given as plate 34 in Bea Brommer, *Reizend door Oost-Indië* [Traveling through the East Indies] (Utrecht/Amsterdam: Spectrum, 1979), p. 41.

5. John Smail, "On the Possibility of an Autonomous History of Modern Southeast Asia," *Journal of Southeast Asian History* 2, 2 (July 1961): p. 75.

6. Jean Gelman Taylor, *The Social World of Batavia: European and Eurasian in Dutch Asia* (Madison and London: University of Wisconsin Press, 1983).

Leur? It is this metahistorical query which I want to give some thought to as a way of stating what I have found most stimulating about Taylor's book.

"Perspective," of course (along with "moral viewpoint," "-centric," "angle of vision," and "objective correlative"), is *the* key term in the historical discourse which Smail inherited from van Leur. One might be tempted to say at the outset that this word entrenches the very problematic which it seeks to uproot, that of the exteriority of the Western observer to the object of his or her historical vision (unlike the more phenomenological word "perception"; yet how many of the historiographical essays in *Perceptions of the Past in Southeast Asia*[7] are perspectives rather than perceptions?). Smail's terminology of vision arises from a central metaphor of near blindness in the texts of J. C. van Leur,[8] who revolutionized the writing of Indonesian history in the late 1930s, shortly before his death: that of a Western observer, standing on the deck of a ship, straining as if in a fog or failing light, to pick out the distinctly individual details of a scene on the "grey and undifferentiated" shores of an Asian island. To put it in the language of the metaphor, van Leur argued that, in order to get a good look at this island, the observer had to jump overboard and head for shore; he could be sure to be rescued and brought to land by an Asian peddler's boat.

I have taken liberties with van Leur's metaphorical coupling of the problem of historical perspective to the view of the Indies from the deck of a ship in order to keep the centrality of the metaphoricity of ships in van Leur's writing clearly in view. Real ships are of course everywhere in his text, and we may find it interesting to note that his only concession to European superiority in Asia before the twentieth century involves a recognition of the military edge held by Europeans because of their technology, including that of the ship.[9] This concession is curious, not because it is either true or false, but because it contradicts van Leur's faith in the "equality" of Asia and Europe. One may suspect that a powerful and tacit tropology is involved in making this contradiction explicit.

As a trope, van Leur's ship is not of one kind but two. On the one hand we have the peddling ship, whose movements in history are metaphors for the intellectual act of sailing out of the gray and undifferentiated fog of colonial historiography into the bright light of a multitudinous world of Southeast Asia, where each detail is autoluminous. Here is van Leur's brilliant summary of the chapter in "The World of Southeast Asia" in which that world is reconstituted, sparkling detail by sparkling detail:

> Countless markets, lying isolated from each other and varying greatly from one another in structure. A few hundred *bahar* of spices, a few thousand bags of pepper, a few hundred packs of cloth, a few dozen *corges* of porcelain, a few dozen picul of wood products on each market. An international trade of person-to-person haggling and retail sales with hand scales or *via* the town weigh-house or the government toll house, carried on in periods when trade

---

7. Anthony Reid and David Marr, eds., *Perceptions of the Past in Southeast Asia* (Singapore: Heineman Educational Books [Asia] Ltd., for the Asian Studies Association of Australia, 1979).

8. Collected in J. C. van Leur, *Indonesian Trade and Society: Essays in Asian Social and Economic History* (The Hague: van Hoeve, 1967).

9. Ibid., p. 189.

> was concentrated in the towns because of the favourable winds and harvests there. When the traders were gone and the money brought along had been put to use or spent, trade came to a standstill.[10]

Each word in this passage is autonomously specific. What links them in a syntax against the shadowy coherence of a Southeast Asian backdrop (in which towns are virtually invisible) is the imagined movement of the peddler and his ship. That movement is recreated as the reader's eye moves from one word to the next. It may be too ironic to suggest that the roving of the eye, wandering from one delightfully exotic fact to the next, retraces Marco Polo's travels. Is it possible that this historian of autonomous Southeast Asia is making us complicit, in the act of reading him, in the historic process which subverted that autonomy?

Van Leur nowhere explicitly states that the metaphorical deck which he urges us to abandon is located, not on a peddler's boat, but on a modern steamship. Yet the opening paragraphs of his 1934 dissertation, in which he sets forth his reasons for challenging the adequacy "of the western European view of history and its categories," imply the presence of the steamship as surely as the passage quoted above contains the sailboat:

> The age of modern capitalism has put us in a position in which we make use of knowledge of the whole world every day. Business and trade have spread a cobweb net over the earth. Industries find all parts of the world opened to them and forced on them as prospective markets. The big-banking system has brought the interests of the most widely distant lands, cities, and ports ... within the sphere of investment and speculation, which in turn has extended its interests to all levels of society. ... And, finally, the present political system of the great powers and the international organization of states mean a consistent *Weltpolitik* in the most colossal form ever seen.[11]

The words and apocalyptic tone of these sentences come straight out of Marx's *Manifesto of the Communist Party*, which van Leur called "that classical example of demagoguery," that "masterly pamphlet."[12] But here they introduce a thesis which defies the hegemonic character of world capitalism and sets out to disprove the intellectual cogency of Marxism for the historical study of Asia. Van Leur argues that the Marxist theory of historical development has imposed this hegemony on the earliest stages of world history, where the "Asian phases" have been placed. But Marx's Asia, van Leur says, "was only brought into the picture as a vague, shadowy concept. His consideration of actual historical processes begins only with the civilizations of the Mediterranean.... The 'course of progress in world history,' then, is based upon the actual preponderance of modern capitalism...."[13]

It is becoming clear that the source of what is gray and undifferentiated about the Indies for van Leur is nothing other than capitalism itself and its intellectual categories, which, standing between the historian and the

---

10. Ibid., p. 219.
11. Ibid., p. 9.
12. Ibid., p. 11.
13. Ibid., p. 13.

differentiated luminousness of Asia, throw the latter into a vague, shadowy penumbra. But it is because capitalism itself, rather than simply Marxism, is the source of darkness for van Leur that he excludes it from the world of Southeast Asia. Its absence is his enabling historical fiction. We see in the following passage, which is important for my discussion of Taylor below, an example of the reasoning which flows from van Leur's pen when he can pretend that capitalism did not exist in eighteenth-century Java. "Is the *milieu* of the Indies in the eighteenth century a reflection of the European world of the *ancien régime*?" he asks:

> It seems to me not. In the eighteenth century, along with the strengthening of the Company's control on Java, came the establishment of a colonial European society. It was a Dutch society only to a limited extent, because of the large number of foreigners and of the stronger, older Portuguese element in the culture of the lower groups, but above everything else because of its character, interlaced to a large extent with fragments of Oriental folkways and social forms. Thus had developed the opulent life of the higher classes in the Indies, with their retinue of slaves and serfs--a life linked to that of the Javanese nobility more than to any other. On the other hand the officials in the lower ranks of the European administration followed a *kampong* way of life, in the cities living side by side with Orientals, Indonesian and Chinese. There was no antithesis Eastern-Western; there was only the antithesis higher classes--lower classes. . . . The seigneurial rule of the Company in close alliance with the princes and lords of Java did not contain any seeds of unrest or disintegration.[14]

In this passage we meet the same illuminating fragmentation and heterogeneity of distinct entities which is characteristic of van Leur's picture of the Southeast Asian peddling world. This benign fragmentation exists both because capitalism has been excluded and in order to prove its absence. If the seigneurial rule of the Eastern-Western elite had been capitalist in character, then it would have given rise not to social distinction but to social disintegration, like that of the *ancien régime*. Not even the antithesis of higher to lower classes can stir revolution in precapitalist eighteenth-century Java.

I disagree with John Smail's reason for thinking that van Leur might never have written "autonomous" historical studies of the Indies in the nineteenth and twentieth centuries, but not with the thought itself.[15] Van Leur could only write the history of a period where capitalism could be said not to exist. When he was faced with a period where he knew it did, or when a historical term or category gave off capitalist-Marxist overtones, he was disparaging. Of the "contemporary part" of colonial history he wrote: "It has been the subject of all sorts of ideological and political interest; De Kat Angelino as well as Sutomo and Sukarno have used it as such. But it has hardly been the subject of real historical research at all. . . ."[16] Or when he encountered Krom's characterization of early Hindu Brahmans as "spiritual advisers," he was forced to remark: "If one overlooks the terminology, which rather leads one to think of confessional labour unions, the concept serves to indicate

---

14. Ibid., pp. 285-86.

15. See Smail, "On the Possibility," p. 84.

16. Van Leur, *Indonesian Trade*, p. 148.

the autonomous rôle of the Brahman priesthood. . . ."[17] These citations suggest that van Leur's concept of autonomy may have been linked to an antipathy to the actual political movements agitating for autonomy in the Indies of his day. It is also not surprising that in the years before his tragic death in the Battle of the Java Sea, his institutional efforts involved setting up a historical section in the Royal Batavian Society of Arts and Sciences, the bastion of classical "Asian" studies in the Indies.[18] At its deepest level, van Leur's historical project was to retreat to a world where, to borrow in ironic fashion the words Marx used to describe the effect of the bourgeois revolution on the means of production, "all that is solid" did not "melt into air," or turn into gray and undifferentiated fog.[19]

If van Leur was in flight from capitalism, jumping from one kind of ship to another, it was always on his mind. We have looked at his consciousness of it in terms of metaphor and of the content of his history. Are there other aspects of his style where it may have found expression? The sources and theoretical underpinnings for van Leur's writing are fully displayed in the notes to the "On Methodology and Theory" section of his dissertation, but I cannot now say how useful it would be to study all of these in depth. There is one reference, however, which intrigued me, for reasons which will soon be apparent. In a note to a sentence about the possibility of comparing the Byzantine to the European Middle Ages, van Leur suggests that Jacob Burckhardt's model of "Renaissance types and patterns" might prove applicable to "the East of an earlier time."[20] Van Leur mentions Burckhardt several times in his annotations, and clearly he found him congenial. This apparently fortuitous connection between the two historians has made me pay attention to what the intellectual historian, Hayden White, has written about Burckhardt's historical style:

> Burckhardt was a Contextualist; he suggested that historians "explain" a given event by inserting it into the rich fabric of the similarly discriminable individualities that occupy its circumambient historical space. He denied both the possibility of deriving laws from the study of history and the desirability of submitting it to typological analysis. For him, a given area of historical occurrence represented a field of happening which was more or less rich in the brilliance of its "fabric" and more or less susceptible to impressionistic representation. His *Civilization of the Renaissance*, for example, is conventionally regarded as having no "story" or "narrative line" at all. Actually, the narrative mode in which it was cast is that of the Satire, the *satura* (or "medley"), which is the fictional mode of Irony and which achieves some of its principal effects by refusing to provide the kinds of formal coherencies one is conditioned to expect from reading Romance, Comedy, and

---

17. Ibid., p. 257.

18. See ibid., p. 257.

19. The sentence "All that is solid melts into air: comes from the *Manifesto of the Communist Party*. See *The Marx-Engels Reader*, 2nd ed., Robert C. Tucker, ed. (New York and London: Norton, 1978), p. 476, and the stimulating discussion of the *Manifesto* by Marshall Berman, *All That Is Solid Melts into Air: The Experience of Modernity* (New York: Simon and Schuster, 1982), pp. 87-129.

20. Van Leur, *Indonesian Trade*, p. 299.

Tragedy. This narrative form, which is the aesthetic counterpart of a specifically skeptical conception of knowledge and its possibilities, presents itself as the type of all putatively anti-ideological conceptions of history and as an alternative to that "philosophy of history," practiced by Marx, Hegel, and Ranke alike, which Burckhardt personally despised.[21]

My point in presenting this long excerpt from White is not to claim too much of a metahistorical similarity between Burckhardt and van Leur but to table enough of White's terminology as it is actually deployed in analysis to make it comprehensible in my own discussion. Like Burckhardt, van Leur was opposed to Marxist interpretations of history, and I have already noted his desire to discriminate individualities. It is also the case that, although he read and admired Weber and Werner Sombart and yearned to find typologies for Asia, van Leur never achieved that kind of formal coherence in his writing. The cycle of monsoons and the crisscrossing pattern of the peddlers' ships are the only forms of coherence in his history. Indeed, if we read through "The World of Southeast Asia," which is a "rich fabric" in the manner of what White would call the satiric mode, we can pick up a tone which may be ironic.[22] Notice, for example, how in the following citations political power and ideology, emanations of capitalism which have no place in van Leur's Southeast Asia, are carefully exorcised by being made to seem absurdly insignificant or exaggerated (the italics are mine):

> Hindu-Buddhism and Islam "were only a *thin, easily flaking glaze* on the *massive* body of indigenous civilization."[23]

> "In Indonesia the *nominal* power the Javanese state Majapahit had exercised . . . was *repulsed*. . . ."[24]

> "The choice fell on Jakarta, as being the place . . . where the Indonesian adversary was *weakest*, a nobleman ruling over a *small coastal town without much trade* and a *small* hinterland. . . ."[25]

> "The power of the Dutch . . . did not constitute any political preponderance in the archipelago. The *might* of the Javanese and the Achinese was *still too unshaken* for that."[26]

Something is going on here which has nothing to do with establishing an "equality" between Europe and Asia. Van Leur is satirizing political power and ideological pretension wherever he finds them. I also think there is irony at work in these sentences because of an undertone of what Northrop Frye, whose *Anatomy of Criticism* is White's principal source for his analysis

---

21. Hayden White, *Metahistory: The Historical Imagination in Nineteenth-Century Europe* (Baltimore and London: The Johns Hopkins University Press, 1973), p. 28.

22. "The aim of the Ironic statement," White writes, "is to affirm tacitly the negative of what is on the literal level affirmed positively, or the reverse." Ibid., p. 37.

23. Van Leur, *Indonesian Trade*, p. 169.

24. Ibid., p. 172.

25. Ibid., pp. 181-82.

26. Ibid., p. 188.

of modes of historical writing, might call "puzzled defeat,"[27] as if van Leur is characterizing historical situations in a way he knows to be false in the long run. If the Europeans are so weak, why do they eventually triumph? If Mataram and Aceh are so mighty, why do they collapse in defeat? If Islam is so flaky, why does it stick? Historians who read van Leur tend to take sentences like the ones I have quoted above as statements somehow empirically arrived at rather than as strategic rhetorical assertions emplotted in a historical fiction of a certain type. Read as satire, van Leur's peddling world of Southeast Asia almost becomes a "fairyland of little people" in what Frye would call a "satire of the high norm,"[28] a parody, that is, of the "heroic" world of kings and capitalists. In a note to the last sentence cited above, van Leur quotes a remark made by Jan Pieterzoon Coen in a letter to the governing body of the VOC, dated January 14, 1619, in which he compared the political ambitions of Aceh and Mataram to those of the King of Spain in Europe. What a richly ironic aside for van Leur the historian to make, given the fact of the tiny Netherlands' decisive victory over Spain at the end of the sixteenth century, the significance of the date 1619 in the history of the Indies and the implicit ("*still* too unshaken") shattered continuity of Javanese and Acehnese power as seen from the perspective of Batavia in 1940! The essential source of satiric irony in van Leur is that, in refusing to admit capitalism into Southeast Asia and in failing to invent a typology of historical stages (his notion of "closed continuity" being a stageless nontypology designed to exclude capitalism for as long as possible), van Leur had no way of explaining how to get historically from Jakarta, that "small coastal town without much trade," to the world-capitalist Batavia of his own era. Van Leur's history does not really contain any cities, and he merely hazards the opinion, in a footnote, that "an analysis of the types of towns in early Indonesia would provide valuable material for the calculation of the possibilities for social and economic development in the course of history."[29] As often as he expressed the desire to talk about indigenous Southeast Asian "types" and to construct a non-Marxist developmental typology he never did. It is an irony which we can enjoy that another satiric historian, Fernand Braudel, who has turned van Leur's peddling Asian world into a world-economy of its own in the seventeenth century, enunciates as his "second rule" of capitalist world economies: "A world economy always possesses an urban pole, a city as the logistical center of its affairs."[30] But van Leur's economic world did not need an urban pole because it was not capitalist.

"When the traders were gone and the money brought along had been put to use or spent, trade came to a standstill." Like Burckhardt's vivid evocations, van Leur's end on a "melancholy note,"[31] an ironic sign of resignation to the impossibility of "every effort to capture adequately the truth of things

---

27. Northrop Frye, *Anatomy of Criticism: Four Essays* (New York: Atheneum, 1967), p. 224.

28. Ibid., p. 235.

29. Van Leur, *Indonesian Trade*, p. 403.

30. Fernand Braudel, *Le Temps du Monde* (Paris: Armand Colin, 1979), p. 17. For a discussion of Braudel's satiric style, see Hans Kellner, "Disorderly Conduct: Braudel's Mediterranean Satire," *History and Theory* 18, 2 (1979): 197-222.

31. White, *Metahistory*, p. 245.

in language,"³² of writing a history of Southeast Asia that was something other than brilliantly, incoherently, evanescently autonomous.

My excuse for writing at some length about how van Leur wrote history is that reading Goenawan Mohamad's words about the "City" made me self-conscious about what I myself am doing here at 11:01 p.m. in Sydney writing a review essay of Jean Taylor's *The Social World of Batavia*. The exercise is helping me to understand the "perspective" of non-Indonesian historians on the history of a place which is only minimally less invisible than the cities of Calvino's novel. Writing about writing Indonesian history has two reasonable objectives. One is to explain to ourselves and to Indonesians like Goenawan Mohamad not *his* history but, without revealing everything to him or to ourselves, something of what we are doing trying to write his history. The other is that, through the application of interpretive methodologies, such as Hayden White's or Northrop Frye's (the list could be a longer one), to the analysis of what has already been written, we can formulate strategies about how and what to write. For if by discovering the metaphors and mode by which van Leur evaded the issue of historic capitalism in Southeast Asia, we can show precisely what he did not say, we can also talk positively about the kinds of topics, the sorts of evidence and thematic emphases which ironic satire is likely to generate. Van Leur's satire thus becomes a guide to what else to look for as well as a model for how to write history in the same mode.

Thus it is that I take the opportunity to say something about Jean Taylor's book, in order to examine van Leur's legacy in the work of a non-Indonesian historian who has studied him, and in order to look beyond that legacy. I am particularly interested in the uses of his faint, and possibly unintended, irony. It is hard to avoid this trope: Taylor returns us to the heart, the ironically invisible capital, of van Leur's problematic.

Taylor invokes the "tempering" perspective of van Leur in the introduction to her book because her aim is to examine "the nature of Dutch society in Indonesia." Reading van Leur has made her anxious to avoid the charge that she is writing "colonial" history, but she intends to give her study of the members of the Batavian European male elite a van Leurian twist, for what will make them significant in a van Leurian sense are their marriages to Asia-born women. "In this book," she writes, "I have taken these family relationships as an organizing center for my study of Dutch colonial society.... My return to the governors-general ... serves to inject into the story of the Dutch overseas the role of Asians in shaping colonial culture."³³

In the opening pages, therefore, Taylor sets the stage for a van Leurian study, but one which could possibly contest his authority. Like van Leur, Taylor will seek to describe the "equality" between Europe and Asia in the Indies until the middle of the nineteenth century. Taylor will follow van Leur as well in setting out, in lively fashion, a rich heterogeneity of facts, which she takes from a miscellany of historical sources. Nor is her book about "Batavia" as such, as little a social history of a Southeast Asian city as van Leur's is an economic one. Yet she has shifted the focus from "little people" to the "high norm," while her promise to talk about women raises the possibility that male norms may be subjected to a feminist critique. At least

---

32. Ibid., p. 37.

33. Taylor, *Social World*, p. xviii.

potentially, van Leur's tacit irony about power and ideology has been given a chance to become an explicit social force within history itself.

Although Taylor's style has something in common with van Leurian satire it is not ironic, her command of the heterogeneity of her sources and their content perhaps still too self-conscious of its origins in the display of learning required for a Ph.D. to become performatively satirical. And where van Leur is actively unconscious of historical capitalism in Southeast Asia, Taylor seems merely indifferent. But the absence of ironic satire is also predictable, as a lost but not irrecoverable modal possibility involved in the shift of focus away from the inherently dispersed and satirizable little world of the peddler to that of a self-Asianizing elite.

Taylor's mode of historical employment is not satire but comedy, the form of fiction in which, as White puts it, "hope is held out for the temporary triumph of man over his world by the prospect of occasional *reconciliations* of the forces at play in the social and natural world."[34] In Chapter One, "Origins of the City of Batavia," Taylor opens her history of the "marriage" of Europe to Asia with an account of the early years of the Batavia settlement. We learn about the VOC hierarchy and the major factors controlling access to its top posts in the early seventeenth century: pure Netherlands descent, European birth, and adherence to the Reformed Church. Housed in their Castle, sealed off defensively from the immediate social environment of West Java even as they plotted their economic offensive in maritime Asia, the male rulers of Batavia controlled all matters of religion and civil life. They also enacted laws, which originated as directives from the Netherlands, to curtail migration of women from the Fatherland and to prevent the repatriation of European men married to Asian or part-Asian women. This civil, sexual, religious, and economic tyranny is comically emplotted as the complex of "parental" and legal obstacles erected by the "old" European order in order to block the transition in Asia "from a society controlled by habit, ritual bondage, arbitrary law and . . . older characters to a society controlled by youth and pragmatic freedom."[35] It is the pragmatic freedom of the households and social style of Batavia's mestizo women which is the ultimate goal of this transition in Taylor's comedy, the "reality" of their adaptation to Asian conditions as opposed to the "illusoriness" of the European male order which it celebrates.

The signs of this comic transition are already there in the early seventeenth century. Soldiers and lower-ranking VOC officials have already gone native and taken Asian wives or mistresses. Their ethnic heterogeneity does not lend itself to satirizing by Taylor or to ironic comment on their indefinable "Europeanness," but serves instead to explain why the institutions and language of the Netherlands failed to take root in Asian Batavia. The new order has clearly emerged by the 1640s, when "the first complaints about the character and style of living of Batavian ladies came from the VOC directors,"[36] and when the Governors-General and their mestizo wives began to affect an "Asian" style of pomp and ceremony. Asianization has now reached the top of the social hierarchy and overthrown its cultural authority. In her second chapter, "Growth of Settlement Society," Taylor says very little about growth because her plot has already reached its essential modal denouement. The horrified commentary

---

34. White, *Metahistory*, p. 9.
35. Frye, *Anatomy*, p. 169.
36. Taylor, *Social World*, p. 36.

by European visitors to Batavia, which Taylor quotes entertainingly, no longer has the force of law. It serves instead to document the triumph of the new order.

That triumph is elaborated upon in Chapter Three, where Taylor sketches the country life of the Asianized elite on their estates, "built beyond the Castle's walls," and standing in comic opposition to it. Batavia itself, as seen through the words of one of her eighteenth-century poets, Jan de Marre, has become a comic Saturnalia, "a reversal of social standards which recalls a golden age . . .":[37]

> O lovely Batavia, that holds me spellbound,
> There your Town Hall with its proudly arching vaults
> Rears its profile! How splendid is your situation!
> Your broad Canals, replenished with fresh water, beautifully planted,
> Need bend before no city in the Netherlands. . . .[38]

Taylor uses this citation tropologically, its ideal Batavia being a synecdoche for mestizo society. In terms of this tropology its does not matter that the Town Hall in Batavia was never the heart of its civic life which, such as it was, was controlled by the Castle, nor that the canals were full of rotting animal corpses and pestilence, an epidemic having broken out in 1732, eight years before the publication of de Marre's poem, when the canals were redug by the uneuphemistically named "mud Javanese." Taylor's tropology also does not invite ironic second thoughts about the timing of the publication of de Marre's *Batavia* in 1740, the year of the massacre of Chinese which led to the destruction of Kartasura, or about what it itself celebrates, the old-order glory of the city as a *Waereldstad* (World City). As we have seen in the case of van Leur, tropes and modes lead to both blindness and insight.

The first four chapters of Taylor's book, based entirely on Dutch sources and tracing the comic growth of Batavia's mestizo world, can be read as a companion piece to M. C. Ricklefs' *Jogjakarta under Sultan Mangkubumi*, another comic history of an Indies society which achieves "autonomy" in the eighteenth century.[39] Working his effects through Javanese as well as Dutch-language materials, Ricklefs is more uproarious and satirical in his ridicule of the old order of Netherlanders, outwitted by the *dolosus servus*[40] of Yogyakarta, Sultan Mangkubumi. In Taylor's Chapter Four, "The Assault on Indies Culture," we also meet the *senex iratus*[41] of Central Java in the 1740s, Baron van Imhoff, whose pleasure retreat at Buitenzorg (not "Carefree," but "Beyond care," for the weekend) was modeled on the Duke of Marlborough's Blenheim and would become, at the beginning of the nineteenth century, the official residence of the Governors-General. Taylor's treatment of the assault on mestizo culture, first by the Enlightened ideas of van Imhoff, then by the reforms of Daendels

---

37. Frye, *Anatomy*, p. 171.

38. Taylor, *Social World*, p. 52. For a longer selection from de Marre's poem, which suggests the possibility of another reading to the one Taylor gives of this excerpt, see E. du Perron, *De Muze van Jan Companjie* [The Muse of Jan Company] (Bandung: Nix, 1948), pp. 153-62.

39. M. C. Ricklefs, *Jogjakarta under Sultan Mangkubumi, 1749-1792: A History of the Division of Java* (London: Oxford University Press, 1974).

40. See Frye, *Anatomy*, p. 173.

41. See ibid., p. 172.

and Raffles, and finally by the resurgence of the old order under the restoration of Dutch rule in 1819, does not abandon the comic mode of emplotment which she sustains with great consistency throughout her book. For Taylor chronicles, not the tragic undoing of mestizo society, but its comic withdrawal into what Frye calls the "secret and sheltered places"[42] of individual experience and consciousness. In Chapter Six, "The Inner Life of Late Colonial Society," she discusses the vicissitudes of Asianness in the novels of Java's nineteenth-century Dutch-language women writers.

I have the sense from reading Frye on comedy and Taylor on Batavia that her history is not one comedy, but a sequence of them, and perhaps the phases of this sequence would become more distinct and distinctly dramatic if she were to rewrite her book with the nature of its narrative mode in mind. But there is another sense in which Taylor's history seems too long, to go beyond a point in the narrative at which it comes up against the limits of its own form, where all the suppressed possibilities it also contains reveal themselves. For me this moment comes in the "Epilogue," which occupies the same relationship to the rest of the book as van Leur's essay "On the Eighteenth Century as a Category of Indonesian History" does to his earlier work. The opening lines of the chapter are the point:

> To recount in detail the final dissolution of Mestizo culture and of colonial society as a whole entails quite a different study from this one, which has focused on the Dutch of Indonesia as a distinct community with values and folk-ways of its own. It requires an examination of the Asian communities of the archipelago on their own terms....[43]

In the Epilogue Taylor comes up against Raden Ajeng Kartini and the "contemporary part" of colonial history the way van Leur crashes into the unthinkable dimension of his "world of Southeast Asia" when he has to explain how the batik of Kartasura or the mythologies of Ronggawarsita represent the equality of the Asian to the European Indies in the eighteenth and nineteenth centuries.[44] Kartini embodies the history of mestizo women Taylor has precisely not written: that of a woman who defied the patriarchal hegemony of her class and colonial masters, whose "mestizo"-ness was expressed by her exquisitely intelligent and multilingual consciousness of her subordination, not by betel chewing and *kabaya*. I am suggesting that Kartini's "history" is too nearly "tragic" in a Furnivallian sense to be ever possible in the comic mode.[45] To the extent that Taylor's narrative leads up to her, and her material provides excellent documentation of the seventeenth- and eighteenth-century origins of Furnivall's "plural society," its mode is put radically in question.

Frye conceives of comedy as occupying a modal space between irony and romance, and his phases of comedy move from the boundaries of one to the other. The form of a romance is a quest. Its characters, arranged "like black and white pieces in a chess game," are either for or against the quest, which

---

42. Ibid., p. 185.

43. Taylor, *Social World*, p. 159.

44. See van Leur, *Indonesian Trade*, pp. 278-79.

45. Cf. Furnivall's despairing vision of degenerate European culture and "feverish" Indonesian nationalism in the Indies in *Netherlands India: A Study of Plural Economy* (Cambridge: Cambridge University Press, 1944), pp. 458-59.

ends with the redemption of society with "the triumph of good over evil."[46] One way Taylor's study could be rewritten to include Kartini would involve thinking about the possibilities of a "nationalist" history in the romantic mode. But I am more interested in the other mode which borders comedy, the one which Taylor shares with van Leur.

The possibility of an ironic rewriting of Taylor's book is already latent in it. It is found in the thematic shift from peddlers to princes, a move which could make van Leur's tacit, ironic recognition of the nexus between capitalism, political power, and ideology in Asia fully explicit. Ironic possibilities are also implicit in Taylor's attempt to bring her project into line with van Leur's, by paying attention, not so much to the Governors-General, but to their wives. From here the historic trail leads, not only from Maria van Aelst to Kartini, but to other invisible dimensions of the female Indies world, to the slaves, for example, who raised the mixed-blood children of the Batavian elite, did their dirty work, and formed their "Asian" retinues. But the slaves of the Batavians also rebelled, and through the history of the Balinese slave Surapati the lines of historical causation run ironically but directly from the Batavian mestizo household to the kraton of Kartasura. The history of the rise of one is inextricably linked to the collapse of the other. The ironic potential of the theme of "mestizo"-ness is also enormous, for it embraces all aspects of racial and cultural relations, of economic, political, religious, and intellectual history, in the Indies. An ironist might reflect on the fact that in the nineteenth-century Philippines, the term mestizo was generally taken to designate a Catholic, Hispanized, entrepreneurial, land-owning Chinese-*Indio* mixed-blood whose culture was becoming distinctly "Filipino."[47] The history that would show why nineteenth-century Java did not have a José Rizal, but rather a Multatuli, a Dipanagara, a Charles te Mechelen, a Sadrach, and a Ho Yam Lo would be ironic indeed.

Such a history would lead us back to the early years of the seventeenth century and the founding of Batavia. It could show, through a rereading of the evidence Taylor presents, just how ironically revealing van Leur's claim about Batavian society in the eighteenth century can become: "There was no antithesis Eastern-Western; there was only the antithesis higher classes-lower classes," he wrote. The fact of the matter is that, as Taylor's material shows, although her comic vision prevents her from interpreting it as such, the antithesis Western-Eastern was hierarchically embedded in the antithesis higher classes-lower classes. Opposed, too, on a scale from higher to lower was the antithesis male-female. This last observation says nothing about how women responded to their subordination, but the history of that response has yet to be written, in any mode.

Fernand Braudel has said that "the real fate of capitalism was determined by its encounter with social hierarchies."[48] Whatever the case may have been before, the fate of Indonesia after 1619 is bound up with the history of how capitalism, interacting with and through the social hierarchy of Batavia, encountered the other social hierarchies of the archipelago. (That history

---

46. See White, *Metahistory*, p. 9, and Frye, *Anatomy*, pp. 186-206.

47. See Edgar Wickberg, *The Chinese in Philippine Life, 1850-1898* (New Haven and London: Yale University Press, 1965).

48. Fernand Braudel, *Afterthoughts on Material Civilization and Capitalism* (Baltimore and London: The Johns Hopkins University Press, 1977), p. 67.

is not over, even though Batavia is called Jakarta again.) Part of the history of capitalism in Indonesia is linked in an important way to that of the landed estates of the Batavian elite in the eighteenth century, which Taylor treats as an expression of the comic triumph of mestizoization. The first ironic point to make is that, like so many other aspects of VOC social life in Batavia, this development has close parallels in the Netherlands, where entrepreneurs were also becoming rentiers in the eighteenth century.[49] This parallelism, as well as all the other similarities, deep or superficial, between "Asian" Netherlanders in Batavia and "Western" Netherlanders in the Netherlands needs to be stated in order to refute assertions about an Eastern-Western antithesis which are false or which do not matter. What matters, in the case of the landed estates, is that they were an expression of what Bernard Vlekke has called "an economic and social revolution which was going to change the destiny of the people of Java"[50] (and not only Java).

At the beginning of the eighteenth century, in what seems to have been an entrepreneurial rather than a rentier-like response to a downturn in the VOC's gross profit on coffee, Batavia's elite began to plant coffee trees in the Priangan countryside near the city. The very first and unsuccessful experiments with growing coffee in Java were carried out by Governor-General Joan van Hoorn at his country estate "Struiswijk," which he inherited from his first wife, Anna Struijs. Van Hoorn subsequently promoted the planting of coffee with the assistance of his relative, the famous Burgomaster of Amsterdam, Nicholas Witsen.

Joan van Hoorn has ironic potential in a possible revision of Taylor's study. Taylor finds him interesting because he was so totally embedded in the "web" of Batavia society at the beginning of the eighteenth century. Yet his relationship to his first wife and to his friend and relative, Witsen, illustrates the functional nature of and difference between local marriages and distant alliances in the eyes of the male elite. Anna Struijs was a capital gain, Witsen a political ally, a man of power and influence in the Netherlands, where all the sons of the Batavia elite were sent for education and advancement. As the master ironist of Batavia's early history has written: "Enthroned above the King of Batavia were of course the Kings of the Fatherland, namely the Regent families, and the highest wish of a Governor-General was naturally to see his children married into a line of Regents."[51]

Even more interesting is what de Haan, in another study which is central to an ironic rewriting of Javanese history, tells us about Joan van Hoorn's father.[52] Pieter van Hoorn believed that the VOC should abandon the Portuguese

---

49. See Peter Burke, *Venice and Amsterdam: A Study of Seventeenth-Century Elites* (London: Temple Smith, 1974), pp. 101-12 and passim.

50. Bernard H. M. Vlekke, *Nusantara: A History of Indonesia* (The Hague and Bandung: van Hoeve, 1960), p. 194.

51. F. de Haan, *Oud Batavia: Gedenkboek* [Ancient Batavia: A Commemorative Volume], vol. 1 (Batavia: Kolff, 1922), p. 139. Cf. Vlekke's chapter on Batavia, "New Aspects of Indonesian Life," *Nusantara*, pp. 185-99, which stays very close to de Haan both in content and ironic tone.

52. F. de Haan, *Priangan: De Preanger-Regentschappen onder het Nederlandsch Bestuur tot 1811* [Priangan: The Preanger Regencies under Dutch Rule to 1811], vol. 1 (Batavia: Bataviaasch Genootschap van Kunsten en Wetenschappen, 1910), p. 93.

system of coastal trading factories in favor of a Spanish form of colonization and economic exploitation. Such an enterprise, van Hoorn thought, required the leadership of a King "with generous powers," rather than a consortium of merchants whose only concern was to maximize quick profits.

Pieter van Hoorn's views were shared by many, including Jan Pieterzoon Coen (who compared the rulers of Aceh and Mataram to the King of Spain and wanted Batavia to be like Manila) and Joan van Hoorn. In his turgid, yet ironically masterful study of the Priangan, de Haan shows how the territorial expansion of the Batavian VOC, beginning in 1684-85 with the defeat of Banten and the pacification of the Batavian countryside (the same pacification program sent Surapati fleeing into Central Java), represented the working out of a double logic which expressed the Company's dual identity as "koopman" (merchant) and "Souverein."[53] As de Haan reminds us in brilliantly ironical asides, the system of forced deliveries developed in the Priangan, indeed its entire institutional and social history, foreshadows the history of Java under the Cultivation System in the nineteenth century. As Fasseur reminds us in his own ironic study of the Cultivation System: "We must also not forget that Van den Bosch had been 'landed nobility' in the countryside around Buitenzorg. In that role his extraordinary social standing among the local population may have been decisive in shaping his view of the relationship between the Government and the indigenous population in general. It would be no exaggeration to maintain that the Cultivation System of Java was, as it were, a 'private estate' writ large."[54] Van den Bosch, of course, also had his King. It would not be outrageous to surmise that when van Imhoff withdrew from the cares of the city to his estate, Buitenzorg, he dreamed of Blenheim, of sovereignty over the whole of Java and maybe beyond.

The walls of Jan Pieterzoon Coen's Castle fell because he planned it that way. The domesticity of van de Velde's Batavian residence, which is largely hidden within the cool, dark interior of the dalem, also includes the man dressed in a top hat and shoes who is doing business with the pigtailed Chinaman, the barefoot slaves watering the dust, and the beggar kneeling at the road's edge, reaching out to a woman with a child. An invisible Castle still stands in Goenawan Mohamad's city, framed by the discourse of his "City." How he would write a history of that Castle, of that "city," is something we can think about more clearly once the invisible structures of our own historical languages and "perspectives" have been made more visible.

---

53. It is interesting that van Leur does not cite *Priangan* at all and Taylor only makes use of its biographical sections.

54. C. Fasseur, *Kultuurstelsel en Koloniale Baten: De Nederlandse Exploitatie van Java, 1840-1860* [Cultivation System and Colonial Profits: The Dutch Exploitation of Java, 1840-1860] (Leiden: Universitaire Pers, 1975), pp. 14-15.

SOUTHEAST ASIA PROGRAM DATA PAPERS

120 Uris Hall
Cornell University
Ithaca, New York 14853

In Print

Number 18 CONCEPTIONS OF STATE AND KINGSHIP IN SOUTHEAST ASIA, by Robert Heine-Geldern. 1956. (Fourth Printing 1972) 14 pages. $3.50.

Number 46 AN EXPERIMENT IN WARTIME INTERCULTURAL RELATIONS: PHILIPPINE STUDENTS IN JAPAN, 1943-1945, by Grant K. Goodman. 1962. 34 pages. $2.00.

Number 49 THE TEXTILE INDUSTRY--A CASE STUDY OF INDUSTRIAL DEVELOPMENT IN THE PHILIPPINES, by Laurence David Stifel. 1963. 199 pages. $3.00.

Number 54 CATALOGUE OF THAI LANGUAGE HOLDINGS IN THE CORNELL UNIVERSITY LIBRARIES THROUGH 1964, compiled by Francis A. Bernath, Thai Cataloguer. 1964. 236 pages. $3.00.

Number 55 STRATEGIC HAMLETS IN SOUTH VIET-NAM, A SURVEY AND A COMPARISON, by Milton E. Osborne. 1965. (Second Printing 1968) 66 pages. $2.50.

Number 57 THE SHAN STATES AND THE BRITISH ANNEXATION, by Sao Saimong Mangrai. 1965. (Second Printing 1969) 204 pages. $4.00.

Number 61 RAJAH'S SERVANT, by A. B. Ward. 1966. (Second Printing 1969) 204 pages. $2.50.

Number 71 AMERICAN DOCTORAL DISSERTATIONS ON ASIA, 1933-JUNE 1966, INCLUDING APPENDIX OF MASTERS' THESES AT CORNELL UNIVERSITY 1933-JUNE 1968, by Curtis W. Stucki. 1968. (Second Printing 1970) 304 pages. $4.00.

Number 72 EXCAVATIONS OF THE PREHISTORIC IRON INDUSTRY IN WEST BORNEO, Vol. I, RAW MATERIALS AND INDUSTRIAL WASTE, Vol. II, ASSOCIATED ARTIFACTS AND IDEAS, by Tom Harrisson and Stanley J. O'Connor. 1969. 417 pages. $5.00 each set.

Number 73 THE SEPARATION OF SINGAPORE FROM MALAYSIA, by Nancy McHenry Fletcher. 1969. (Second Printing 1971) 98 pages. $2.50.

Number 75 WHITE HMONG-ENGLISH DICTIONARY, compiled by Ernest E. Heimbach. Linguistics Series IV. 1969. (Second Printing 1979) 497 pages. $6.50.

Number 82 MAGINDANAO, 1860-1888: THE CAREER OF DATO UTO BUAYAN, by Reynaldo C. Ileto. 1971. 80 pages. $3.50.

Number 83 A BIBLIOGRAPHY OF PHILIPPINE LINGUISTICS AND MINOR LANGUAGES, with Annotations and Indices Based on Works in the Library of Cornell University, by Jack H. Ward. Linguistic Series V. 1971. 549 pages. $6.50.

Number 84 A CHECKLIST OF THE VIETNAMESE HOLDINGS OF THE WASON COLLECTION, CORNELL UNIVERSITY LIBRARIES, AS OF JUNE 1971, compiled by Giok Po Oey, Southeast Asia Librarian. 1971. 377 pages. $6.50.

Number 85   SOUTHEAST ASIA FIELD TRIP FOR THE LIBRARY OF CONGRESS, 1970-71, by Cecil Hobbs. 1971. 94 pages. $3.50.

Number 87   A DICTIONARY OF CEBUANO VISAYA, Vols. I and II, by John U. Wolff. 1972. Linguistics Series VI. 1,200 pages. $8.00.

Number 88   MIAO AND YAO LINGUISTIC STUDIES, Selected Articles in Chinese, Translated by Chang Yu-hung and Chu Kwo-ray. Edited by Herbert C. Purnell, Jr. Linguistics Series VII. 1972. 282 pages. $4.00.

Number 89   A CHECKLIST OF INDONESIAN SERIALS IN THE CORNELL UNIVERSITY LIBRARY (1945-1970), compiled by Yvonne Thung and John M. Echols. 1973. 226 pages. $7.00.

Number 90   BIBLIOGRAPHY OF VIETNAMESE LITERATURE IN THE WASON COLLECTION AT CORNELL UNIVERSITY, by Marion W. Ross. 1973. 178 pages. $4.50.

Number 91   SELECTED SHORT STORIES OF THEIN PE MYINT, Translated, with Introduction and Commentary, by Patricia M. Milne. 1973. 105 pages. $4.00.

Number 92   FEASTING AND SOCIAL OSCILLATION: A Working Paper on Religion and Society in Upland Southeast Asia, by A. Thomas Kirsch. 1973. 67 pages. $5.00.

Number 98   THE CRYSTAL SANDS: THE CHRONICLES OF NAGARA SRI DHARRMARAJA, translated, edited and with an introduction by David K. Wyatt. 1975. 264 pages. $6.50.

Number 101   AN ANNOTATED GUIDE TO PHILIPPINE SERIALS, by Frank H. Golay and Marianne H. Hauswedell. 1976. 131 pages. $5.00.

Number 102   NO OTHER ROAD TO TAKE, Memoir of Mrs. Nguyen Thi Dinh, translated by Mai Elliott. 1976. 77 pages. $6.00.

Number 103   DIRECTORY OF THE CORNELL SOUTHEAST ASIA PROGRAM 1951-1976, compiled by Frank H. Golay and Peggy Lush. 1976. 88 pages. $3.00.

Number 106   COMMUNIST PARTY POWER IN KAMPUCHEA (CAMBODIA): DOCUMENTS AND DISCUSSION, compiled and edited with the introduction by Timothy Michael Carney. 1977. 86 pages. $4.50.

Number 109   THE STATUS OF SOCIAL SCIENCE RESEARCH IN BORNEO, edited by G. N. Appell and Leigh R. Wright. 1978. 117 pages. $5.75.

Number 111   CAMBODIA'S ECONOMY AND INDUSTRIAL DEVELOPMENT, by Khieu Samphan, translated and with an introduction by Laura Summers. 1979. 122 pages. $5.75.

Number 113   MEMOIRS OF THE FOUR-FOOT COLONEL, by General Smith Dun. 1980. 147 pages. $6.00.

Number 114   LAWYER IN THE WILDERNESS, by K. H. Digby. With a preface and notes by R. H. W. Reece. 1980. 123 pages. $5.75.

Number 115   THE MANIYADANABON OF SHIN SANDALINKA, translated by L. E. Bagshawe. 1981. 132 pages. $7.00.

Number 116   COMMUNICATIVE CODES IN CENTRAL JAVA, by John U. Wolff and Soepomo Poedjosoedarmo. 1982. 188 pages. $7.50.

INDONESIA, a semiannual journal, devoted to Indonesia's culture, history, and social and political problems.

    *No. 1, April 1966, *No. 2, Oct. 1966, *No. 3, April 1967
    *No. 4, Oct. 1967, *No. 5, April 1968, *No. 6, Oct. 1968
    *No. 7, April 1969, *No. 8, Oct. 1969, *No. 9, April 1970
    *No. 10, Oct. 1970, *No. 11, April 1971, *No. 12, Oct. 1971
    No. 13, April 1972, No. 14, Oct. 1972, $4.50 each, $8.00 both
    No. 15, April 1973, No. 16, Oct. 1973, $4.50 each, $8.00 both
    No. 17, April 1974, No. 18, Oct. 1974, $4.50 each, $8.00 both
    *No. 19, April 1975, No. 20, Oct. 1975, $4.50
    No. 21, April 1976, No. 22, Oct. 1976, $5.00 each, $10.00 both
    No. 23, April 1977, $5.00, *No. 24, Oct. 1977
    *No. 25, April 1978, No. 26, Oct. 1978, $6.00
    No. 27, April 1979, No. 28, Oct. 1979, $6.00 each, $12.00 both
    No. 29, April 1980, No. 30, Oct. 1980, $6.00 each, $12.00 both
    No. 31, April 1981, No. 32, Oct. 1981, $6.50 each, $12.00 both
    No. 33, April 1982, No. 34, Oct. 1982, $6.50 each, $12.00 both
    No. 35, April 1983, No. 36, Oct. 1983, $7.50 each, $14.00 both
    No. 37, April 1984, No. 38, Oct. 1984, $7.50 each, $14.00 both

STUDY AND TEACHING MATERIALS

Obtainable from Southeast Asia Program
120 Uris Hall, Cornell University, Ithaca, New York 14853

THAI CULTURAL READER, Book I, by Robert B. Jones, Ruchira C. Mendiones and Craig J. Reynolds. 1970. (Second revised edition 1976) 517 pages. $7.50.

THAI CULTURAL READER, Book II, by Robert B. Jones and Ruchira C. Mendiones. 1969. 791 pages. $8.25.

INTRODUCTION TO THAI LITERATURE, by Robert B. Jones and Ruchira C. Mendiones. 1970. 563 pages. $7.00.

A.U.A. LANGUAGE CENTER THAI COURSE, by J. Marvin Brown, Books 1, 2, 3. $4.50 each. Tape Supplements for Books 1, 2, 3, $2.00 each. SMALL TALK (Dialogue Book A), $5.00. GETTING HELP (Dialogue Book B), $5.00. BOOK R (Reading and Writing Text), $5.00. BOOK W (Reading and Writing Workbook), $5.00.

BEGINNING INDONESIAN, by John U. Wolff. 1,124 pages. Part One, revised 1977, $12.50. Part Two, reprinted 1974, $12.50. INDONESIAN READINGS, 1978, $12.50. INDONESIAN CONVERSATIONS, 1978, $12.50. FORMAL INDONESIAN, 1980, $12.50. Tapes available at extra cost.

BEGINNING INDONESIAN THROUGH SELF INSTRUCTION, by John U. Wolff, Dede Oetomo, and Daniel Fietkiewicz. 1984. 900 pages. $25.00. Tapes available at extra cost.

INTERMEDIATE SPOKEN VIETNAMESE, by Franklin Huffman and Tran Trong Hai. 1980. $10.00.

Maps

Central Thailand. 7 x 10 inches; scale: 34 km to 1 inch. Price $.25 each; $1.00 set of five.

    A. 1. Jangwat Outline Map. 1955.
         2. By Amphoe. 1947.
         3. Population Density by Amphoe. 1947.
         4. Proportion of Chinese by Amphoe. 1947.
         5. Concentration of Chinese by Amphoe. 1947.

Thailand. 13 x 22 inches; scale: 50 miles to 1 inch, except B-10 as noted. Price $.25 each; $1.00 set of six.

    B. 6. By Amphoe. 1927.
         7. Population Density by Amphoe. 1947.
         8. Fertility Ratios by Amphoe. 1947.
         9. Concentration of Chinese by Amphoe. 1947.
        10. Untitled (Amphoe Outline Map). 16 x 44 inches, in two parts, each 16 x 22 inches; scale: 27 miles to 1 inch.

Maps and Gazetteer for 1964, 1969, 1974. Maps of Ethnic Settlements of Chiengrai Province, North of the Mae Kok River, Thailand. Prepared by L. M. Hanks. 1975. 35 pages. $8.00.

CORNELL MODERN INDONESIA PROJECT PUBLICATIONS
102 West Avenue
Ithaca, New York 14850

In Print

Number 6   THE INDONESIAN ELECTIONS OF 1955, by Herbert Feith. 1957. (Second Printing 1971) 91 pages. $3.50. (Interim Report)

Number 7   THE SOVIET VIEW OF THE INDONESIAN REVOLUTION, by Ruth T. McVey. 1957. (Third Printing 1969) 90 pages. $2.50. (Interim Report)

Number 16   THE DYNAMICS OF THE WESTERN NEW GUINEA (IRIAN BARAT) PROBLEM, by Robert C. Bone, Jr. 1958. (Second Printing 1962) 182 pages. $3.00. (Interim Report)

Number 25   THE COMMUNIST UPRISINGS OF 1926-1927 IN INDONESIA: KEY DOCUMENTS, edited and with an introduction by Harry J. Benda and Ruth T. McVey. 1960. (Second Printing 1969) 177 pages. $5.50. (Translation)

Number 32   PRELIMINARY CHECKLIST OF INDONESIAN IMPRINTS DURING THE JAPANESE PERIOD (March 1942-August 1945), by John M. Echols. 1963. 62 pages. $1.50. (Bibliography)

Number 37   MYTHOLOGY AND THE TOLERANCE OF THE JAVANESE, by Benedict R. Anderson. 1965. (Third Printing 1979) 77 pages. $5.00. (Monograph)

Number 39   PRELIMINARY CHECKLIST OF INDONESIAN IMPRINTS (1945-1949): WITH CORNELL UNIVERSITY HOLDINGS, by John M. Echols. 1965. 186 pages. $3.50. (Bibliography)

Number 43   STATE AND STATECRAFT IN OLD JAVA: A STUDY OF THE LATER MATARAM PERIOD, 16TH TO 19TH CENTURY, by Soemarsaid Moertono. 1968. (Revised edition 1981) 180 pages. $6.50. (Monograph)

Number 44   OUR STRUGGLE, by Sutan Sjahrir. Translated with an introduction by Benedict R. Anderson. 1968. 37 pages. $2.00. (Translation)

Number 45   INDONESIA ABANDONS CONFRONTATION, by Franklin B. Weinstein. 1969. 94 pages. $3.00. (Interim Report)

Number 46   THE ORIGINS OF THE MODERN CHINESE MOVEMENT IN INDONESIA, by Kwee Tek Hoay. Translated and edited by Lea E. Williams. 1969. 64 pages. $3.00. (Translation)

Number 47   PERSATUAN ISLAM: ISLAMIC REFORM IN TWENTIETH CENTURY INDONESIA, by Howard M. Federspiel, 1970. 250 pages. $7.50. (Monograph)

Number 48   NATIONALISM, ISLAM AND MARXISM, by Soekarno. With an introduction by Ruth T. McVey. 1970. (Second Printing 1984) 62 pages. $4.00. (Translation)

Number 49   THE FOUNDATION OF THE PARTAI MUSLIMIN INDONESIA, by K. E. Ward. 1970. 75 pages. $3.00. (Interim Report)

Number 50   SCHOOLS AND POLITICS: THE KAUM MUDA MOVEMENT IN WEST SUMATRA (1927- 1933), by Taufik Abdullah. 1971. 257 pages. $6.00. (Monograph)

Number 51   THE PUTERA REPORTS: PROBLEMS IN INDONESIAN-JAPANESE WAR-TIME COOPERATION, by Mohammad Hatta. Translated with an introduction by William H. Frederick. 1971. 114 pages. $4.00. (Translation)

Number 52   A PRELIMINARY ANALYSIS OF THE OCTOBER 1, 1965, COUP IN INDONESIA (Prepared in January 1966), by Benedict R. Anderson, Ruth T. McVey (with the assistance of Frederick P. Bunnell). 1971. 162 pages. $6.00. (Interim Report)

Number 55   REPORT FROM BANARAN: THE STORY OF THE EXPERIENCES OF A SOLDIER DURING THE WAR OF INDEPENDENCE, by Major General T. B. Simatupang. 1972. 186 pages. $6.50. (Translation)

Number 56   GOLKAR AND THE INDONESIAN ELECTIONS OF 1971, by Masashi Nishihara. 1972. 56 pages. $3.50. (Monograph)

Number 57   PERMESTA: HALF A REBELLION, by Barbara S. Harvey. 1977. 174 pages. $5.00. (Monograph)

Number 58   ADMINISTRATION OF ISLAM IN INDONESIA, by Deliar Noer. 1978. 82 pages. $4.50. (Monograph)

Number 59   BREAKING THE CHAINS OF OPPRESSION OF THE INDONESIAN PEOPLE: DEFENSE STATEMENT AT HIS TRIAL ON CHARGES OF INSULTING THE HEAD OF STATE, Bandung, June 7-10, 1979, by Heri Akhmadi. 1981. 201 pages. $8.75. (Translation)

Number 60   THE MINANGKABAU RESPONSE TO DUTCH COLONIAL RULE IN THE NINETEENTH CENTURY, by Elizabeth E. Graves. 1981. 157 pages. $7.50. (Monograph)

Number 61   SICKLE AND CRESCENT: THE COMMUNIST REVOLT OF 1926 IN BANTEN, by Michael C. Williams. 1982. 81 pages. $6.00. (Monograph)

Number 62   INTERPRETING INDONESIAN POLITICS: THIRTEEN CONTRIBUTIONS TO THE DEBATE, 1964-1981. Edited by Benedict Anderson and Audrey Kahin, with an Introduction by Daniel S. Lev. 1982. 172 pages. $9.00. (Interim Report)

Number 63   DYNAMICS OF DISSENT IN INDONESIA: SAWITO AND THE PHANTOM COUP, by David Bourchier. 1984. 128 pages. $9.00. (Interim Report)

Number 64   SUHARTO AND HIS GENERALS: INDONESIA'S MILITARY POLITICS, 1975-1983, by David Jenkins. 1984. 300 pages. $12.50. (Monograph)

LIST OF CONTRIBUTORS

Terance Bigalke is Assistant Director of the Midwest Universities Consortium for International Activities (MUCIA).

John Bowen is a Lecturer in Social Studies at Harvard University and Research Associate at the Harvard Institute for International Development.

Tony Day is a Lecturer in the Department of Indonesian and Malay Studies at Sydney University.

Howard Federspiel is a Professor of Political Science at the Ohio State University at Newark.

Thomas Hudak is an Assistant Professor of Linguistics at the University of Kentucky.

Sidney Jones is a Program Officer at the Ford Foundation.

Audrey Kahin is Editor of Cornell's Modern Indonesia Project.

Paul Stange is a Lecturer in Southeast Asian Studies at Murdoch University.

www.ingramcontent.com/pod-product-compliance
Lightning Source LLC
Chambersburg PA
CBHW080635230426
43663CB00016B/2880